Tell
Me
Who I Am

Tell Me Who I Am

Alex and Marcus Lewis
with Joanna Hodgkin

HODDER &
STOUGHTON

First published in Great Britain in 2013 by Hodder & Stoughton
An Hachette UK company

1

P.176 'Indoor Games near Newbury', from *Collected Poems*, by John
Betjeman © 1955, 1958, 1962, 1964, 1968, 1970, 1979, 1981, 1982, 2001
Reproduced by permission of John Murray (Publishers).

Picture Acknowledgements
All photographs are from the author's collection. Additional acknowledgements: 7
(middle left & bottom right)/ photos Ken Niven, 8 (middle)/ photo Hugo Dixon.

Every reasonable effort has been made to contact the copyright holders, but if
there are any errors or omissions, Hodder & Stoughton will be pleased to insert
the appropriate acknowledgement in any subsequent printing of this publication.

A CIP catalogue record for this title is available from the British Library

Hardback ISBN 978 1 444 75726 2
Trade Paperback ISBN 978 1 444 75727 9
Ebook ISBN 978 1 444 75729 3

Typeset by Hewer Text UK Ltd, Edinburgh
Printed and bound by Clays Ltd, St Ives plc

Hodder & Stoughton policy is to use papers that are natural, renewable
and recyclable products and made from wood grown in sustainable
forests. The logging and manufacturing processes are expected to
conform to the environmental regulations of the country of origin.

Hodder & Stoughton Ltd
338 Euston Road
London NW1 3BH

www.hodder.co.uk

We want to acknowledge the extraordinary individuals who happened to enter our lives almost like guardian angels just when we needed them most: the Hudsons, the Brockways, the Richardsons, the Taylors and the Handleys who made all the difference in our childhood. Also our long-suffering business partner and friend, James Burton. Without all your help, we would not have made it through.

To you, to our siblings Amanda and Oliver, and to our wives, this book is dedicated with gratitude and love.

'I am not what happened to me. I am what I choose to become.'

C G Jung

Contents

Contents

Introduction

I recognised them at once. Two men with the same beaky, attractive features and eager grins, both wearing shirts printed with small blue flowers. Not exactly the same, but similar. (Had they randomly chosen floral shirts for this meeting, or was this one of those recurring twin coincidences that are more than mere coincidence? The mysteries of identical twinship are, to an outsider, infinitely fascinating.)

Over the next hour I got an impression of them which grew and developed over the following months, but never fundamentally changed. They were and are two of the most engaging and likeable people I've ever met: funny, vulnerable, open, entertaining, self-absorbed and yet in some strange way selfless as well. And they have an underlying innocence that is truly remarkable. I knew the outlines of their story, and knowing what I did, I was astonished by the speed with which they were prepared to trust their history to me, a complete stranger. Just as they now trust their history to you, the reader of this extraordinary saga.

At the end of that first unforgettable afternoon, Alex said to me, 'I want to write this book because I want to know who I am.'

Because at that stage of his journey, he reckoned he only knew about 30%: the rest was confusion, a cacophony of overlapping narratives, sometimes contradictory, sometimes a blur, sometimes downright wrong. *Game on*, I thought. The storyteller in me recognised this would be a major undertaking. Forget the urge to name the murderer or follow the hunt for true love and happiness: the quest to uncover his hidden identity was as powerful a motivation as I've ever known. And the process of writing the book became a key element in the book itself.

Which makes it a different kind of narrative. If you are looking for a straightforward kind of account, stop right here. Alex and Marcus's story is infinitely more complex and interesting than that, and for the sake of clarity, it is divided into three parts.

The first section pieces together the world of family, home and friends that Alex discovered when he woke from his coma in the late summer of 1982 with his memories erased, never to return. With his twin Marcus to guide him, he was slowly able to create a personal history and a sense of self that carried him through for more than ten years.

Then, at the age of thirty-two, he discovered that a large chunk of his early life had been omitted from the picture Marcus had helped him to assemble. Painfully, doggedly, he started the process again, gradually piecing together a new version of his story. This process forms the second section of the book.

The third part covers the revelations that emerged, sometimes with shocking suddenness, while we worked together on the book. During long sessions in my flat, over meals and endless cups of tea, interrupted by phone calls and visits and the random minutiae of daily life, with laughter and strong emotion and a constant struggle to nail down a kind of truth, we forged a new narrative. It has been an astonishing journey for all of us.

It's a journey in which we've all had much to discover. Though I've worked with people with troubled pasts before, I am far from an expert. One of the things that has struck me most forcibly throughout Alex and Marcus's story is the way the child who experiences major trauma holds different and apparently contradictory realities in their mind and heart at the same time. This was what Marcus taught us: that he both knew, and did not know, what was buried in their past. On one level he remembered daily; on another level he had managed to completely forget. Thus his apparently contradictory statements: 'It never happened to me.' 'I never thought about it.' 'I always knew I'd have to tell him.' 'It was always there.'

All true.

Because some children survive from day to day by having no past. Yesterday is a blank and Now can be erased if it becomes too much to bear. If the present can be wiped and the past is a moveable feast, normal definitions of Truth and Lies are an irrelevance. This was endlessly fascinating, but also a challenge. One of their closest friends said to me, 'I wondered how this woman was ever going to write their story: one twin can't remember anything and the other never tells the truth!'

And yet Marcus, whenever he strikes a core of truth, is one of the most courageously honest people I know.

Still, for readers who have grown up in a mostly happy family, this can be hard to disentangle. But stay with it. Through Alex and Marcus, and their extraordinary quest, there is much that touches all our lives.

The second thing I've learned is how complex the ties of family, love and betrayal can be. Quite early on in our discussions, Marcus mentioned being struck by an interview he'd heard on the radio. A young woman who had been subjected to years of beatings from her father was asked how she felt about him now that he was dead. She said simply, 'I miss him.' Not the beatings, obviously, but the chance to have a decent parent, now gone forever. The interviewer was startled, but Marcus knew just what she meant.

There are individuals in this book who have done wicked and cruel things to those they should have been protecting, but there are no monsters. It would have been easier, perhaps, if we could dismiss the villains in this tale as monsters, but that would be to miss the point entirely.

This is a story that is far from over, and far from complete. It's a truism that even in a relatively uncomplicated family there will be differing perspectives, contradictory memories, conflicting versions of characters and events. In a family like Alex and Marcus's, a single final true account is a chimera, forever out of reach. This is their reality and it will always be fluid.

But for me, perhaps the most remarkable gift from working with them has been an affirmation of the endless resources of the human spirit. Despite what they suffered as children, they have gone on to achieve so much. They are successful entrepreneurs, respected around the world for the hotel they have built on a magical island. They have a huge, loyal circle of friends, some of whom have known them for thirty years. They grew up with secrets and lies, yet they are open and, in some fundamental way, completely honest. They are loving husbands and fathers who have broken the chain of secrets and self-interest.

Their history throws up endless questions: what is the alchemy that makes one person choose to destroy the lives of those closest to them while others strive to create something inspirational? What are the forces that really shape us?

Every person's history is unique, but it is hard to think of two lives with as many extraordinary elements as theirs: memory and identity, twinship and torn loyalties, truth and fiction, low life and high society.

This is their world. It is a world I have been privileged to share in for a while.

Read it, and be amazed.

Joanna Hodgkin
London
March 2013

Prologue

The first time my life changed direction I was three weeks old. My father and I were in an accident: for a few days we were both on life-support machines. The second time I was eighteen and another accident radically altered my life; the after-effects are with me today. I lost my first eighteen years, and they never returned. The third time, although not an accident, was the most dramatic. I was thirty-two and discovered extraordinary intrigue in my family and I had to start again. This time around, recovery was never going to be straightforward.

This could have been a dark story. But through it all, my twin brother Marcus has made all the difference. As babies we were hardly ever separated and as children we were always together. As adults we have worked together and sometimes gone our separate ways, but the bond between us has never been broken. With the help of Marcus, and my wife Camilla who has been my rock throughout this, I have come through.

It was only after doing a Radio 4 interview about a snippet of my life that I realised why I needed to tell this story. The response to that brief interview showed me how my story might make a difference to many people who've lived in silence too long. If any of this resonates with your experience then this book is especially for you.

Alex Lewis

PART I

The First Story

I

'O Brave New World'

Guildford Hospital, August 1982.

Marcus Lewis sat beside the metal bed in the corner of the ward. He was hunched forward, watching for the smallest sign. His brother had lain there for over a week. Alex was immobile, unreachable, his eyes closed and his breathing shallow – just as he had been since the last night of July, when he had fallen off the back of a motorbike, smashed onto the tarmac and fractured his skull. By the time the first morning of August dawned, he had slipped into unconsciousness.

The face Marcus was looking at was his own face, reflecting back his features, handsome, with dark hair and eyes that had been quick to smile, but subtly altered now, gaunt and pale in the aftermath of the accident. He and Alex were identical twins, always together, mirroring each other's gestures, laugh and voice. Even their close friends had difficulty telling them apart. Marcus was talking to Alex as he had been all week, chatting about their home and friends, what he had been doing, what people had been saying. Nothing all that important. Just keeping the channels of communication open.

In the ward, nurses and auxiliaries carried on with their daily tasks: checking blood pressure and handing out meals, dealing with visitors and examinations. The squeak of trolleys and screens, footsteps on linoleum, the clatter of crockery, the murmur of voices. Since the accident, Marcus's life had narrowed to the micro-world of this ward, this chair, this small patch of floor and this narrow space beside his brother's bed.

The doctors had done what they could to prepare him and their mother Jill for the worst. They had assured them that Alex would come round eventually – but what would he be like? Would he still be Alex? The head injury was severe, and complicated by the fact that he had fractured his skull as a baby. There was a chance he would be permanently brain-damaged, perhaps even a vegetable. Their mother was growing desperate. But Marcus was certain that behind the mask of unconsciousness, Alex remained essentially the same as always. He knew because the unspoken thread of communication that connected them as twins had never been broken. He knew in the same way that he had known, waking early in the morning of 1 August, that something terrible had happened to Alex.

Born within five minutes of each other, alike as two peas in a pod, they had a connection beyond words.

Marcus had sat beside his brother's bed for hours every day. Long hours of waiting and worry.

And then after several days, without warning, Alex opened his eyes. He looked directly at his twin. And he spoke. His voice was faint, and croaky from lack of use. But the words were clear.

'Hello, Marcus,' he said.

The effect was electric.

All around them, the room erupted in pandemonium. Nurses and doctors stopped what they were doing and gathered round the bed. Their mother raced over from the nurses' station. She was overjoyed. Alex had come round! He could speak! He recognised Marcus and he was going to be all right!

Alex held his brother's gaze. He frowned. The noise was bothering him.

Jill, their mother, was never a quiet woman, even under normal circumstances. Now her raptures at the recovery of her son echoed through the ward. But soon her joy turned to dismay. Something was wrong. What was happening? Why wasn't he thrilled to see her? She couldn't make it out at all.

Her precious son had recognised his twin at once.

But he did not seem to know who she was.

Everyone was crowding round the bed. Alex spoke again to Marcus, but this time his voice was tinged with fear: 'Who is that woman?'

'That's our mother,' Marcus told him.

The information did not make any kind of sense. As far as Alex was concerned, the middle-aged woman who was creating such a hullabaloo was a total stranger. He'd never even seen her before.

He didn't remember anything.

For Alex – even now, thirty years later – that moment of emerging from unconsciousness marks the start of his known life. Day one. A new beginning. 'My earliest memory, and I'll never forget it, is seeing Marcus. And then seeing this hysterical woman round the bed. A very tall, loud, quite large lady with dark hair, running round the room quite hysterically.'

Jill refused to accept that her son did not know who she was.

By this point she was shouting, 'Hello, darling! Hello, hello, HELLO!'

When the medical staff realised her behaviour was distressing their patient, they asked her to step outside the room for a bit. She refused, and tried even harder. She had a fluting, upper-class voice; the sort of voice that expects to be heard. And obeyed at once.

'Of *course* he knows who I am! He's my son! Hello, darling. *Hello!*'

Eventually they persuaded her to leave, and Alex slipped back into unconsciousness.

Already the pattern had been established. Alex never remembered his mother and she never accepted that he could recognise his twin brother, but not her.

But that's exactly what had happened. At that moment in the hospital room, Alex had opened his eyes on a world where everything and everyone – apart from Marcus – was strange and unfamiliar. He didn't even know his own name. He was drowning in confusion, and Marcus was his only chance of staying afloat. He depended on his twin for everything.

In August 1982, when they were both eighteen, Marcus became, in effect, his memory. As Alex says now, from the moment he emerged into consciousness, 'I lived my life through Marcus.'

Marcus had to tell him everything. About his home, his friends, his family. His life. Who he was.

Well, almost everything.

There was never a moment when Marcus made a conscious decision to withhold some crucial information about their early life. To begin with, it never came up. He was too busy dealing with practicalities. But, as he steered his brother through the days, there were memories he never shared, uncomfortable truths he glossed over, gaps that he allowed Alex to fill with 'normal' family details. Alex never had a clue that their family was very far from normal.

Marcus acted out of love. He also acted to protect himself.

He might have been doing Alex a favour.

Certainly Alex, by losing his memory, gave his twin an unexpected gift and made it possible for Marcus not to lose his own memory, exactly – that luxury was denied him – but to bury it. To bury it for years.

For more than a decade Alex pieced his story together, never imagining that the picture that emerged was only half the truth.

The good half.

The rest stayed where Marcus felt it belonged. Hidden away.

2

Memory Bank Deleted

One tries to imagine, but it is almost impossible. What would it be like to have no memories at all from the first eighteen years of your life?

Just imagine if you had no memories of the house or flat you grew up in. No memories of playing in parks or gardens. No memories of that first scooter, falling off your bike, TV dinners or family meals.

No memories from school, of friends or teachers, favourite lessons, canteen dinners or the cycle of the seasons. The smell of the changing rooms and sport on cold afternoons. Playgrounds and corridors, boredom and occasional excitement. The first day of the holidays.

No memories of treats or trips, a visit to the zoo or waking up on Christmas morning. No memory of favourite toys or comics. No memories of the TV programmes that all your contemporaries watched, the catchphrases they still use sometimes. The pop songs your generation grew up with; the films that shaped you all.

No memories of the day your siblings were born, of the friends who visited the house, your godparents, the pets who were a part of the family, the neighbours and the odd characters in the village.

No memory of falling in love for the first time, or your first date.

No memory of birthdays.

No memory of games or jokes.

No memory of learning to drive.

No memory.

Imagine. It wasn't just Alex's memory that had been wiped out by the head injury, but his entire fund of knowledge about who he was. A thousand little daubs of colour contribute to the self-portrait we all carry with us through our lives, a self-portrait that changes and develops with every success or failure, every new friendship or achievement or loss. Or simply with the passage of time. It might not be accurate — it never is completely accurate — but it is essential. It tells us who we are.

Partly it's how we see ourselves mirrored in the opinions of others: 'I've missed you.' 'Trust you to . . .' 'You're so bossy!' 'I like you because . . .' Partly it's the way we reflect ourselves back to ourselves: 'I'm always clumsy!' 'Just like me to be left out.' 'People think I'm tough, but I'm more sensitive than they imagine.' Perhaps most significant of all are those secrets we keep from everyone else, even our closest friends; those hidden thoughts, embarrassing memories, hopeless daydreams we sometimes find it hard to admit even to ourselves.

All those pointers, all these descriptive voices, had vanished; Alex was born at the age of eighteen into a silent and empty inner world, a landscape without signposts, and he had to start again from scratch. What kind of a person was he? Was he exactly like his twin Marcus, or were they different, and if so, how?

Over the weeks and months and years that followed, Alex didn't just have to piece together the narrative of his life. He had to create a sense of himself, a portrait that captured what it meant to be Alex Lewis.

The scene his newly opened eyes looked out on was endlessly confusing. For months he existed in a kind of mental fog. Everything he saw and touched was unfamiliar. He was like a small child. The nursing staff had to teach him how to walk again, how to go up and down stairs, how to dress himself and use the bathroom. To begin with, even his speech was limited. Only the words a child knows were available to him.

The hospital ward was the only place he knew. Slowly he was getting to recognise the doctors and the nurses. But all too soon the medical team decided he was ready to be sent home. They assumed he would be pleased – surely everyone wants to get back to their family – but for Alex the prospect was alarming. Home? He had no idea what that meant.

The scary lady who kept insisting that she was 'Mummy' came and collected him in her car. He sat huddled in the passenger seat and wondered where he was going. His arm was still in plaster and his head felt strange. Soon they had left the town and were driving through the green lanes of late summer to a picturesque Sussex village. The car pulled up in front of a long, low, old-looking house surrounded by a large garden.

'We're home!' she cried.

Duke's Cottage.

Home?

Alex climbed painfully out of the car, crunched over the gravel and edged through the front door. He found himself in a large hallway with a long dining table along one side. The house was dark with low, beamed ceilings and lots of rooms with hidden corners. The whole place was filled with clutter. Everywhere you looked antiques and junk were heaped together. They told him this was because their mother Jill was an antique dealer and had a stall in Portobello market every Saturday. The words 'Portobello market' meant nothing to Alex, though apparently he had gone with her to help many times.

A tall, elderly man came out of one of the rooms and greeted him formally. He learned that this imposing gentleman was his 'Daddy'. His father shook Alex by the hand and then retreated into his gloomy, panelled room. He seemed distant and a bit frightening, but for all Alex knew, this was how all fathers were. It was easier to connect with the children: his sister Amanda, who was eight, tall and fair-haired, and little Oliver, the baby of the family, who was just six. With the adaptability of children, they accepted the changes in their big brother, and they didn't seem so threatening to him.

Everyone recognised Alex, but to him they were all strangers. Apart from Marcus. People assumed he'd get his memory back slowly, but he never did. Not even a hint of a memory.

Without Marcus, it's hard to know how Alex would have managed. For a long time, his whole life was about survival. Getting through the day. Managing simple tasks. Even now, his memory of those first months after the accident is muddled. Everything was a blur, with Marcus the only fixed point in the chaos.

3

'MarcusandAli'

'I told him everything he needed to know,' says Marcus. 'Everything. His girlfriend, his jobs, who our friends were, where we lived, where our bedroom was. Everything. This is the house. This is the kitchen. This is the bathroom. This is Oliver. This is Amanda. Everything from the day we got home. And I had to keep repeating it.'

The twins had always done everything together. Neighbours remember that when they were children, you never saw one without the other being close by. So much so that their names became blended into a single word: Ali'n'Marky, MarcusandAli. They'd always been a team, so at first Alex's total dependence on his twin wasn't all that noticeable. Except that he himself had changed.

He was much thinner and more frail-looking. His wrist had been broken in several places when he came off his bike and it remained in plaster for months. He was confused all the time and agitated, and he couldn't cope with more than one or two people at a time. Questions upset him, and any kind of banter, raised voices or play-fighting distressed him horribly. He cried frequently, quick immediate tears like the tears of a small child, tears that overwhelmed him, then vanished as fast as they'd appeared. Sometimes he didn't seem to know what was going on at all and moaned in incoherent distress. If the tension became too much, he simply lost consciousness entirely and collapsed.

And at Duke's Cottage, he was often anxious. For one thing, his mother kept insisting that of course he knew who she was. Jill was a flamboyant woman who wore flouncy skirts and dramatic clothes she'd picked up in charity shops. She had a loud style that was all her own; a way of imposing herself on any situation and sweeping aside all opposition. And right now the topic that most absorbed her was Alex's so-called amnesia. She refused to let the subject drop. 'Okay,' she kept saying, 'you've forgotten everything else. But you do remember Marcus. *And me!*' She kept trying to imprint that on him. She was his mother. So he had to know her. He was just pretending. Now he must stop and admit that he knew who she was.

But Alex didn't. He couldn't, and wasn't able to pretend that he could. But she never gave up; she was convinced that if she just spoke loudly enough, he'd have to agree.

Worse still, Jill downplayed the severity of his injuries. According to her, he'd had a nasty bump on the head and was a bit confused. 'Oh, Alex is just a bit quiet,' she'd tell friends, when they commented on her sickly-looking son. 'But he's all right really.'

He was anything but 'all right'. The memory loss was bad enough, but Alex had no way of knowing that he was trying to write his own story in a household where fact was indistinguishable from fiction. Reality was whatever Jill decided it was and never mind the facts. Later, his younger brother Oliver was to sum up the difficulty by saying, 'We grew up in a house of ill-truths.'

Alex was struggling to disentangle the facts, but at Duke's

Cottage that was a dangerous undertaking. So it was par for the course that Jill insisted that her children were happy and Alex was fine, just a bit of a bump, no matter all the evidence to the contrary.

This was the only way of operating that Marcus had ever known and he had not yet started to question it. He knew perfectly well that Alex's memory loss was real, because he spent so much time filling in the gaps for him, and did so for years. But he quickly fell in with the official version of events. He picked up on Jill's cue and soon stopped mentioning the accident or the fact that Alex had lost his memory. As Marcus says now, once the initial trauma was over, 'we tended to get on with our lives and not make such a big deal of it. We just moved straight into coping mechanism and pretended it had never happened. Get on and deal, see your friends and go out . . .' It was what they'd always done. Knowing how to lie was a necessary survival tool in their family.

And because the public version was that Alex had never lost his memory, no follow-up care was provided. So far as they can remember, Alex was never examined by neurological experts, or given any kind of professional help. He just had to cope as best he could. Now that Alex and Marcus have children of their own, they are baffled by this lack of care. Why on earth didn't their mother move heaven and earth to get Alex the specialised help he so desperately needed? It's what any normal parent would have done. But at the time, like so much else that had happened in their lives, they just accepted it. With no way to make comparisons, they presumed that this was how any family would have dealt with the crisis.

4

Bramley Grange Hotel

Shortly after his return from hospital, a woman called Pam Taylor turned up at Duke's Cottage. Alex, of course, had no idea who she was, but she seemed competent and kind. She told him he had been working in her hotel at the time of the accident. She quickly assessed the situation at Duke's Cottage and announced that she was going to take Alex back with her to the hotel where he could be looked after properly. He later learned that Pam had never had a very high opinion of Jill's maternal abilities, and she could see that Alex was not getting the help he needed. Help which she knew she could provide.

Jill didn't argue, so Pam loaded the bewildered young man into her car and drove him back with her to Bramley Grange Hotel. It was confusing and frightening for Alex, but then everything was confusing and frightening and, as usual, he just did as he was told. Marcus had encouraged him to go, knowing the Taylors were good and caring people. And perhaps deep down, some echo of a memory told Alex that this was someone he could trust.

It turned out to be a good move. Bramley Grange was a large, rambling hotel just south of Guildford. Alex had been working there for about six months at the time of the accident. At first he had worked in the kitchen, but Pam and her husband

Ken soon spotted that he had good people skills and they moved him to work in reception and in the restaurant.

Pam and Ken Taylor had good reason to be confident that they could provide Alex with a safe haven. They had gone into the hotel business in order to give their daughter a secure home. Gail had been born three months prematurely and weighing under a kilo; in 1951 that meant she was not expected to survive. But she did. The doctors said she was sure to be brain-damaged and that her parents should forget about her. They refused. At a year it was discovered that the large amounts of oxygen she'd received in the incubator had destroyed her sight. The experts were agreed: Gail was 'useless, a complete write-off, blind, epileptic, spastic and a cabbage' – but still her parents refused to give up on her. By the age of nine, she was unable to speak and screamed at the slightest upset.

But Pam knew her daughter could understand what was said to her, and finally she tracked down a speech therapist who was prepared to take her daughter on. Gail learned to talk, and from then on her progress was extraordinary. The 'cabbage' turned out to have an exceptional memory and a brilliant ear for music. She learned languages, gained friends all over the world through her skill as a radio ham and impressed all who met her. But she would need physical help for the rest of her life.

The Taylors had become hoteliers so they would always live and work in an environment where their daughter would be close by and cared for.[1]

---

1 Gail has told her life-affirming story in the remarkable book *My World*, published in 2007 with a foreword by Sir Harry Secombe.

Alex and Gail had got on well before the accident and now that they were both so dependent on others, though in very different ways, their friendship deepened. Although Alex could not remember Gail or the hotel, he felt much more secure there than he had done at Duke's Cottage. Bramley Grange was safe and happy in a way that 'home' never was. He spent most of his time with Gail. All the staff seemed to know him; they acknowledged his handicap and were kind.

Gail and her parents remained his lifelong friends. At the time, Alex just accepted everything as part of the muddle he was living through, but the Taylors' extraordinary generosity was part of a pattern that had existed ever since the twins were small. No one ever realised quite how damaging their family life was, but many people were aware that their needs were not being met at home. For a long time, friends had been stepping in to fill the breach, just as Pam and Ken Taylor were doing now.

And it wasn't just because the boys needed help. As children, Alex and Marcus possessed a particular charm. Some adults even referred to it as charisma. Of course, there was the novelty value of being identical twins, but it was more than that. They were funny and affectionate and good company. They both had an appealing kind of innocence; an extraordinary capacity to trust people. They were impossible to ignore. They were quirky and entertaining and had a gift for wriggling their way into people's hearts. Quite simply, people loved them.

And that made all the difference.

5

Our Kind of People

Time was elastic for Alex. After a few weeks – or was it months? – he returned to Duke's Cottage. Better able to look after himself, he began to trace the outlines of his world.

'Mummy' was at its centre. Jill was fifty, a striking woman, six foot tall with long dark hair that was turning grey and a dramatic manner that was all her own. Always the centre of attention, she had a large circle of friends and a knack of turning any gathering into an instant party. The one word that is used about her repeatedly is *fun*. Jill Dudley was fun. Loud and exuberant and often outrageous.

She seemed to have no inhibitions, and talked loudly and frequently about her favourite topic, which was sex. She appeared to assume that everyone shared her obsession, which her children's friends, especially the young men, thought was wonderful, so free and easy and bohemian. Sometimes it was embarrassing for the twins, especially when she had had a few drinks and started making references to their 'willies', but Jill was unstoppable. It was best just to laugh along with everyone else.

Also, she was grand. She'd been a debutante in 1949 and had done the season, and she was enormously proud of the fact that she was related to Clement Attlee, Prime Minister of

Great Britain just after the war. She let it be known that she was his great-niece, though actually she was a distant cousin. A staunch Tory, she was obliged to gloss over the inconvenient fact that Attlee was a lifelong socialist and a Labour Party icon. His fame as the architect of the Welfare State was another unfortunate detail she liked to skim over, but still, a famous relative is an asset and Jill never allowed boring facts to get in the way of a good story.

Her closest friend was now a countess. Cynthia, who was sometimes referred to in the tabloids as 'the Big Cyn', had made a couple of judicious marriages before finding her present husband. When his father died, they would become Duke and Duchess. Jill and Cynthia threw parties together at their London flat, and Marcus and Alex had been brought in to serve drinks and canapés to the guests from an early age. In some ways that had been a useful training: they were both superficially confident in almost every social situation, though it took Alex quite a while to recover his confidence after the accident.

Their mother was posh, and they lived in a rambling Elizabethan house with a huge garden, but money always seemed to be scarce. Jill bought all her own clothes, and those of her children, at charity sales. As she had size 10 feet, she could never find suitable shoes, so she wore sandals in all weather, her toes and heels spilling over the ends. She always had cash in her handbag, but that was needed to buy antiques. The twins were never given pocket money, despite all the chores they did around the house. Jill was not the kind of mother you ever asked for things.

'Daddy' was just as forceful. Jack Dudley was in his mid seventies when Alex had his accident. To begin with, when he came back from the hospital, Jack seemed remote. He had been a chartered accountant, and though he was officially retired, he still kept two or three clients, mostly relatives. He had his own study on the ground floor, and next to that was the drawing-room, where children were not welcome. A separate staircase led to his bedroom, which connected to Jill's bedroom through a shared bathroom, and he and Jill ate their meals separately, so at first Alex did not see much of him.

The twins shared a small, chilly bedroom on the ground floor beyond the kitchen. For most of their teens they'd been relegated to an outside shed near the house. Jill insisted on calling it an annexe, but it was flimsily built and unheated, without power points or plumbing of any kind – spartan in the extreme.

Jack was every bit as grand as his wife. So grand, in fact, that his close friends dubbed him 'Lord' Dudley, a nickname he obviously relished. As the weeks passed and life at Duke's Cottage reverted to type, Alex discovered another aspect of his father's character: he was a bully. Jack had been instructed not to shout at Alex when he first came back from hospital, since raised voices distressed him so much, but Jack soon went back to his old ways. All his children were scared of his rages, though he never resorted to physical violence. He didn't need to. Jack Dudley's anger was terrifying enough without that.

And it wasn't just his family who feared him. Even his friends were wary of his caustic wit. Jill turned fear of her husband into a drama, a way to heap responsibility for everything negative onto his shoulders: for instance it was Jack's fault that the twins still didn't have keys to their own home. 'Don't make Daddy angry!' was a constant refrain.

At some stage, Alex discovered another aspect of his family's history: Jack Dudley, the man he and Marcus always referred to as Daddy, was not actually their father at all. He was their step-father and their mother was his fourth wife. Their real father had been a man called John Lewis who had been in a car accident when they were three weeks old. Apparently the fatal crash had happened when he had gone to pick up Alex from hospital. Marcus, who'd had some kind of infection, had not been well enough to go home, so he had stayed in the safety of the hospital, but Alex had been thrown from the car and fractured his skull. That was one of the reasons the hospital had been so concerned about his recent injury: it was a second trauma to his brain. The boys knew almost nothing about their real father, who had died in hospital a week after the collision: there was only one photograph, which showed a kindly, gentle-looking man, quite unlike the ferocious Jack. Jill never talked about him. And they never asked.

Gradually, Alex discovered that his family was as full of shadowy corners as the old, rambling house they had grown up in. They had a grandmother, Jill's mother, who lived in a huge house on the outskirts of Newbury. Granny and Jill were very close, though the old lady was a chilly and eccentric woman whose real passion was her dogs. She bred Chihuahuas and the house was full of small, excitable, noisy dogs – as many as sixty at any time – which she exhibited and doted on, dressing them up like dolls and lavishing her affection on them. Although most of the dogs were supposed to be confined to one section of the house, there were usually about six that were her particular pets, so the mayhem and the smell spread everywhere.

The twins' uncle was even more of a mystery. William was three years older than their mother, but a bitter feud existed between them. Jill and her mother had cut him out of the family years ago. William's annual attempt to talk to his sister on her birthday cast a shadow over the whole day. Sometimes he turned up at Duke's Cottage, but he was never allowed in. His five sons were also ostracised and Marcus and Alex were forbidden from contacting them.

On one occasion, when they were in their early twenties and happened to be at home for the weekend, Jill mentioned casually that one of their cousins had just died of a brain tumour.

'What happened? When is the funeral?'

Jill refused to tell them. She was surprised, then angry, at their concern. And as they had no way of contacting their uncle or their cousins, there was nothing they could do.

No reason was ever given for this hatred, though there was a rumour that William had, in some way, been responsible for their real father's death.

But how? John Lewis had died in a car accident. William had been nowhere near. How could he be blamed?

Don't ask.

Marcus and Alex knew instinctively that asking questions was off-limits. And Marcus was good at making the family stories entertaining.

For instance, he told Alex about one day when they must have been about thirteen. There'd been a ring at the door and he'd gone to answer it. A young woman holding a mixed-race baby stood outside and introduced herself. 'Hello. I'm your sister.'

Startled, but assuming it must be some kind of joke, Marcus went into the house and said to his parents, 'There's a woman at the door and she says she's my sister.'

'Ah yes,' said Jack calmly. 'That must be Molly.'

Molly turned out to have been the daughter of a woman Jack had been in love with just after the war. Her mother died when Molly was small, and after that she was cared for by her maternal grandparents and educated in a convent. She had become a nun herself as soon as she was old enough, and went out to Africa to work in a mission. After several years there, she had fallen in love with a local man and her little son was the result.

Jack was old-school enough to disapprove of a non-white grandson, though he blamed his outrage on the fact that his grandson was illegitimate – as was his daughter – and so Molly did not stick around for long. Before she went, she confided in Alex and Marcus that when she was a child in the convent her father saw her only twice a year, when he'd take her for tea at the Savoy. She thought he must have spent more on those expensive teas than he spent on her all the rest of the year.

Molly disappeared again, and for years they had no more contact with her.

Random comings and goings. Alex was finding it hard to piece it all together.

6

And Friends

O n Christmas Day 1982, five months after the accident, Alex put on a black tie and a dinner jacket. The whole family were dressed up in their formal clothes and assembled in the hall. They drove the short distance to a beautiful old house that belonged to close friends. Ian and Laura Hudson greeted Alex warmly, and Marcus seemed to be completely at home with the family.

Lunch was a formal affair for upwards of twenty people, all the men and boys in black tie, the women in silk and velvet. The alcohol flowed. After lunch there was the traditional game of charades which the whole extended Hudson family thoroughly enjoyed. The Duke's Cottage visitors were the audience; they laughed uproariously at everyone's attempts to mime words, but never joined in. None of them were comfortable with theatrical games. Like many people who grow up in families where dissembling is an everyday survival tool, they found play-acting for entertainment just about impossible.

In the evening, the Dudleys returned to Duke's Cottage; excessive alcohol never prevented them from getting behind the wheel of a car, though Jack had been convicted of driving while over the limit a while back, and had lost his licence for a year. Alex and Marcus stayed behind and played billiards with Ian and Laura's children, then stayed the night. This had been a family tradition for years.

Marcus explained to Alex that Ian and Laura had played a special role in their lives ever since Jill married again and came to live in Sussex. They had spent almost every weekend with the Hudsons, and they had provided them with a secure home-from-home. Alex soon discovered that if he needed advice, or even practical help, it was Ian and Laura he needed to turn to, not his parents.

And it wasn't just the Hudsons. One of Jack's oldest friends, Jack Brockway, and his second wife Deirdre, also gave sanctuary to the boys. Deirdre was a practical and generous Australian; she had no children of her own, but she adored arranging treats for Alex and Marcus. When they were younger she had taken them to see the Trooping of the Colour, and visited Hamleys with them on birthdays.

Gradually Alex was learning the characters in their world, but the process continued for years. Not a scrap of memory from his first eighteen years ever came back, and the gaps constantly had to be filled by Marcus. They lost count of the number of times they'd pause in a doorway before pressing the bell.

'Tell me again who we're visiting,' Alex would say.

Marcus would quickly give him a thumbnail sketch: names, ages, their connection, how they'd met. By the time the door opened, Alex would be able to greet their hosts like old friends. (Which, of course, is what they were.)

He was learning to cover up the memory loss, to say, 'Oh yes, I remember that!' when all he remembered was the account that Marcus had given him. But it was easier than having to explain his handicap all the time.

Alex was discovering that real affection and happiness were to be found away from his family circle. In the years leading up to his accident, he and Marcus had naturally been starting to stretch their wings, moving away from the people they now refer to as their 'guardian parents', the Hudsons and the Brockways. They'd established their own circle of friends. For most of their childhood they had been content with each other's company – Marcus'n'Ali, AlexandMarcus – but on New Year's Eve 1980, when they were both sixteen, a neighbour's son invited them to go with him to a large party a few miles away. It turned out to be a decisive event.

By this time they'd both bought mopeds with the money they'd made doing odd jobs in the village. They set off in the dark and arrived at a stunning Arts and Crafts house called Long Copse set on the side of an escarpment, with huge vistas across the countryside as far as the South Downs. Even better, from Marcus and Alex's point of view, the teenagers in the family – Sam and Ellen Handley – had the run of a cottage behind the house, and also a large barn, which was where the party was being held.

They made a dramatic entrance, two identically good-looking brothers with all the sophistication of teenagers who have got their own wheels before anyone else. Everyone was impressed by their self-assurance and their ability to get on equally well with adults and people their own age. The twin thing made it fun as well. The only way anyone could tell them apart was because they were wearing different ties, but halfway through the evening they switched. Or did they? No one could be absolutely sure.

The crowd of privileged youngsters at the party welcomed them into their circle of friends, and a new stage in their life began. Ric, Caz and Jo, together with Sam and Ellen, became central for them. The Handleys' house at Long Copse became a kind of refuge; Sue Handley thought nothing of setting one or two extra places at supper, and soon she was doing it more often than not.

When Alex had his accident, his friends were all understandably concerned. He had been going out with Caz, but her mother had died a few months before and her father moved away, so their relationship ended, though they remained friends. As soon as he was back on his feet, his friends carried on much as before, helped by the tricks Marcus and Alex were evolving to cover up the memory loss. When they gathered in the pub, Marcus made sure they didn't all talk at once, or play-fight, because that would upset him, and if he got too stressed Alex still went out cold. Some friends were anxious about his thinness and the way he sometimes seemed to lose the plot and not know what was going on, but they never guessed the full extent of his disabilities.

On the contrary, they soon realised there were advantages to this new changed Alex, who no longer drank very much. It made him an ideal designated driver when they all went out: the fact that he was still having occasional blackouts and had been advised not to drive for a bit was easily ignored, and often Alex was persuaded to remain at a party long after he would have preferred to leave, because his friends wanted him to ferry them home.

Now his friends are appalled to remember how they exploited his problem; partly it was just the normal callousness of teenagers to whom everything is pretty much a laugh. But partly they were taking their cue from Marcus and his family. If his own mother thought Alex was fine, then surely it was OK to assume that he was? And Alex relied on his friends. Even if their actions were sometimes thoughtless, they gave him the love and approval that was strangely lacking at home.

The summer of 1982, the summer of Alex's accident, was for many of their new friends their last summer at home: they would soon be leaving for university and the predictable ladder into the professions, medical school or the law, the City or teaching.

None of these options were available to the twins.

7

A Wasted Education

One of the difficult aspects of their childhood that Marcus could not possibly cover up was their lack of a proper education. They had gone briefly to a prep school in the village where they had struggled academically and had eventually been diagnosed as dyslexic.

This discovery coincided with a time of financial difficulty for the Dudleys, and it gave Jack the perfect excuse to remove them from private school and send them, at the age of eleven, to the local comprehensive. There they were put in the bottom stream and learned nothing at all. When they left at sixteen they were barely able to read and write. Marcus, who had most difficulty academically, had discovered that the one lesson where he could do well and earn praise was woodwork. He went to Godalming College and studied joinery and gained a single qualification: O-level Woodwork.

It might not have seemed like much at the time, especially not compared to their privately educated friends who were gathering impressive bundles of A levels, but Marcus had found something he could shine at. Until then, lessons had just confirmed his view of himself as crap at everything, especially when coupled with Jack's constant put-downs at home. Now, at last, there was a chance of doing well at something.

Alex was not yet prepared to give up entirely on school-work. In the years before the accident he had worked hard at sixth-form college, but to no real purpose. As Marcus says, 'He worked his arse off to see if he could pass any exams – and still didn't get any qualifications.' Alex moved into catering – he'd already worked on Saturdays in a nearby pub – and went to work at Bramley Grange. At the time of his accident, it looked as though being a waiter was the most he could hope for.

Dyslexia has had a massive impact all through their lives. It helped sour their relationship with Jack, for whom 'dyslexic' was just another word for stupid, and it corroded their self-confidence all through their formative years. Paradoxically, it was one of the reasons they gave such an assured impression when they roared up to the Handleys' New Year's Eve party. Marcus is clear that as dyslexics they'd become adept at glossing over their difficulties – both in the classroom and out of it. They either had to create a convincing façade or sink without trace – and they had no intention of doing that.

Their struggles with the written word made even the simplest tasks impossibly hard, and Marcus can still be reduced to tears of frustration when faced with a form to be filled in, or a sheet of instructions. To this day he maintains that dyslexia has been the single dominating fact of his life, far more damaging than anything else he's been through. But he is also the first to admit that there have been unexpected advantages: the conventional route was closed, which forced them to work harder, to take risks and to seize unexpected opportunities. Often with dramatic results.

But as Alex was readjusting to life after his accident, the future looked bleak. He was still at home, just when all his friends were heading off to university. He was dyslexic and he had no real marketable skills.

How was he ever going to make a life for himself?

8

The Gift of a Future

To be fair to her, Jill did make one attempt to get help for Alex, and it was to have far-reaching consequences.

'Come on, darling,' she announced one morning. 'We're going to see my friend Vivien. Maybe she can help you get your memory back.'

With no idea what to expect, Alex got into the car with his mother.

Vivien Kay was someone Jill had known off and on for years. When they first met, Vivien had been involved with horses, but now she had established herself as a healer. Admirers credited her with all manner of unusual powers, and it occurred to Jill that she might be able to hypnotise Alex into at least remembering who his own mother was. The rest of his memory loss she could live with, but his refusal to recognise her still felt like a rejection, and that was intolerable.

So they drove to Dorking, where Vivien was based. Alex was confused by everything. It was only a few months after his accident, and his whole life was still a hopeless muddle.

Both he and Vivien remember that first meeting vividly.

'He was completely out of control,' she says now of the traumatised eighteen-year-old who was brought in to her consulting room. 'He was literally lurching down the hallway, looking for the door, looking for the door handle, not wanting to do things wrong. Because there was a part of him missing.'

Vivien is a large, forceful woman with greying hair and a direct manner. A controversial figure, with no time for conventional therapeutic methods, she was to go on to play a critical part in the family's story. At that first meeting she noticed that Alex's face was convulsed by frequent uncontrollable spasms and she did a quick assessment. She did not try to hypnotise him, nor did she help him to recover his memory; instead, she did something that was perhaps even more important: she gave him hope. She let him know that he did have a future, that his life was going to get better, that he was going to achieve things and have a family of his own. For Alex, at that dark time, her confidence in him was a lifeline.

She sat with him for a while, as the images came into her mind, and then she did him a reading, predicting various events in his future. 'You will work at sea,' she told him. 'You and Marcus will have your own business by the time you're thirty, and you'll marry and have two children.' All that seemed impossible from where he was at the time, but Alex wrote it all down carefully on a scrap of paper.

On the drive back to Rudgwick, Alex and his mother didn't speak much. Maybe she was disappointed that he still couldn't remember anything. 'It's going to work out, Mum,' he told her and his new confidence seemed to cheer her up.

He says now, 'I held onto my piece of paper and kept it for the rest of my life.' It meant everything to him because, as he explains, 'in that state of mind you worry that it's going to happen again; that you'll fall over, hit your head.'

The familiar past that we all take for granted was a luxury Alex did not have. Always he was haunted by the fear he'd lose his memory again, and he started taking photographs of all the events in his life and sticking them in albums, a page for each month, an album for each year. There had been hardly any photographs from his childhood to help him fill in the gaps. Only one picture of his father, and hardly any of their life before they moved to Rudgwick; for Alex, taking photos and storing them felt like a kind of insurance. Gradually the fat albums stretched across his shelf. They were reassuring. Looking at them he knew that if he ever lost his memory again, he'd have a visual record to refer back to.

What is striking when one looks through those albums now is how filled with laughter and fun Alex's life appears. Every coloured snapshot shows him and his friends having a good time. They look like young people who have everything going for them and who know how to enjoy themselves. A circle of friends who lead a charmed life.

Anyone looking at the photo diaries would imagine that Alex and Marcus were a couple of privileged young men without any worries. There's no hint of the blank that formed Alex's inner world, or the fog of darkness that never cleared. And no hint either of the secrets that Marcus had locked away in the deepest recesses of his memory.

They look as if they had the world at their feet. And before too long, that was how it began to feel: they were about to spread their wings and explore. It was time for them to start to break away from their home and establish their independence.

But for Marcus and Alex this process was already complicated. They were identical twins: how do you separate yourself from someone who is in so many ways your mirror image? Now everything had been further complicated by Alex's accident, and his continuing dependence on Marcus. And for Marcus, the process of self-discovery was coloured by events of which Alex could not remember.

9
Gordon

On a Spring morning Marcus and his mother parked the car outside a standard industrial unit on the outskirts of Haslemere. Marcus, age eighteen, was nervous, dressed in his business suit and tie. Gordon Richardson, a cabinetmaker, wanted an apprentice; if Marcus got taken on, it would be his first real job.

The door opened and a man of about sixty with greying hair looked out. Marcus liked the look of him at once.

'Marcus Lewis?' he asked. 'Please come in.'

Gordon was somewhat taken aback when Jill swept into the office after her son and plonked herself down beside him. He was more surprised when the interview began.

He asked Marcus about his interest in carpentry.

'Oh, he loves wood!' declared Jill triumphantly, before Marcus had a chance to open his mouth.

'Ah, yes. Good. What sort of pieces have you made?' Again Gordon directed his question at Marcus.

'He's made lots of things,' Jill said. 'He's frightfully gifted. He's—'

'Mrs Lewis, do you think it would be possible for me to talk to your son on his own? If you wouldn't mind just waiting outside for a little while . . .'

Reluctantly, Jill was persuaded to retreat to the car. Alone together, Marcus and Gordon discovered they had a real rapport. Marcus showed him some of the pieces he had done at the college, and by the time he stood up to leave he knew he'd got the job.

Marcus had struck lucky. Quite simply, as he says now, 'Gordon changed my life.'

His new employer was an unusual man who had worked for many years in a senior position with a large multinational company, before changing direction entirely. Now he was devoting himself to his real passion, which was making fine furniture. Over the following years he shared his knowledge and love of cabinetmaking with his young apprentice.

It didn't stop there. Gordon was appalled by Marcus's ignorance – not just his problems with reading and writing.

'How can you not know about *any*thing?' he asked.

Radio 4 played all day in the workshop, and for Marcus it was a revelation. Politics, geography, literature, sociology, history and philosophy, it was all coming at him over the airwaves and he soaked it up. 'Radio 4 was a massive turning-point,' he says, the real start of his education. He discovered that Gordon was a sceptic, as he was himself, and their shared rationalism strengthened the bond between them.

It got better. When Marcus had been working with him for nearly two years, Gordon fell in love with a woman who just happened to be a gifted teacher. Gill was working with Vietnamese refugees, teaching them to read and write in English, but she soon realised that Gordon's young apprentice needed her help just as much as the refugees did, so she sat down and went through the basics with him. 'We started at the beginning,' says Marcus, 'all the "cat-sat-on-the-mat" stuff.'

And then, just when Marcus was beginning to grow in skill and real confidence, Gordon drew him aside.

'Gill and I are going to get married,' Gordon told him. 'We plan to move up to Scotland. I've found an old farm that I can do up, where I can have a workshop and a garden. We're leaving Haslemere.'

Marcus was dismayed. He loved his job, he loved Gordon and he loved the whole experience of being with them and broadening his mind. And now, just like that, it was all to be snatched away.

Gordon showed him a photograph of a tumbledown group of farm buildings, but Marcus was still finding it hard to take it all in.

Gordon said quietly, 'There's a lot of work to be done. It's just a wreck. Marcus, Gill and I would like you to come with us. It's a hell of a long way away, but you can live with us and help do the place up. That is, if you want to.'

It was an extraordinarily generous offer from a middle-aged couple who were still quite new to each other. In part it's a tribute not just to their big-heartedness, but also to Marcus himself, and his ability to slot into a family very different from his own. Looking back, Marcus thinks that Gordon was aware that there were problems at home, and was keen to get him away from the negative influence of his family.

His mind in turmoil, Marcus returned to Duke's Cottage.

'Mum, Gordon and Gill are going up to Scotland and they've invited me to go with them.'

Jill's response was unequivocal. 'How ridiculous! Of course you can't go. You have to stay at home.'

'But what can I do here?'

'You can find work in the village. Maybe one of the farmers needs help.'

Farming? Marcus didn't have to think it over for long. *Fuck it*, he thought, *I'm out of here.*

Jill was outraged, but he stuck to his guns.

Leaving Alex was not a problem. It was nearly two years since his accident and he was coping much better with daily practicalities. Their closeness was a continuous fact that he and Alex had always taken for granted, though they're aware that sceptics find it hard to accept; it was in no way dependent on seeing each other, or even talking. It was – and is – just a constant sense of connection.

Leaving Oliver and Amanda was more difficult. Marcus knew, as Alex did not, that the household was an unhealthy one for children, and he had to smother his feelings of guilt in order to make the break. But he had to get away.

Marcus packed his gear into his little Mini, said his good-byes and set off. The journey to Kirkudbrightshire took the whole day and Marcus remembers it as one of the most terrifying experiences of his early life.

The problem was his dyslexia. From Sussex to the Borders is a long journey under any circumstances, but for Marcus it was a nightmare. The work he'd done with Gill unravelled under pressure, and road signs became meaningless jumbles of lines and circles. One of his friends had made him a set of flashcards with the names of places along the way printed in clear letters.

He remembers that he had to keep 'pulling over on the motor-way and playing Snap with my flashcards,' trying to match the squiggles on the cards to the squiggles on the overhead signs. Sometimes the sign didn't match any of his cards, and then he'd have to drive blind until he found one he recognised.

Even when he arrived at the right village, his troubles were still not over. He saw an elderly man in rough clothes and pulled to a stop.

'Excuse me, I'm looking for a little farm called Barlochan. You wouldn't happen to know it, would you?' he asked politely.

The man nodded and 'Caneeahseeahochahoochahhahnoo!' came out of his mouth. Marcus stared at him blankly before driving on. The same thing happened with the next person he asked. 'I thought, where the hell am I? None of these people even speak English!' He found Gordon's farm eventually, but it was a while before he learned to make sense of the local accent.

In some ways, living with Gordon and Gill in Palnackie was like being on a retreat. The girl he'd been involved with visited a couple of times, but it was such a long way from Sussex that the relationship ran out of steam. Most of the time it was just Marcus and the Richardsons, and that suited him fine. For the first time in his life he was living in a proper home, with adults who treated him both as an adopted son and as an adult.

He and the Richardsons spent the first four months work-ing on the garden: they cleared away tons of rubbish, created a rock garden, planted dozens of trees, made dry-stone walls. When they started on the buildings, Marcus worked alongside

Gordon and learned all the skills that would stand him in such good stead in the future: plumbing, roofing, tiling, plastering and decorating, as well as the fine cabinet work he was already becoming accomplished at. And in the evenings there would be books and discussion. Secure with his adopted family, for two years he blossomed.

And then, suddenly, it was over. One evening when their work was done, Gordon sat him down. 'You need to move on, Marcus,' he told him. 'You can't stay with us for ever. It's not right. It's time you tried something different.'

Marcus was devastated.

'What have I done wrong?' he kept asking. 'Why do you want to get rid of me?'

Gordon and Gill told him repeatedly that they were far from wanting to be rid of him, but they could see that for his own sake he needed a new challenge. Marcus couldn't accept this. It was years before he realised they'd been telling him the truth: that they were turning him out into the world for his sake, not theirs.

He loaded up his Mini once again and drove south. Miserably he went over and over in his mind what he could possibly have done to make them reject him.

But as the years went by, the bond with Gordon and Gill never wavered. They continued to be the mum and dad Marcus had always longed for, and today Marcus's children call the elderly couple in Kirkcudbrightshire Granny and Granddad. Visits to the house and garden that Marcus helped to create, and to see the hundreds of saplings he planted now tall trees, are a regular treat for his family.

10

Morels

This time it was Alex in suit and tie, driving through the Sussex countryside with his mother. It was only a year since his accident, and he was still confused, still pretty much doing whatever was expected of him, without the resources to make any real decisions for himself. 'I've got you a job interview,' Jill had announced that morning. 'So you'd better look smart.'

They parked outside a restaurant in Haslemere called Morels. Jill swept Alex inside and greeted the owners, a French couple called Jean Yves and Mary-Anne.

'This is my son, Alex,' she told them airily. 'And I want you to give him a job.'

Which they did. Now, Alex thinks it was because they thought he was a member of the aristocracy. Morels was one of the leading restaurants in Surrey; Jill and her friends often ate there and their table was always booked in the name of 'Lord' Dudley. To them it was a joke, but not one the Morels were in on.

'They were expecting me to be the honourable something or other,' says Alex. He liked the Morels straight away; when he realised the job came with accommodation, the prospect was even more appealing. He'd be able to leave home. His mother hadn't figured that out when she took him along for the interview, and she was none too pleased that he was about to fly the coop for a second time, but it was too late for her to back out now. Marcus was still working with Gordon nearby.

Alex started work right away. Naturally, Jill had not mentioned either his dyslexia or his memory loss, and nor had he; but it meant he had to work twice as hard as anyone else if he was going to keep his double handicap hidden. He was still suffering the after-effects of his accident: apart from the single fact of knowing who Marcus was, no memories had come back from his first eighteen years, but more troubling were some of the strange mental sensations, like falling, like spinning, like losing control, that he never spoke about. He'd tried talking about it once to Marcus, but his twin had been embarrassed, thought he was being weird, so Alex kept quiet. Sometimes he feared he might be going crazy.

Covering up the dyslexia was hard enough. It was a struggle just to read the menu, and the labels on the wine bottles were often incomprehensible. He had to devise strategies for coping.

When he was with customers, he scribbled their orders onto a notepad, and once he was safely back in the kitchen he retreated to a corner and copied the order down from the menu on a fresh piece of paper. He chucked the rough version in the bin and gave the correct one to the chef. It was time-consuming, but as a dyslexic he was used to having to work harder than anyone else to achieve the same results.

The memory loss had to be hidden as well. One of the reasons the Morels had taken him on was because he knew many of his customers, local folk who were part of the Dudleys' social set.

Or rather, they knew him.

Alex, of course, didn't recognise anyone, but he quickly learned the art of pretence. A couple would come in through the door and exclaim, 'Alex, how lovely! We saw your parents only last week!'

And Alex, who had not the faintest idea who they were, would greet them like old friends and then quickly check their names on the reservation list so he was able to carry on the charade. It was exhausting, but it worked.

He and Marcus had always done it. All identical twins know the routine. A total stranger comes up to you in the street and embraces you like an old friend. Explaining they've got the wrong twin takes time and often causes embarrassment, so it's often simpler just to say, 'Oh hi! And how are you? Yes, all fine . . . see you around.' And continue on your way.

About six months after he'd started work at Morels he was on a zebra crossing when he bumped, quite literally, into a girl with ginger hair. He apologised and was about to move on when she exclaimed, 'You're Alex! We were at college together.'

'Oh yes, I remember you now,' said Alex, feigning delight, though of course so far as he was concerned she was a complete stranger.

They chatted for a while, then met up again a day or so later. Her name was Katrina and she was working in a flower shop nearby. After a while, pretence was impossible: he admitted to her, in confidence, that he'd lost his memory completely and explained how difficult that made everything. She accepted it all, which meant a lot to him. They started going out and stayed together for a couple of years, eventually getting a flat together. 'Katrina was important in my life,' says Alex now. 'The first serious girlfriend, the first person I lived with. A lot of firsts.' Years later, when her first son was born, she asked Alex to be his godfather.

In lots of ways, his time at Morels was positive and enjoyable. He was away from Duke's Cottage for the first time that he could remember, he was finding his feet in the outside world, and he was with a group of people with whom he got on well. Every evening the staff sat down and had a meal together before the first customers arrived, a relaxed and sociable interlude before the evening's work. Alex had money of his own and was beginning to feel the first stirrings of freedom.

But under the surface, he existed in a kind of no-man's-land that he had no way of explaining, even to himself. He felt strange, different from how he imagined 'normal' people must feel. Something was holding him back and stopping him from letting go and enjoying himself the way other people seemed to, but he had no way of understanding where these disturbing sensations came from, or what they meant. All the superficial laughter and the fun was shot through with something bleaker. 'I was just existing. It was a sort of limbo. I went to work, went to parties, met people. But nothing had much meaning to it.'

He covered it well, but those years were, for him, quite dead in terms of feelings or emotion.

At work, no one guessed what he was battling with. He was promoted to maître d', meeting and greeting people and making them welcome. It helped that he had lived and socialised with the kind of people who formed the clientele and, as he says, 'knew what they were about', even if their names and faces meant nothing to him.

Less helpful was the fact that Jill continued to visit Morels with Jack and their friends. After a few drinks, her distinctive flutey voice could be heard all over the restaurant. 'This is my son!' she wanted everyone to know. 'Isn't he wonderful? Look how well he's doing! Alex, darling, you're amazing!' She made a huge fuss of him and, not surprisingly, he found the attention deeply embarrassing. Still, he knew there was no way of stopping her. With Jill, you just had to laugh and pretend you thought it was funny.

A more rewarding customer was Lawrence Portet, Captain of the *Queen Elizabeth II*. Over several visits, Alex got to know him and his wife, and on one occasion mentioned that he'd like to work on the ship. Captain Portet didn't say anything at the time, but when he came back a month later, he asked Alex if he had been serious.

'About what?' asked Alex, who had forgotten their earlier conversation.

'About working on my ship.'

'Well, yes. I am.'

Captain Portet pulled out a business card, scribbled a name on the back and told Alex to write to the person on the card and mention his name.

Alex debated for a while: he was happy at Morels, but the

QE2 would be a whole new adventure. He phoned Marcus in Scotland and his twin encouraged him to go for it. As so often, he turned to family friend Laura Hudson for advice, and she helped him draw up a CV and an accompanying letter. He went for an interview and the following day was informed he'd got the job.

One of Vivien's predictions was about to come true.[2] And working at sea would give Alex his first real taste of freedom.

2 About half her predictions were right, the others were either wrong or have not materialised yet.

11

The QE2

T he moment he stepped on board the *QE2*, Alex entered a strange and exotic world. A quarter of a mile long, the luxury liner carried 2,000 passengers who were looked after by 2,000 staff. There were four restaurants for the guests and Alex was put to work in the second one, 'Tables of the World'. The waiters worked in pairs and each pair covered eight tables. To begin with, Alex found it a real struggle. Under pressure, his memory often let him down, and when he got into a muddle, some of his fellow staff members laughed at him, which he hated. But he was determined to stick it out, and life improved once he was paired with Frank, an old hand who had worked on liners for many years.

Frank took Alex under his wing and showed him how it all worked. As Frank wanted an easy life, Alex did all the running back and forth to the kitchens while his partner tended the diners.

Frank was straight, but three-quarters of the staff on board were gay. Jill had warned Alex that this might be a difficulty for him. It was Alex's first exposure to a gay community and to begin with he found the frequent overtures problematic. He could not remember ever having to fend off this kind of unwanted attention, though he learned quickly how to handle it. After a little while he found a group of like-minded friends to hang out with during his free time, and things improved.

In the windowless bowels of the ship below the waterline, the staff had their own community: cinemas, pubs, gyms, canteens, even a morgue and a tiny prison. There were huge and frequent parties, with a great deal of dressing up. As Alex says, 'I've lived *Priscilla Queen of the Desert* on a major scale. It was a real eye-opener.' It was also a big drinking culture, but Alex had to be careful. The head injury – which, of course, he never mentioned – meant he could only drink in moderation.

The routine was eight weeks working followed by four weeks off. The company flew them back to the UK from whichever port they had docked at when their eight weeks were over. After his first break, Alex realised that the real money was to be made from tips, and to get those Frank told him he needed a gay partner in the dining room. Being a waiter on a liner like the *QE2* was a totally different deal from working in a restaurant on land: as each pair was looking after the same group of people three times a day for five or ten days at a time, providing a good show was as important as serving food. And at cabaret, the gays had the edge. So Alex teamed up with a waiter called Ginella (real name: David) and while Alex scurried back and forth to the kitchen, Ginella put on an extravagant show for the guests at their tables. The tips rolled in.

During the eight weeks of work, the hours were long, but Alex was used to hard work, and he enjoyed being so far from home. More importantly, this was a job he'd got for himself.

As he says, 'I wasn't beholden to my parents for the first time. They couldn't get to me.' On the ship, there was no chance of them turning up and embarrassing him in front of the other guests.

Thanks to all the cash tips, Alex and his friends from the ship enjoyed themselves whenever the *QE2* pulled into port and they had time on shore. They had the money to do what they wanted; they hired luxury cars and boats, and once they even organised a helicopter. They tried out jet-skis and speed-boats, zipping in and out of far-flung ports.

Being away for such long periods put an impossible strain on Alex's relationship with Katrina and it soon fizzled out, though they remained friends. Still, there was plenty of fun to be had with four weeks of shore leave. As soon as he got back to England after a couple of months on board, Alex would dump his kit at Duke's Cottage and head off to London to hang out with his friends. Most of the Long Copse crowd were students by now; there was always a spare bed or a bit of floor for him to crash on and they were always delighted to see him. If Marcus was around, then so much the better.

One of Alex's most vivid memories from the *QE2* is of the passengers the staff nicknamed 'jumpers'. Luxury liners are apparently a popular destination for would-be suicides, especially when the cruise was scheduled to pass through the warm waters of the Caribbean. The staff all knew what it meant when the ship abruptly tilted strongly to the right. It would stay that way for quite some time as the huge ship turned to go back the way it had come.

The first time it happened, Alex was shocked. He ran to the side to peer over the rail into the darkness to see if he could spot the unfortunate woman in the churning water below. By law, the captain was obliged to turn the boat around and search for the jumper, but it was always hopeless. As Alex says, if someone leaps into the water from the decks, fourteen floors up, they get sucked under by the ship's wash the moment they hit the ocean. Besides, the *QE2* is so vast it takes 12 miles for it to turn around 180 degrees. In time, Alex grew more blasé, but never to the extent of the old hands.

On one occasion, as he remembers with amusement, Frank was serving a table of New Yorkers when the ship suddenly listed hard to the right. A woman in the party asked, 'Frank, what's happening?'

Suave as ever, Frank said, 'That would be a jumper, madam,' and then, without missing a beat: 'More peas?'

Today Alex laughs when he recalls this exchange. But there were times throughout those apparently contented and busy years when, without ever being able to explain his unhappiness, he himself experienced an almost overwhelming urge to join the jumpers leaping into oblivion.

12

The University of Travel

Marcus got straight to the point. 'Come and join me,' he said. 'I'm in Australia. You'll love it here.'

Marcus had been travelling for nearly a year when he contacted his twin. He'd set off with the Hudsons' daughter Julia, who was almost like a sister, and they'd spent a couple of months on a kibbutz. Then they'd followed the *Lonely Planet* trail through India, Thailand and Indonesia, having amazing adventures along the way, and finally settled in Sydney. Julia was ready to head back to the UK via the States to be with her boyfriend, but Marcus had got the travel bug and had no intention of going home yet. He was finding ways to support himself, and he was gaining in experience and confidence all the time.

Besides, there was nothing to tempt him home. For most people, leaving the security of their family and travelling across the world is scary as well as exciting; for Marcus it was home that had always been unsettling. Some of his adventures along the route had been life-threatening – like the time the driver lost control of his bus on a perilous mountain road in China and smashed into the rock face – but he was enjoying himself, and relishing the chance to share the lives of people so different from those he'd grown up with, both the locals whose world he glimpsed as he travelled, and the young westerners he met along the way.

Alex left the *QE2* in the autumn of 1986 when all the staff were sent home while the liner was converted from steam to diesel. Marcus didn't want Alex to get drawn back into the Duke's Cottage world. He wanted him to discover for himself the excitement and challenge of travel. And though since his accident he had never been as adventurous as Marcus, Alex agreed to join his twin in Sydney.

They were as far from Rudgwick as it is possible to be on this planet, and their enormous capacity for enjoyment had full rein. Both had secrets they could share with no one else, not even with each other, but it didn't stop them from having good times whenever they could. Life was for living, and they intended to live it to the full.

There was so much to explore. Alex says now, 'People ask, "Did you go to university?" And I say, "No. We went travelling." Call it what you like, this was our university. Discovering our boundaries and possibilities.'

Jill and Jack never helped out financially, so once the money the twins had saved ran out, they had to find ways to support themselves. And here, their dyslexia was both a hindrance and a spur to branching out. Unlike their friends, they were unable to get office work, so to begin with they worked in factories, as labourers or in restaurants. The twins both took long hours in their stride. Often they were working two jobs, one by day and another in the evening.

But when Marcus went to New Zealand, to work in

Auckland, he had a flash of inspiration that led to the first of their entrepreneurial schemes.

His Swedish girlfriend, Sophie, and her friends were all long-haired blondes, but in New Zealand they couldn't find the cloth-covered hairbands they used to tie back their hair. The next time Marcus was in Australia, he tracked down a woman who manufactured these hairbands and bought up her entire stock. He emptied his rucksack, filled it with hairbands, with just a couple of T-shirts on top in case customs got curious, and then headed back to New Zealand, where he laid out his wares on a colourful sarong on the pavement. Business was brisk. He'd bought them for a dollar each and sold them for two.

He phoned Alex. 'Get all the cash you can scrape together, go and find the hairband lady and buy up as many as you can. Forget clothes, just fill your rucksack with hairbands and come on out.'

Alex did, and the 'Hairband Twins', as they were known, soon became a familiar sight on the corner of the Auckland street. Their mother had always been a brilliant saleswoman, and Marcus could remember watching her on her stall in Portobello Road on Saturdays all his life. He'd heard the patter and absorbed her technique, and now he put it to good use. They sold thousands of them, and their hairband money financed their travels for more than a year.

But first, there was one ambition they wanted to fulfil: they were longing to go white-water rafting along the famous Shotover River. The best company was very expensive and they were reluctant to blow all their hard-earned cash on a single trip. So they went to the organiser with a proposition: if they filled a tour, could they go for free? The manager said, 'You've got to fill three tours first.' OK then. They went back onto the street, spent a few days signing punters up for the trips and got their two free places.

The trip began with a breathtaking journey up the steeply wooded gorge in a tiny helicopter. They donned helmets and life jackets, listened to the instructions and set off in two eight-man canoes. It was exhilarating, thrilling and exhausting – all they'd hoped for.

It wasn't until the journey was complete that disaster struck.

Having reached the calm water at the end of the run, Alex and some of the others took off their helmets, plunged into the river and swam in the placid water near the canoe. Alex floated a bit further than the others, and the next thing he knew he was being dragged under the surface by a hidden eddy. His head hit a submerged rock and he blacked out.

The current dragged him downstream for a hundred metres before anyone could reach him. He was unconscious when they pulled him out; his heartbeat had dropped to almost nothing. The organiser panicked and was running to call an air ambulance.

'No!' shouted Marcus. 'You don't have to do that. He's going to be all right. Trust me.' He straddled Alex's stomach and pressed hard. 'Come back, Ali!'

Alex choked, spewed up river water and opened his eyes.

'There,' said Marcus. 'I told you he was all right.'

Alex was still spluttering and shaky.

'Are you sure?' everyone wanted to know. 'Don't you think we should call a doctor to check him over?'

But as far as Marcus was concerned, the drama was over and of no further interest. And as soon as Alex could struggle to his feet, he agreed. The enduring closeness between the twins has never involved any kind of mollycoddling, none of the usual 'Are you OK?'s or 'Can I help?'s, and sometimes it can seem to outsiders that the twins are almost callous with each other.

Alex has banged his head and almost drowned? So what, he's fine again now. Let's go and have a drink.

Marcus gashes his hand open on a piece of glass? Here, wrap a bit of cloth round it and come and help me carry this wood.

They're tough on themselves and tough on each other. For them, it's the same thing.

After the rafting trip, they headed off in different directions for a while. For both of them, but more especially for Marcus, it was vital that each twin should forge their own trail.

One day when they had been travelling round New Zealand in opposite directions and out of touch for several weeks, Marcus got a lift into a small town in the North Island called Rotorua. He'd never been there before, but as soon as he arrived in Rotorua, he walked the short distance to the bus stop and sat down, because, as he says, 'I knew Alex was going to get off the bus.'

And sure enough, after half an hour, a bus trundled in from the opposite direction, the door opened, and Alex stepped down. Marcus said a brief hello and they went off to get a drink together. Neither of them were the least bit surprised at the time, but years later Marcus remembered that day and wondered, 'Why did I think *for a minute* he was going to get off that bus?' When it happened, however, there had been no conscious thought. It just happened.

Not long afterwards, they left New Zealand and went their separate ways. Marcus was bolder, keener to step off the beaten track: he travelled extensively through China and discovered that there his dyslexia did not seem to be an issue. In fact he found Chinese pictograms more comprehensible than his more academic friends did. It was a revelation, and a great boost to his confidence. 'As a dyslexic, you're always one step behind everyone else. In China, I was one step ahead.'[3]

In China and Tibet, Marcus had extraordinary adventures and for long periods of time he was able to forget all about Duke's Cottage, his family and the secrets he kept locked away. Thanks to his travels, he gained an understanding of other lifestyles; he spent several weeks living simply with a family in a remote part of Nepal, and then in Tibet he travelled with a group of Buddhist monks, sharing their hardships. These were all experiences that were to serve him well when, ten years later and on another continent, he embarked on the extraordinary project that was to become the twins' greatest achievement to date.

For Alex, not surprisingly, travel was more of a challenge. His courage was of a different order: doubly handicapped by memory loss and dyslexia, knowing he could black out at the most inconvenient of moments, he had to draw on reserves of

3 Although dyslexia is not unknown in China, it is far less common. And dyslexics rarely find their condition a handicap to learning Chinese as a foreign language.

courage most of us never need. And to some extent, he was living a lie. His girlfriend during this period had no idea about the accident or its consequences. On the rare occasions that anyone asked him about his childhood, he recycled Marcus's memories as if they were his own.

Most of the time he travelled alone. Since the accident, he'd been anxious around strangers; now he had to learn to be more outgoing. As he says, 'You'd be on your own, arriving in a hotel in Delhi, for instance, full of backpackers your age.' He found that pretty daunting. He'd have to find his way about, then go to the bar and 'hold your breath and go in and talk to someone. Otherwise you'd be on your own.' He and Marcus, like many twins, loathe solitude. 'You can't be on your own,' he says. 'It's just not something you do.'

Friendships made on the road led to unlikely opportunities. In a run-down hotel in Hong Kong, Marcus bumped into a friend he'd met in Tibet called Migo, who suggested he might want to work for a while in films. Why not?

Their first film was supposedly set in Vietnam, with Marcus and his friends David Clark and Robert Nias cast as a trio of American soldiers on patrol. When they were shot, they had been instructed to detonate the pigs' blood capsule strapped to their chests and fall down dead. They decided to see who could spin out his death throes for the longest time. The shot rang out, the pigs' blood exploded with a mass of fake gore and they staggered in circles. They stumbled to their knees, got up again and pirouetted slowly, then staggered some more, until the irate director screamed, 'Cut! *You die more quickly!*' Shaking with laughter, they all stood up, and the sequence had to begin again. But they had worked out that after a certain period in a film, they couldn't be fired without huge expense, so they continued to milk their death agonies to the full, and dubbed their hapless director 'Mr You-Die-More-Quickly'.

Next came a ninja movie. For the flying scenes, Marcus was strapped into a harness on the end of a rope that was slung over the branch of a tree. At their cue, a dozen strong men hauled on the other end of the rope so that he whizzed up into the tree. A mattress was strapped to the trunk to cushion the impact, but sometimes the mattress was in the wrong place and then, '*Whack!*' says Marcus. 'You'd hit the tree.'

Dying grunts and flying ninja: Marcus was up for any adventure on offer.

13

Breakaway

It's one thing to break away from home by travelling across the globe; it's quite another to break with old habits of compliance and avoiding confrontation, of being dutiful sons and seeking approval.

Dawn was just spreading across the sky as Marcus and Alex walked to the children's playground near their lodgings in the Redfern district of Sydney. Alex was unhappy, but resigned. No one was about and the playground was empty, so they sat down on a couple of swings. It seemed like their travels were at an end.

'We'll have to go home,' Alex said. 'They're both ill and they need us to look after them. We can't just abandon them. We don't have any choice.'

'Why not?'

'They need us.'

'No, they need a nurse, not us.'

Jill had contacted them that morning. Jack had just been discharged from hospital; she was having trouble with her hips and couldn't manage his care. She told them their adventures were over and they were needed at Duke's Cottage. 'Come back at once,' she insisted.

'Why?' asked Marcus again. 'They wouldn't do it for us if it was the other way round. You know they wouldn't. And they haven't even offered to pay our fare!'

'They probably can't afford it,' said Alex. 'You know how tight money always is at home.'

'That's bollocks,' said Marcus. 'They live in a bloody great house; Amanda and Oliver go to private school. Daddy buys expensive wines whenever he wants. They can spend money if they want to. If they need nursing, then they will have to hire a nurse who can do the job properly.'

'But we can't just say no.'

'We have to, Ali. We're happy here. We've got jobs, we've got girlfriends. This is our life. Our one chance. If we go back now, that's it. One-way ticket. We'll get sucked back in to Duke's Cottage and working for them all the time and our travelling will be over.'

'They're our parents,' said Alex. But his statement lacked conviction. While they'd been travelling, they'd had a chance to see how other families operated. At the beginning of their time in Australia, the Hudsons had flown out to visit them and Julia. At the time it was so unlike anything that Jill or Jack would do that the twins were amazed. Still, they were beginning to see that their parents did things differently from most people's.

Back and forth they debated. Alex was racked with guilt. The thought of his parents in pain and struggling to cope made him want to give up everything and get a flight back to England, but deep down, he recognised that Marcus was on to something.

'If we go back now,' said Marcus, 'God only knows how long we'll be stuck in Duke's Cottage working as their unpaid skivvies. We have to say no.'

'Are you sure, Marky?'

'One hundred per cent.'

'OK then.'

They slid off the swings, went to the payphone and dialled the number. They could hear the phone ringing in Duke's Cottage, then Jill's familiar voice answering.

'Mum? It's Marcus. Ali and I have made up our minds. We're not coming back. Not yet at any rate.'

'What? I don't believe it! You *must* come back. We need you!'

'No, you don't. You can hire a nurse. If Daddy needs proper care, a nurse will know what to do better than we would.'

'This is outrageous. Come home at once!'

'Sorry, Mum. We're staying put.'

'Don't you dare. Just do what we tell you!'

Marcus put down the phone.

Alex felt bad about it for days, but even so, this first act of deliberate rebellion felt to him like 'a light-bulb moment'. Guilt was not a problem for Marcus. His life was just starting to open up. He was spreading his wings, and gaining in confidence all the time. And, as he says now, the decision was easier for him because he was privy to information that was hidden from his twin.

What neither of them knew was how their decision would affect Amanda. Their sister was thirteen years old at the time. Oliver was away at boarding school and for most of the time she was alone in the house with her parents and utterly miserable. The prospect of having her big brothers come back had been keeping her going. When they wrote and confirmed that, contrary to Jill's instructions, they were staying where they were, she was desperately disappointed and seriously considered ending it all.

The twins' freedom came with a high price in other, more obvious ways. Some months later, Alex was alone in Kuala Lumpur when a bank delay meant he ran out of money. His wallet empty, he had no cash at all. It was the scariest experience he'd had in all the years of travelling. He was completely alone and destitute in a strange city, with not even the money for a phone call. In desperation, he went to a phone box and asked the operator to put a reverse-charge call through to Duke's Cottage, so he could ask for a temporary loan. He heard Jack pick up the phone.

'Hello, I have a reverse-charge call for you from Kuala Lumpur. Will you accept the call? Your son says he has no money and is sleeping on the street.'

Jack didn't hesitate. He didn't even tell Jill. He just said, 'No, I'm not interested. I'm not accepting the call.'

The line went dead.

Alex was forced to spend several nights sleeping on the streets of Kuala Lumpur with the beggars. Or rather *not* sleeping, because he was terrified someone would steal his rucksack. One day some tourists he met took pity on him and gave him food. All the while he was incredulous, hurt and angry to think his parents were callous enough to let him remain alone and hungry and in danger on the street.

The situation was resolved when he phoned the Hudsons. Ian instantly accepted the call, and said, 'Yes, of course. I'll get it off to you right away. Are you sure you're all right?' He wired out the money without delay.

The contrast with his own parents' behaviour could not have been more stark. Normal parents. Normal behaviour. Why weren't Jill and Jack like that?

14

Twin Decs

By the end of 1987 they were both ready to come back to England, but they did not return empty-handed. Marcus travelled to China on a 'luxury' liner – all flaking tiles and peeling paint – with his friends Dave and Jo. He bought up as many quilted jackets as he could take with him and took the Trans-Siberian Railway back, arriving just in time to spend Christmas with friends in London. Meanwhile Alex had found a shop in Jakarta selling beautiful batiks; he got the owner to put up the closed sign, bought up the entire stock and shipped it home. Once back in England, they sold the batiks and Chinese goods in Camden market for a good profit. Then they looked around for another way to support themselves.

They travelled down to Duke's Cottage and visited their parents. Oliver and Amanda were overjoyed to see them. As usual, anything remotely unpleasant was glossed over. No one mentioned their decision not to come home, nor the fact that there'd been no communication for months, nor the way that Jack had refused to take Alex's call. Get on and deal. Don't talk about it. Let's just have a drink and a laugh.

And Jill put her contacts to good use. One of her old flames offered them his Chelsea flat for a peppercorn rent, but in return he wanted them to decorate it. He'd always been kind to them, and they stayed in his flat till his death. It became another of the party houses that they and their friends had all over London. The twins partied hard and they worked hard.

Their friends, the Brockways, who had enjoyed treating them when they were children, asked them to decorate their house. By the time the work was done they realised this was something they could do well, and also, as Marcus says, that 'people loved having us do their houses because we were posh.' One could add: hardworking, reliable and entertaining as other factors in their favour. But their next commission ended in disaster.

John Scot was another friend of their mother's; he'd bought a string of properties in Notting Hill Gate in the fifties at a knockdown price. One of his houses needed decorating and Alex and Marcus agreed to do the work. John insisted they write a proper quote before he gave them the job. A friend helped them draw it up, and, as they were keen to get the job, they pitched the bill for their time quite low. When the decoration was done, they handed him the first invoice, and then a second one to cover all the paint, wallpaper and equipment they'd bought.

John Scot was not impressed. 'No, boys,' he said. 'That was included in your quote. You need to learn this lesson. *That* is what you quoted and *that* is what I'm paying.'

As Alex says, 'We walked out of there with our tails between our legs.' They'd lost money on the job and realised they needed to be more professional. In fact, they were grateful to John for the lesson. 'Tough love,' Marcus calls it, adding, 'We never made another mistake with a quote.' They continued to work for him over the years as jobs came up.

They called their business 'Twin Decs'. They bought a van and painted their name on the side, which provided unforeseen benefits: occasionally, when visiting Glastonbury, they were mistaken for DJs and waved in without charge. They worked hard and Twin Decs built up a good reputation.

Even Jack Dudley was impressed with their achievement. One morning when they happened to pass him in the hallway at Duke's Cottage, he said briefly, 'You've done well, boys. I'm proud of you.'

The comment was made almost casually, but Alex and Marcus 'took it in and held on to it'. They'd been waiting for his praise since he first became their 'Daddy', when they were barely eight years old, and those few words meant a huge amount to them both. Especially now that he was dying.

It was prostate cancer. Jack had always loathed doctors and hospitals and had suffered in silence for months; by the time the cancer was diagnosed it was virtually untreatable. His fingers and toes swelled so much he needed help with dressing and undressing. Alex and Marcus helped him whenever they were at Duke's Cottage. The rest of the time it was left to Jill. In spite of all their rows, the couple kept a bond of affection and she nursed him devotedly. At least, it looked that way. As Marcus says, with Jill it was always impossible to know how much was done for show, and how much was sincere. She was an infinitely complex person.

As was Jack. In the final weeks he could no longer climb the stairs and slept in a bed in his drawing-room. He began to express remorse to Jill for his harshness towards her. Alex and Marcus happened to be visiting just before he was admitted to a hospice near Horsham. To everyone's amazement, he demanded that the local vicar come to visit. Apart from weddings and funerals he'd never gone to church, but now he wanted to unburden himself.

The priest arrived. 'I've been a bad man,' Jack told him bluntly. 'I want to confess my sins before I die. I don't want to go to hell.'

The study door closed on the two men, and no one heard what passed between them. Alex and Marcus reflected that perhaps Jack's fear of hell was not so out of character after all. In spite of his academic achievements and his sharp intelligence, he had always had a superstitious streak. Marcus told Alex about the occasion, before they bought Duke's Cottage, when he'd refused to get out of the car to view a property. 'I'm not going in,' he said. 'It feels bad. I know it's haunted.'

What were the misdeeds that were weighing so heavily on Jack's conscience as he prepared for the end? Was he regretting his unkind treatment of Jill's twin sons, or perhaps his neglect of the motherless daughter he'd abandoned to the nuns?

He died in a hospice near Horsham. When he'd been laid out the family were told they could say a final farewell. Alex was deeply moved, and went to sit beside the body for a while, and before he left, he kissed the cold face of the old man who had been such a scourge while he was still alive.

Marcus refused to go into the room. He may have made a show of sorrow, for his mother's sake, but all he felt at Jack's passing was a profound sense of relief.

15

Masonic Funeral

Jack's death was to be a revelation in several ways.

They had always known he was a Freemason. Lodge visits were a regular feature of his week. But they had never realised what an important figure he was in the Masonic world. The Masons took over the organisation of his funeral, though in fact every detail had been planned by Jack himself. When the day came, family and friends, including Jill and her children, were ushered into a side aisle, leaving the main part of the church available for the Masons.

Ian Hudson, one of Jack's closest friends, remembers, 'I almost felt out of it! 80% of the people there were Masons.' There were so many that they took up the whole central area of the church, ranked in order of seniority. Alex and Marcus watched with fascination as leading figures from public life, men they'd seen on the television news, walked solemnly into the church and took their seats.

The funeral address, which Jack had apparently written himself, was given by Tommy Johnson, a wine-seller friend who had occasionally travelled to the Continent with Jack on cooking holidays. He emphasised the central place of Masonry in Jack's life. 'After his family,' he told the congregation, 'the most valuable element in his life was being a Mason . . . He was a member of many Lodges and other Masonic bodies, and if I single out the Imperial Mark Lodge (of which he was secretary for over twenty years) it is because this Lodge seemed most exactly to reflect his temperament.' The speaker also commented that although Jack was likeable and much loved by his friends, 'he could on occasion be difficult, even awkward . . . He seemed almost to thrive on abuse.'

A curious way for a man to want to be remembered at his own funeral.

At the end of the service, the coffin was taken away by the Masons while the family returned to Duke's Cottage for the wake. As Alex says, 'Daddy went left and we went right.'

The second revelation was that at Duke's Cottage everything continued much as before. Ever since they could remember – and for Alex, of course, that was only since he was eighteen – Jill had portrayed her husband as the bogeyman who insisted on all the rules and restrictions that had governed their lives.

But after Jack's death, the twins still weren't allowed a key for the front door and they still weren't able to visit without making an 'appointment'. This had become an iron rule. Alex remembers an earlier occasion when he drove down from London, arriving about eleven o'clock. The lights were still on when he knocked, but his parents refused to open the door because they said he hadn't made an appointment. He had to sleep in the car and was only allowed to enter the house the following morning.

The blame for these restrictions had always been put firmly on Jack. It was Jack who wouldn't let them have a key; Jack who got upset if they turned up without an appointment. Everything bad was due to Jack.

But even now that he was dead, nothing changed.

If anything, with Jack no longer there to restrain her, Jill's behaviour became even more eccentric. She found it impossible to cope with any administrative task and found ways to get neighbours and friends to help out. Even opening the post seemed to require the assistance of an elderly neighbour, who became a daily visitor to the house.

On a weekend visit in 1993, Alex's frustration spilled over into fury, and when he got back to London he sat down and wrote his mother a rare, and revealing, letter. He began by apologising for his behaviour: 'I'm really writing to say to you that I'm sorry I shouted at you. I don't remember ever doing that and I'll try not to do it ever again. You see, I have a great deal on my mind and I have not been myself for a while, not that any of you would notice because I don't show it.'

He listed some of the reasons he'd been out of sorts, then he wrote, 'And maybe I got angry on Saturday because I feel I should have the same freedom in our house as Amanda and Oliver do. I don't know why, but it seems to me that you feel somewhat uneasy when we arrive unannounced or with a friend, or when we are in the house without you, or being there for any length of time without you knowing we are there.'

Alex ended the letter with these words: 'It is as if you have things in the house you do not want us to look at.'

It was a comment only Alex could have made. Memory loss had gifted him a kind of innocence and he was starting to ask the questions that his siblings never could.

He wanted a key, not just to the house, but to the story of their family. Jill's refusal to let either of the twins have access to their own home was hugely symbolic, a part of her insistence on secrecy and silence.

But Alex was beginning to ask uncomfortable questions. The fact that nothing had changed after Jack's death planted the first seeds of doubt and unease in his mind.

Doubts and unease that never quite went away.

16

Birthday Alarms

Their mother might have been defensive of her own privacy, but she had no regard at all for her sons'.

After Jack's death, Alex and Marcus were working hard at Twin Decs and making a success of it. They had a wide circle of friends with whom they liked to relax in the evenings, many of them people they'd known since the Long Copse days. But they lost count of the times there'd be a ring at the door late at night, they'd go down to let in a friend and find Jill on the doorstep. Hair wild, enormous glasses balanced on the tip of her nose, feet crippled by tiny sandals, she'd sweep past them and shout jubilantly, 'Coo-ee! It's me-ee! Oh good, are you having a party?'

Then she'd hobble up the stairs as quickly as her painful hips would allow, and throw herself into the gathering with a loud, 'Here we all are!' She'd be unstoppable, already well over the limit and helping herself liberally to any alcohol in sight. Alex and Marcus would cringe, but, as they'd always done, they'd pretend they thought it was funny.

'Well, you're a lovely couple,' she'd exclaim to some unsuspecting friends. 'But you'd be much better with him! I think you ought to swap.'

Tall and imposing, she'd sometimes pick a girl up and carry her bodily across the room to plonk her down in front of whoever she'd decided was her Mr Right. It was outrageous, but Jill got away with it precisely because she was so extreme, no one had ever come across anything like her before. Besides, she was hilarious and unpredictable and created a kind of crazy firestorm that was impossible to resist.

But finally Alex and Marcus couldn't stand it any more. They screwed up their courage and confronted her.

'Mum, you have to stop turning up without being invited like this. We've got to have our own lives. It's just not fair.'

Jill was disbelieving, then angry, and then deeply hurt. But for once the twins stuck to their guns.

Jill's friends were starting to drift away. She was lonely without Jack, and she always demanded more of people than they could give. One person she made heavy demands of at this time was Vivien Kay, the healer who had given Alex hope for the future in the year after his accident.

Vivien was living not far from Rudgwick. She had always had a welcoming, open home, but even she found Jill's habit of dropping in and demanding a free counselling session impossible, and after a while had to ask her to phone first. Jill wanted healing for free, and she wanted feeding because there was no longer anyone at home to cook for her. Vivien felt sorry for Jill, and realised that she was beginning to be fearful for the future, but she was also aware that she was in the presence of a person who was fundamentally not at peace with herself.

A curious incident occurred on the twins' thirtieth birthday at the end of January 1994. This is one of the events that

Marcus is puzzled by, since it doesn't sit comfortably with his rationalist philosophy.

Jill was due to come to London to take them out for a birthday dinner at the River Cafe. Alex and Marcus derived a lot of pleasure from choosing the most expensive restaurants for these annual outings, since by now Jill's stinginess was legendary.

'We knew it hurt her,' says Marcus gleefully, because she'd physically recoil when she walked into a restaurant, checked out the ambience and realised how much the evening was likely to cost. 'We loved passing her the bill.' He and Alex hoot with laughter at the memory. 'She'd lick her fingers as she counted out each £50 note.'

On this particular evening she was late. As this was fairly typical, they weren't concerned until half an hour after she'd been due to arrive.

'She's a bit late,' Alex commented, starting to get irritated.

Marcus said, 'No. It's more than that.'

They phoned Duke's Cottage. No reply.

Another fifteen minutes passed but there was still no sign of her.

'This is really out of order!' said Alex, by now thoroughly annoyed. 'We're going to miss our reservation if she doesn't get here soon.'

'No,' said Marcus. 'It's serious. She's had an accident.'

'What do you mean?'

'I can't explain. But I can see her. She's fallen down the stairs at Duke's Cottage.'

Alex stared at him. 'Are you sure?'

'I don't know. But we have to check.'

They phoned the house several times; no reply.

'We have to get someone to go round,' said Marcus. 'Something is definitely wrong.'

'They'll think we're nuts!' protested Alex.

Marcus insisted they phone a local doctor to ask if he would drop round to the house. Alex thought this was a bit far-fetched, but they did phone, and got through to the doctor's wife, Mrs Grant.

She said her husband was out but she would go round.

As soon as Mrs Grant pulled into the driveway of Duke's Cottage, she realised that something was wrong. The doors of Jill's car were open, and the front door was too. She went inside and found Jill lying unconscious at the foot of the back stairs, just as Marcus had predicted.[4]

But, he says, 'I was wrong,' because she hadn't, as he'd thought, fallen down the stairs. She had been setting the answerphone when she had some kind of fit and collapsed back against the bottom stair. Mrs Grant called an ambulance and got her to the hospital.

Their timely intervention probably saved Jill's life. She had a series of tests and the doctors discovered that her blackout had been caused by a brain tumour. In the spring of that year, she had an operation to remove it. Afterwards, Alex and Marcus went with her to see the surgeon and hear the result.

---

4 Mrs Grant maintains there was nothing remotely strange about this sequence of events: Jill was late, and Marcus was concerned, so she agreed to go to the house. No need for further explanation. As Marcus says, 'She went round there for one reason and I asked her to go for another.'

The doctor worked from a private clinic; they remember that his bedside manner left a lot to be desired.

'It's been very successful,' he told them. 'Thanks to my skill, approximately 95% of the tumour has been removed. Your mother is really very lucky indeed.'

'OK,' said Marcus, and then, aware that Jill was listening and not contributing very much to the conversation, he asked tentatively, 'Do you think it will affect her life expectancy at all?'

'Of course,' said the surgeon breezily, without any preamble. 'She's probably got about twelve months.'

For Jill, still weak after the operation, this was the first time she'd heard that her illness was fatal. She was sixty-three.

For several months she refused to accept his prognosis.

She had chemotherapy and her hair fell out. Amanda was now twenty. She'd gone abroad as soon as she'd left school and had been living in India for a couple of years, but she came back and stayed at Duke's Cottage to help Oliver look after their mother. Jill had discovered that cannabis eased her symptoms and she and Amanda would go together to buy the drug. Her children noticed with some amusement that she was obviously no stranger to drugs – though until now she had always told her children she was anti-drugs – but she never grasped the convention that joints were for sharing. Once one had been handed to her, she hung on to it, puffing happily, until the next person insisted she pass it on.

Jill continued to run her Saturday stall in Portobello market almost to the end of her life. She still demanded, and almost always got, complete obedience from the twins. Alex and

Marcus would be summoned whenever she needed their help setting up or dismantling her stall, and they always dropped whatever they were doing and came to help. After so many years of conditioning, old habits died hard.

As her condition deteriorated, Jill needed more care than Amanda and Oliver could provide. Naturally she was 'too poor' to afford live-in help. During the last months of her life, it was Alex and Marcus who paid the nurses' wages.

Alex realised the end was getting close. One afternoon when he was driving her back from the hospital, he said, 'What about William? This feud has gone on almost all your life; it's time to be reconciled. Let's go over to his house and you can make your peace. After all, he's your brother.'

She stared at him for a moment, utterly astonished. 'Why?' she asked. 'Why would I do that?'

'He's your brother.'

'Absolutely not. No. Never.'

Alex saw it was hopeless. But she wasn't finished. 'You have to promise me, Ali, really promise, you won't let him come to the funeral. William must not come to my funeral, do you understand? Promise me!'

'OK, OK, I promise,' said Alex. He remembered the old rumours, that William had somehow been to blame for his real father's death thirty years ago. But he knew better than to ask. Right now his mother was so frail that all his instincts were to protect her.

They drove the rest of the way home in silence.

Whatever the truth about her feud with her brother, Jill intended to carry her hatred to her grave.

17

Beginnings and an End

Early in 1995 Jill agreed to give Alex and Marcus some capital so they could take advantage of a business venture James Burton had suggested. They wanted to buy a derelict property in Brixton and do it up. Ian Hudson, who had been acting as her informal financial adviser since Jack's death, had persuaded her that this was a good scheme.

'We'll go to the bank,' she told them. So they drove with her to a bank in Guildford, and helped her inside. These days she was quite frail, and looked much older than her sixty-three years.

Right away, they noticed something strange: the staff all treated this crippled woman, with her charity-shop clothes and her huge feet spilling out of tiny sandals, with great deference. Clearly, they knew her well and she was a special customer.

'I want to withdraw some money,' she said and named a large figure. 'In cash. Now.'

Alex and Marcus held their breath. It must be the illness that was making her confused. The cashier was going to turn her down and there'd be a scene . . .

'Certainly, Madam,' said the cashier, without even a flicker of surprise. 'Would you care to step this way?'

They were ushered politely into a private room and after a few minutes the entire sum was brought in and counted in front of them.

Clearly, the woman who had always maintained that the cash in her handbag was all she had in the world possessed resources they had never imagined.

The twins bought their first property with James Burton in January 1995, Twin Decs became Lewis Burton and they were launched on a new and exciting business.

In February, Jill, now very ill, went into a hospice, the Old Rectory in Ewhurst. Her children took turns to sit with her, and friends remember how heartbroken her sons appeared to be: they wanted their mother to see them settled with families of their own. They wanted her to know the joys of being a grandmother.

On the first of March, while her children had stepped outside her room so the nursing staff could turn her over in her bed, Jill died. As Alex says now, 'She decided to leave while we were outside the door.'

When he saw what had happened, Alex broke down in tears and was inconsolable. Though he had always felt a kind of distance from her, and had never connected with her again after the accident the way he had connected with Amanda and Oliver, she was his mother. Eccentric and embarrassing, perhaps, but all the same a constant and powerful presence in his life, and now she was gone.

He was engulfed with sorrow.

And then, even as he sobbed by his mother's bedside, he realised that he was grieving alone.

Marcus, Amanda and Oliver no longer showed any emotion. They had appeared to be distressed while she was dying, but now it was as if a switch had been thrown, or perhaps a spell had been broken. Beside their mother's corpse, they were calm, almost matter-of-fact.

'Come on, Ali,' said Marcus. 'Let's go home. There's nothing more we can do here. The nurses will take over now.'

He seemed brisk, almost cheerful. Alex couldn't understand it at all.

They drove back to Duke's Cottage, turned the key in the front door and let themselves in. When Jill went into the hospice, they'd had keys made. It still took a bit of getting used to, this freedom to come and go as they pleased.

The hallway was dark, cluttered with boxes of antiques, piled high with junk. The whole house had become shabby over the past few years, carpets threadbare: no money, apparently, for repairs or decoration. There was dust everywhere.

They went through the breakfast room to the kitchen and opened the fridge door. It felt strange. They could help themselves to anything they wanted. Ever since they could remember, Jack's food had been sacrosanct: no one could touch it. And after he died, Jill hardly ever bought anything, preferring to get friends to feed her if she could. Now it was piled high with food they had bought themselves and they could pick and choose without fearing the consequences.

'There's Daddy's wine in the garage,' said Marcus hesitantly. 'Shall we open a bottle?'

Even now, with both parents dead, it still seemed like they were crossing a line to be able to help themselves. Almost as if they kept expecting to hear Jack's terrifying explosion of rage or Jill's shrill cries of poverty, or 'You mustn't do anything to upset Daddy!'

They sat down round the table in the breakfast room, opened a bottle of Jack's vintage claret and had their first meal together as orphans. There was the funeral to be planned. Would there be enough cash left to pay for it? And all the stuff in the house would have to be sorted. Some of it was priceless, some of it rubbish. How would they know how to deal with everything? And there was so much of it! Where should they start?

Amanda had been away from her life in India long enough. As soon as the funeral was over, she intended to leave. She wasn't interested in anything in the house. As far as she was concerned, Alex and Marcus could do what they wanted with it all. But Oliver was nineteen and about to go to university. Alex and Marcus, so handicapped with dyslexia, envied him this opportunity, but they were proud that their little brother was being so mature at this difficult time. They'd keep the house as long as possible so he'd still have a home.

Alex listened with growing disbelief as the conversation moved back and forth between the three of them. Their mother had only been dead for a couple of hours, and here they all were discussing practical problems as if losing your mother was something that happened every day. He couldn't make out what was going on.

'That's when I started thinking something was odd,' he says, 'because nobody was bothered about it. Nobody cried about it for an instant, or even talked about the fact that she'd just died.'

Their apparent callousness made a deep impression on him. 'It was so strange. *I* was bothered that she'd died. Nobody else was.'

He puzzled about it for weeks, and then pushed it to the back of his mind. It was nearly two years before he uncovered the reason for what looked at the time like coldness on the part of his siblings.

18

The Ring

It was a sweltering hot day. Alex and Marcus, together with Oliver and Amanda and the ever-stalwart Ian Hudson, were sitting in the solicitor's office waiting for the will to be read. Years before, Jill and Jack had asked him to agree to act as guardian to their children if they were to die, so he was now officially Oliver and Amanda's guardian. Soon after their mother's death, Alex and Marcus asked him and Laura to become their parents officially, a recognition of their unwavering kindness and support.

As always, Ian was immaculately dressed – a suit-and-tie man at all times – but today even he was sweating.

'Do you mind if I remove my jacket?' he asked.

No one minded. Ian loosened his tie and smiled encouragingly at them all. The solicitor read out the terms of the will. It didn't take very long. There were no individual bequests. Everything Jill had was to be divided equally between her four children, making allowance for the money that Alex and Marcus had already received to set up Lewis Burton. Ian was to look after Oliver and Amanda's money until they were old enough to take charge. There were no surprises in the division of her money.

The surprise was how much she'd been worth. Even Ian was shocked.

The woman who had always hunted down food that was out of date and marked down, who had bought clothes for herself and her children at car boot sales, who had made her struggling friends pick up the tab whenever they went out for a meal, the woman who had smuggled chicken bones out of restaurants in her handbag 'for soup', the woman who had let Oliver's nanny pay for his birthday party out of her own wages, had all this time been a person of considerable wealth.

Amanda couldn't stand it. She stood up and left the room. She remembered how she had scrimped and saved and done odd jobs in the village in order to buy herself a pair of jeans when she was fourteen years old. They had been the first new item of clothing she'd ever had. All the humiliation of wearing second-hand clothes when her privately educated friends had everything new, all that penny-pinching and obsessing about cheapness, it had all been a sham.

Amanda was so angry, it was a while before she could be persuaded to come back in so the meeting could conclude.

By that time they were all angry and amazed. Each one had their own memory of Jill's duplicity. Even Ian, generous to a fault, couldn't help remembering Christmas after Christmas when he and Laura had welcomed the Dudleys to a lavish lunch party and Jill had, without fail, turned up bearing a single bag of past-their-sell-by-date satsumas as the family's contribution. You'd have to be a saint not to feel a twinge of irritation, knowing how Jill's unspent cash had been mounting in her bank account all the while she was proclaiming her poverty.

Until that boiling hot session in the solicitor's office, Alex and Marcus had been wondering how to pay for the funeral. Now they realised it was death duties they should have been worrying about. Marcus and Alex discovered that funeral expenses could be offset against inheritance tax, so they decided to give her a good send-off. Alex's grief at losing his mother had passed, or been buried – it was hard to tell which – and he and Marcus slid back into coping mode, making-the-best-of-it mode, the way they always did.

It was summer. Jack's roses were in full bloom and the garden at Duke's Cottage was looking its best. A friend of their mother's had advised them not to have the reception in the house, since priceless tiny treasures lay everywhere, so they hired a marquee, brought in caterers and invited all her friends, the people she'd known through her lifetime in the antiques trade, neighbours, all the people who had enjoyed her ebullience and high spirits while she was still alive.

To their dismay, when they looked around the church at the mourners, they saw the tall, unmistakeable figure of her brother William, a thin grey rat's tail of a ponytail hanging down his back. He had heard about her death from someone who had spotted the announcement in *The Times*. In spite of Alex's promise, it was going to be impossible to throw him out. William joined the crowd walking back through the village to the house. Alex and Marcus had a quick debate and, as usual, turned to Laura Hudson for help.

She approached William, who was enjoying the lavish hospitality and talking animatedly to a Rudgwick neighbour. 'William, I'm sorry, but Ali and Marcus have asked me to drive you to the station. Jill was very clear that she didn't want you to come today and—'

'No, I'm not going,' said William.

Laura persisted, and eventually persuaded him to go with her to Horsham station. On the drive back to Rudgwick, she opened all the windows to release the smell of alcohol that had filled the car.

Alex and Marcus still had one more request of Jill's to carry out before they could relax with their friends for the rest of the afternoon. Although her will mentioned no individual bequests, she had told them a few weeks before her death that there was one exception: the huge diamond ring she wore at all times must be given to her closest friend.

Cynthia was by now a Duchess. She was an elegant, imposing woman, hair immaculate, beautifully dressed. Marcus remembered the evenings at her flat in Gloucester Road, when as children he and Alex had put on their smartest clothes and handed round drinks and canapés at the parties she and their mother used to throw. They'd known her a long time, but she had never been the kind of woman they could feel relaxed with, as they could with Deirdre or Laura.

She had given the eulogy in the church, and, as with everything she tackled, she did it with poise and professionalism, though some people noted that her praise of Jill was a little lukewarm. She came back to Duke's Cottage, but did not intend to linger. She came over to say goodbye to Alex and Marcus, and to offer, once again, her condolences.

'Before you go,' said Marcus, 'there's just one thing.'

'Mummy wanted you to have her ring,' said Alex. He'd

had it with him all through the service, and now he handed it over.

Cynthia looked surprised, then pleased as she slipped the ring into her pocket.

Marcus said, 'Mummy told us you'd know what it was about.'

'Yes,' was all she said.

She left soon afterwards. For some reason, this exchange stayed with Alex and Marcus, and puzzled them.

The bequest of Jill's most valuable and most personal item of jewellery, the enormous ring that had been a gift from Jack before their marriage, carried a significance that observers recognised, but could only guess at.

It was one of the mysteries that Jill left behind her.[5] One of many, as Alex and Marcus were to discover.

5 This transaction struck all who saw it as significant. If this were a novel, a neat explanation would emerge in due course, but in real life some loose ends are impossible to tie up.

19

Family Urns

The caterers cleared away the debris, the marquee was taken down, and Alex and Marcus threw themselves into their new business venture with James Burton. Oliver went to university and Amanda returned to her life in India. In their different ways, they all adapted to the new situation. They were all now orphans, but Ian Hudson was always around to offer advice and help them sort out the financial legacy Jill had left.

Marcus and Alex decided to make the most of the opportunity. During the week they worked flat out in London, but on Friday evening they drove down to Sussex and filled Duke's Cottage with their friends. It felt liberating. After all those years of being banished to a chilly back bedroom or an unheated annexe, all those years of never setting foot in Jack's drawing-room or study, now they had the run of the whole place and could do as they liked. And what they liked most was throwing parties and enjoying themselves with people they loved.

For their friends, many of whom they'd known since that first New Year's Eve party at Long Copse, the whole situation was a novelty, an extraordinary period in their lives. Jill's children were the first of their generation to be left without parents, with all the freedom and responsibility that implied, and for everyone in their circle this was an exhilarating and uncharted journey. Oliver was mostly living in Rudgwick at this time, enjoying the freedom of the big old house, and he helped with the sorting.

They didn't start on the job of sorting the house out straight away – it was too daunting and for the time being they were content just to relax and luxuriate in their new-found independence. Besides, it was the only home Oliver had ever known and they were in no hurry to sell the place, though death duties would mean they'd have to do so eventually.

But they did clear out some rooms, and realised how weird Duke's Cottage had become. One of the upstairs bathrooms was impossible to enter because Jill had stuffed it full of clothes from charity auctions and car boot sales. Old clothes in the bath, old clothes on the basin and the toilet, old clothes stacked up almost to the ceiling. As a penny-pinching exercise it didn't make any sense. Even at knockdown prices, these mountains of clothes must have cost her more than a few new ones would have done. Most of them she'd never worn.

They remembered Jack's frustration at her inability to understand basic household economics: she'd travel miles to buy petrol a penny cheaper than at the local garage, and never factored in the extra cost involved in driving there. But at some level she must have been more savvy than anyone guessed, or how had she ended up worth a small fortune?

They hired a skip and lobbed hundreds of old coats and cardigans and skirts inside, scrubbed the bathroom down and made it usable. From then on, there was always a skip parked on the gravel in front of the house, and it always filled up quickly.

Their friends pitched in. As they began going through the mountains of stuff that Jill had accumulated during a lifetime of antique dealing and hoarding, they started to make some remarkable discoveries.

The annexe, like the upstairs bathroom, was full of old clothes. Female friends like Caz, who'd been Alex's girlfriend at the time of his accident, and Ellen Handley from Long Copse, had a great time sorting through the mounds of clothes, deciding which to throw in the skip and which to keep. The whole room stank of damp and mould, but in among the rubbish there were treasures worth keeping.

It was the same story all through the house. They pulled open the door of one cupboard and cartons of cigarettes tumbled out. Stacks of them, still wrapped in their duty-free cellophane and never touched. Some of the brands were so old they were no longer on the market. They carried them in triumph down to the breakfast room and the smokers divvied them up. This was turning into a treasure hunt.

But there was no way they could rush the process. Priceless antiques were jumbled together with worthless tat; a cardboard box full of chipped crockery might be hiding a Lalique vase at the bottom. The sheer quantity of stuff made it a monumental task. Tote boxes, carrier bags, cardboard boxes and holdalls were crammed into every room of the house and the huge attics that filled all the space under the roof. And it wasn't just the house. There was the annexe, the sheds, all the outbuildings, the garage . . .

Jill had been a squirrel, hiding precious things away so they turned up in all the most unexpected places. A friend who had visited her in hospital just before her brain tumour operation remembered that as Jill had been drifting in and out of consciousness, she'd muttered woozily, 'There are earrings in the grandfather clock.'

And she'd been right. They searched every drawer, inside every nook and cranny. Everywhere. A friend noticed that a curtain was hanging oddly, went to investigate and felt something squashy in the hem. When they unpicked it they found a wad of £50 notes hidden inside. After that the hunt was on. Every curtain in the house was shaken and explored and several more notes were discovered. And not just in the curtains. They found fifties in the oddest places, in jars and pots, even under loose floorboards. Never knowing where the next heirloom or pile of cash might be hidden, they had every incentive to be thorough.

Oliver was helping them tackle the garage when their labours turned surreal. He let out a cry of surprise.

'Look at this!' he yelled.

'What is it?' Alex and Marcus rushed over.

In amongst the heaps of old tins of food, useless jars, empty bottles and pots was an urn with a passport on top.

'Jesus!' exclaimed Alex. 'It's Uncle Stuart!'

They looked at each other in amazement, then kept on looking. Sure enough, in another box they 'found Aunty Joan in an urn.' Clearly their mother had collected her uncle and aunt's ashes from the crematorium, but omitted to do anything further with them and so they got buried under the mounds of junk in the garage. The craziness of it all began to appeal to their sense of humour and they stowed 'Uncle Stuart' and 'Aunty Joan' in the narrow cupboard in their mother's bedroom where they had temporarily put her ashes.

Jill was on the top shelf, Uncle Stuart underneath and Aunt Joan at the bottom.

The family vault was in Ardingly and Jill had left strict instructions that her ashes were to be interred there. So Marcus and Alex dutifully drove down to Ardingly to arrange the triple interment of their mother, their uncle and their aunt. The vicar, who was new to the parish, looked through his records and, to their astonishment, retrieved yet another urn from a cupboard. This one contained the ashes of Jill's mother, Rosalind Wakefield. So now, said Marcus, they had 'another bloody urn' to deal with. They realised it must have been the cost of interment that had stopped Jill from burying her relatives: opening the tomb turned out to be an expensive business, and after that there was the lettering to be paid for.

While that was being organised, they took their grand-mother's ashes back to Duke's Cottage and put her in the tall cupboard with her brother, her sister-in-law, and now their mother as well. Jack's ashes had already been scattered among his beloved roses, a cost-free solution that Jill clearly had no problem with. By now Alex and Marcus regarded the whole business as a brilliant joke. One weekend Alex showed a new girlfriend round Duke's Cottage. 'This is where we used to live,' he told her. 'This was our room. This was our mother's room. Oh, and I haven't introduced you to the rest of the family.' He opened the cupboard door, revealing the four urns stacked neatly one on top of the other. 'This is my mum. This is Aunty Joan and Uncle Stuart. And here's Granny.'

According to Alex, she just stared at him, speechless, and the relationship petered out soon afterwards.

20

Dukestonbury

Duke's Cottage had become a party house. Alex and Marcus were enjoying the place while they could, but now they began to think big.

In 1996 the organisers of Glastonbury decided that they and their fields needed a year off, and the festival was cancelled. This gave the twins an idea: why didn't they organise their own event in the huge garden behind the house? They wanted to do something spectacular before the house had to be sold. It would be an unforgettable party and they'd call it Dukestonbury.

They started planning with their usual energy and enthusiasm. 500 invitations were printed and circulated around their friends and friends of friends. They got a Brixton associate to organise the bouncers. They hired bands and waiters, ordered a marquee, learned what they had to do to stay legal, all this while carrying on with their work doing up properties in Brixton.

'Do you notice something?' Marcus asked Alex one morning as they went out to their van.

'What?'

'We're being followed.'

'Really?'

'Yeah. It must be the police.'

In 1996, rave culture had alarmed the authorities so much that legislation had been passed to clamp down on them, as the twins well knew. But Dukestonbury was going to be on their own property, and they weren't charging for entry. The police spent a week tailing them in the belief that the twins must be involved in drugs and that they could nail them that way. Marcus almost felt sorry for the sleuths: it must have been very boring, traipsing from one building site to another after a couple of drug-free developers.

The police called them in anyway.

'This stops here,' the cop told them.

Alex and Marcus sat in an interview room in Wandsworth police station while a fatherly sergeant informed them that the whole enterprise had got out of hand, it was likely that thousands of people would turn up on the day and they needed to close the whole thing down right now. The twins listened politely. But a lawyer friend had already told them to find out whether the police were issuing them with a legally enforceable demand, or if it was simply a request.

'Right. Over to you.' The cop ended with a flourish. 'Now you're going to close it down.'

'Are you ordering us to stop, or are you asking?'

The man stared at them. He hemmed and hawed for as long as he could, but then he had to admit, 'We're *asking* you to stop.'

'In that case, no,' said Marcus. And they left.

Dukestonbury turned out to be a strange hybrid. In some ways, as Marcus says, it was 'a full-on, hard-core, no-nonsense, can't-pretend-it-was-anything-else rave' with pounding music and most of the guests high on drugs. But it was a rave like no other. The guests who turned up at Duke's Cottage clutching their precious invitations couldn't make it out at all. They were met by waiters in tailcoats and white gloves who offered them a flute of champagne. A classical string quartet played beside the pond with its water lilies, and the woods at the far end of the garden were thrown into sharp relief by dramatic lighting, courtesy of a friend who ran a professional lighting company. There was a big double marquee, Persian rugs spread over the lawns, as well as burger vans and a candy-floss stall in the driveway. For Oliver and his friends, who had just finished their first year of college, it was stunning. A police helicopter circled overhead, but when the local police tried to enter, the Brixton bouncers courteously explained that they couldn't enter a private party without a warrant. Local people who turned up hoping to get in were turned away.

The DJs were friends Ian Hume and Sancho Panza, who still play the Notting Hill Carnival. They faded through the classical string quartet, the music getting harder and harder through the night. It wasn't finally switched off till nine the next day. As the morning sun spread across the gardens, guests emerged from the woods where all sleeping tents had been erected, and straggled across the lawns in search of breakfast. The party had been a total success, far bigger and more imaginative than anyone had been expecting. For the twins it was what they call a Wow Moment – the first time they really began to shake off their sense of being less able than their friends, that feeling of inadequacy that dyslexics often spend their whole lives trying to overcome. OK, so maybe they'd never make it to university, but they sure could organise a hell of a party.

The following year Dukestonbury II took place, with about twice as many guests as before. As Alex says, that was when their long-suffering Rudgwick neighbours finally lost the plot. But by then the twins' years in Duke's Cottage were drawing to a close.

21

Discoveries

Alex and Marcus decided it was time to get serious about sorting the contents of the house. They were never going to get the job done if they only did it at weekends, even with all their friends piling in to help. They had to take two months off work and get systematic.

Jill had created an aura of myth around her collection of miniatures, which was well-known in the antiques world. Rupert Toovey, the leading Sussex auctioneers, had spent months sorting through her collections: snuffboxes and thimbles, doll's house furniture and curiosities. She'd been fascinated by anything small and had an excellent eye for treasures. Once all those pieces had been taken away to be catalogued, there was still a mountain of stuff to be dealt with. And amid the laughter and jokes shared with friends, Alex and Marcus were catching glimpses of something darker.

Oliver had started seeing a therapist. To Alex, that made sense. He'd lost both his parents and was about to lose his home. You could see why he needed someone to talk it all through with. But Marcus? When Alex realised that Marcus was seeing the same person as Oliver, that didn't add up at all. 'Because I know my brother inside out,' says Alex. 'And I thought: why would he want to go and see a therapist? We haven't had that bad a life!'

Have we?

The niggling questions that Alex had started to ask when he noticed the way his siblings reacted to their mother's death refused to go away.

And the things they found as they continued to clear the house were bizarre. Sometimes disturbing.

Jill's bedroom was filled, like the rest of Duke's Cottage, with dark brown antiques, chests of drawers, a writing desk, tall cupboards. An en-suite bathroom led off it, and beyond that was her 'dressing room' with a single bed where Jack had slept more and more often towards the end of his life. One wall of that room was entirely taken up with an enormous built-in cupboard with sliding doors.

They pulled back the doors and set to work. First they found more cartons of cigarettes. Then they uncovered boxes full of Easter eggs. Dozens of them in all shapes and sizes. As they pulled them out and the pile grew on the floor, they realised that they'd found every Easter egg they had ever given their mother: she must have thanked them, then stashed them away, never to be eaten, never to be thrown away. The chocolate was grey with age and inedible, so, puzzled but determined to make a joke of it, they chucked the historic eggs onto the skip.

Then, right at the bottom of the cupboard, they found an old shoe box. They took off the lid and pulled out a bundle of envelopes. Every envelope was addressed to Jill's children: Alex Lewis, Marcus Lewis, Alex and Marcus Lewis, Amanda,

Oliver. The dates on the envelopes went right back to early 1965, the twins' first birthday.

Alex opened an envelope at random and found a card inside: *Happy Birthday to Marcus and Alex with love from Aunty Isabel.* A ten-shilling note fluttered to the floor. He looked at the date on the envelope. Their father's sister must have sent it for their third birthday. Jill had never shown it to them, never given them the money, never even spent it herself.

Oliver opened the next one. It contained a WH Smith gift voucher from his godfather. A voucher that was more than ten years out of date.

The shoe box was crammed with cards and gift vouchers Jill's children had never received: a ghost history of their childhood, the affectionate gestures of relatives and friends they'd been denied. All safely stored away.

But why? What had been going through Jill's mind as she squirelled their cards and presents away birthday after birthday, Christmas after Christmas? Stuffing bundles of cash in the hem of curtains or under floorboards at least had a weird kind of logic – the instinct to hoard against hard times – but old birthday cards sent to her children? And discontinued currency? Why didn't she want them to know that people were thinking of them, spending money on them? What was that about? Their mother's pointless meanness was horribly unsettling for them all

They climbed the stepladder that led up to the attic. The space under the roof was lit by a single weak bulb and the ceilings sloped, so you could only stand upright in the centre; the air was thick with dust and cobwebs. And the floor was covered in boxes, of course. Tote boxes and carrier bags, old suitcases, piles of junk everywhere.

Most could be thrown away. But in among all the boxes and junk they found their mother had also kept all her correspondence. Every letter sent by her school friends while she was a day girl at St Gabriel's in Newbury. Letters from the nuns and circulars from the Old St Gabriel's Association. Copies of letters she had written to her parents when she was working away from home. Letters from her mother, from her father, from her friends. Letters from the husband who had died when her babies were three weeks old. Letters from Jack. Letters from lovers.

Many lovers. Well, Jill had never made any secret of the fact that she'd led a colourful life after her first husband's death and before she met Jack. But a whole bunch of letters, written on airmail paper in a distinctive curled hand, were in Italian and they dated from 1963, the year before Alex and Marcus were born. They put them to one side and asked a friend to translate them. It became obvious that Jill had been having a passionate affair with this man, whose name was Aste, at the time they were conceived.

The implications were huge. Alex and Marcus had to face the possibility that this unknown Italian was in fact their biological father. And, looking at the other letters from 1963, there were other potential candidates as well.

For Alex, this was when, in his words, 'we started doubting if we were who we were.'

At the time he pushed the doubts to one side. There was still a vast amount to be sorted and Duke's Cottage had to be sold to pay the death duties: time was running out.

His mother's bureau was full of tiny drawers and in one of those he found a key. When Caz and her friends had finished clearing the clothes out of the wardrobe in Jill's bedroom, he noticed a small door at the back.

'It must be Narnia!' he joked as he tried out several keys. The one he'd found in her bureau worked and the door opened easily.

He closed it again at once. It was full of sex toys and kinky underwear.

A friend called Clare had been sorting clothes into piles.

'What's up?' she asked.

'You have a look,' said Alex.

She went into the wardrobe and opened the secret door. 'Jesus!' she exclaimed, and then said quickly, 'Don't worry, Ali, I'll deal with this. It's OK for me. She wasn't *my* mother.'

A little later he watched while Clare dragged a couple of black bin-bags down the stairs and hurled them into the skip without a word. There are things you don't want to know about your mother's private life.

The most disturbing discovery of all was a photograph Oliver found in their mother's bedside drawer. It showed Alex and Marcus when they were about ten years old, perhaps younger. They were naked and their heads had been cut off. Two small headless boys, front view, no clothes.

Oliver called his brothers and handed it to them without a word. Her twin sons displayed as faceless bodies. For once, their ability to turn almost anything into a joke failed them. As the house was emptied of a lifetime's possessions, something dark was coming to the surface.

Alex couldn't make it out at all. Like so much else, he simply pushed it to the back of his mind. That had always been his survival technique. He and Marcus never spoke about the things they were finding, not seriously anyway.

And then, in among the endless papers and junk, Alex came across a business card that was to have a huge impact on their lives. It gave the name and phone number of Vivien Kay, the healer Jill had taken him to see after his accident, more than ten years previously. Alex decided to go and see her; he thought she might be able to give him some advice about what to do with all the stuff that needed sorting.

Which, in a way, was exactly what Vivien did.

22

Carol Vorderman and Mysteries

An unusual snapshot has survived that shows Alex and Marcus as they were on the eve of the revelations that would turn Alex's world upside down: a ten-minute documentary about them that was made just after the sale of Duke's Cottage and transmitted at the beginning of December 1997. It was one of the *Mysteries* series fronted by Carol Vorderman in which 'real-life mysteries are put under the microscope'. It focussed on Alex's accident and the way Marcus had 'known' about it at the same time: his premonition, and the uncanny way in which some twins seem able to communicate.

This was not their first television appearance. In fact by the end of the nineties they were well on the way to becoming professional media twins. The reason was simple. Marcus's long-term girlfriend was a lively and striking-looking New Zealander called Fran. Her first job in the UK was as a researcher on Esther Rantzen's *That's Life!* programme. Each week featured an item broadly classified as 'human interest' and Fran was one of a team who were supposed to come up with ideas and 'feeders' for a topic. Occasionally she found herself at a loss.

'I'm going to get fired if I can't think of something!' she'd wail to Marcus on a Friday evening. 'You and Ali have to help out.'

'How?'

'Well, you're twins, aren't you? People are always fascinated by twins. We can work it up.'

'Are you sure?'

Apparently she was. The brothers agreed to appear in a programme exploring the experience of identical twins. They were nervous, not knowing what to expect, as they sat down under the studio lights, one on each side of Esther Rantzen, in front of an audience entirely composed of twins. It must have gone off all right, because the next time Fran was desperate for feeders, they went on again, this time talking about head injury and memory loss. The third time Fran appealed to Marcus, he remonstrated with her.

'Hang on a minute! Don't you think the viewers might just possibly notice that it's the same two brothers being wheeled on all the time?'

'That doesn't matter. *Please*, Marcus, say you'll do it!'

So he and Alex duly took part in a feature on dyslexia. They were the token man-in-the-street dyslexics; Susan Hampshire and Duncan Goodhew were the celebrity dyslexics. It turned out to be a useful finale to the twins' *That's Life!* career: Susan Hampshire gave them a copy of her book, *Susan's Story*, about her own struggle with dyslexia. Over the next few months they both read it, slowly, but to the end, which for them was a milestone: the first book they ever read right through. But not the last.

Now, the ever-optimistic Fran was working on a programme called *Mysteries* that featured events apparently not explicable by mainstream science, so it was only a matter of time before Marcus and Alex reprised their earlier TV appearances.

★   ★   ★

The programme begins with the *Mysteries* music pulsing spookily in the background while an urgent voice intones: 'An accident leaves a boy critically ill. Did his twin brother know about it in advance?' On a grey October day, Carol Vorderman strolls casually past a circular slide while two ten-year-old twin boys wearing identical check shirts whizz past. She says, 'Although there seems to be a bond between brothers and sisters, when you look at twins, especially identical twins, there often seems to be something that goes much deeper . . .'

Marcus then speaks and talks about the way he and Alex had grown up together, had done everything together, to the extent that 'it was difficult to do anything without him. He was part of me. He was my other half.' He looks slightly uneasy as he speaks, not entirely confident of the role he is supposed to play.

A kindly neighbour from Rudgwick confirms his state-ment. 'You never expected to see them apart, and you never did. I can't think of them without each other.'

The film then cuts to a busy hotel kitchen, an actor playing Alex earnestly stirring a big pot while a couple of other simi-larly white-coated actors with chef's hats look vaguely busy in the background. Marcus's voice explains that at the time of the accident, Alex was working as a trainee chef, while Marcus was learning to be a cabinetmaker. This is illustrated by the Marcus actor planing a length of timber in an empty room.

Marcus then talks about the night of Alex's accident. He'd been sleeping, but woke suddenly with 'a feeling about Alex that was very strong. And that feeling was very negative. I knew,' he says, 'there was some reason I felt like this.' He is then heard saying to his mother, 'Mum, Mum, something's happened to Alex.'

But she assumes he's had a bad dream and sleepily tells him to go back to bed. 'She couldn't understand,' says Marcus. 'It's not something you do at eighteen, wake your mother up because you've had a nightmare.' But sleepless, a troubled actor-Marcus is shown gazing pensively at old snapshots of himself and Alex until suddenly the night-time silence is shattered by the ringing of a telephone.

'The moment the phone rang,' says the real Marcus, 'was when I knew I was right.' And he adds, with some satisfaction, 'I wasn't going mad.'

There is plenty of anecdotal evidence for this kind of experience. The next person to speak is Dr Elizabeth Bryan[6] who at that time was a consultant paediatrician at Chelsea and Westminster Hospital and a worldwide specialist in twin studies. She expresses herself carefully: 'I have met a number of twins who have had feelings of great distress which later has been found to be time-related to when their twin has had an accident or has even died.' She acknowledges that 'there is something very special in the bond that identical twins have,' before admitting with a gentle smile, 'perhaps one day we'll understand it, but I don't think we do now.'

---

6 Dr Elizabeth Bryan was a pioneer of twins studies, and transformed the way parents of multiple births are helped. She founded the Twins and Multiple Births Association (1978) and the Multiple Births Foundation (1988) and became President of the International Society of Twins Studies. She died in 2008.

The scene shifts to the hospital ward where Alex has been lying unconscious for several days. A doctor explains that with such severe head injuries, some degree of permanent brain damage would have been a real possibility. Marcus sits next to his brother's bed.

'Footy on the weekend, Ali?' he asks, though without much hope.

Their mother, who looks blonde and pretty and not at all like their real mother, is chatting to staff a little way away.

Alex opens his eyes.

'Hello, Marky,' he says.

'Alex?' Actor-Marcus looks pleased. The viewer sees his face blurring and multiplying to show how he must have appeared to a woozy Alex surfacing from the coma.

Their mother races over to the bedside, but Alex just looks bewildered. 'Who is this woman?' he asks, shrinking away to the furthest side of the bed. 'Get her away from me!'

'He didn't know who our own mother was,' Marcus explains.

Present-day Alex is now shown for the first time. He is wearing glasses and an Aran sweater and he radiates a kind of trustworthy innocence. He says, sounding amazed by his own story, 'I woke up not knowing my own name or who I was, yet looking at someone else and knowing his name. That, to me, is extraordinary. Beyond medicine. Beyond what is possible. But it happened.'

A sceptic appears in the form of Dr Robin Luff, who says that Alex's recognition of his twin and his confusion about his mother was probably just due to the fact that Marcus had been talking to him all the time while he was unconscious, and was nothing to do with the nature of his memory loss at all.

But Alex is clear that he has never recovered an iota of memory from before the accident, and he explains the part Marcus played in his recovery: 'What Marcus did for me in those early days was to fill in the gaps. I always say to people, "I remember this," but I'm only remembering what Marcus has told me. So I've basically got his memories in my mind.'

The final shot shows them sitting side by side. No one would have the slightest difficulty telling them apart at this period in their lives. Marcus's hair is slicked back and he looks rather shifty, whereas Alex is serenely confident, in spite of having no memory. They both agree that the accident, and Alex's memory loss, have made them even closer than they were before.

And then Marcus volunteers a final comment that sounds spontaneous. 'I always did resist,' he says, 'the temptation to tell you things that weren't quite true to make myself look better.'

Alex looks a bit startled by this statement, but he obligingly laughs.

Marcus persists, 'I always told you straight up, honest!'

The programme ends with brotherly merriment.

Why did Marcus go to such trouble to insist on his honesty?

Six months later, it would have been impossible to make that programme. The careful narrative that the twins had created together since 1982 was about to be blown apart.

23

Vivien

Alex drove to a small house in Putney and rang the bell. He was apprehensive, not knowing what to expect, and almost turned round and went back to his car. This felt too much like a step into the unknown for comfort. But he knew he needed a sense of what the future held for him. Fifteen years before, Vivien had given him hope for the future. She'd said he would work at sea, and he had, and that he and Marcus would have their own business by the time they were thirty. That had happened as well. Maybe she could work her magic again.

Right now, his future seemed like a blank. Duke's Cottage had been sold, and the business they'd set up with James Burton was being wound up. They were going to keep the properties and rent them out, but the building side of things would stop. What was next?

Vivien opened the door and showed him into her front room. He'd forgotten what she looked like, but now saw that she was pretty much what you'd expect a visionary and healer to look like: reassuringly large, with long dark hair streaked with grey. She looked kind, but with an edge of danger, like a motherly, slightly unpredictable gypsy from a film.

Alex cleared his throat nervously and said, 'I want to know what my future is.'

She stared at him for a moment, then asked, 'Where are you going?'

He was puzzled. Was she referring to his life plans, his actions that day, his general intentions? But that was what he'd come to talk about. He asked, 'What do you mean?'

She said, 'You've just left your body.'

Her statement took his breath away. For years, since quite soon after the accident, he'd had horrifying experiences that he'd never talked about with anyone. He had once tried to tell Marcus, a year or so after the accident, but Marcus hadn't wanted to know about it: he was wary of anything that sounded a bit weird, which had only added to Alex's fear that he was not normal.

In the beginning, when he was stressed or had a slight bump on the head and blacked out, there was nothingness, but after a few months that nothingness was replaced by a sensation of spinning out of control. It was as though he was spiralling at great speed into an infinite vortex, faster and faster, with no way to stop. To anybody who was with him it looked as though he was completely motionless, but for Alex it felt as if he was hurtling into an abyss at terrifying speed.

Once he came back from the hospital there had been no aftercare. Why would he need it? His mother insisted he was fine, and his friends had grown used to what they called his 'funny turns'. That was just how his life was.

And now, here was this woman calmly telling him she could see what was happening in his mind. Maybe she had sussed his secret: he was mad and all his deepest fears were about to be confirmed.

Hardly daring to admit it, he said, 'This is what I do. Am I weird?'

'No,' she told him. 'It's called astro-travelling.'[7]

Alex's amazement grew. 'You mean, it's got a *name!*'

'Yes. And people spend years meditating to be able to do just that.'

For Alex, this was one of the most extraordinary moments of his life: this woman was telling him that the horrors he'd silently endured for so long actually had a name. Did that mean other people felt like this too? That he wasn't alone and about to be carted off in a straitjacket?

He admitted, 'I haven't slept for years and years because I'm afraid that when I sleep I arrive on the ceiling.'

There, he'd said it.

'Yes.' Vivien accepted everything he said as if it was the most natural thing in the world. 'You're in your astral body, but we've got to stop it because it's tiring you out and I need you in your body to talk to.'

That session with Vivien was a milestone. The out-of-body experiences had been terrifying in themselves, but even worse was the fear that the accident had made him a little bit crazy. To discover that his weird secret had a name, that it was something other people might even try to achieve, was a revelation

---

7 The psychological term for this kind of 'out-of-body' experience is dissociation. It is sometimes a consequence of head injury, but can also be a defence mechanism during extreme trauma, especially in childhood.

and a new beginning. A load that he'd been carrying in secret for more than ten years started to shift.

Alex had grieved when Jill died, but for the most part he was cut off from his feelings. He knew how to act the part, as his calm demeanour on the *Mysteries* programme showed, but for him the reality was very different: a kind of numb nothingness. He filled his days with work and socialising, parties and busyness, but none of it felt real, or meant much to him at all. He says, 'At that time I had very little emotion. Never attached to anything. Had a girlfriend – leave a girlfriend. Nothing really mattered. We had a company, we worked together, we had friends, but I had no sense of feelings.'

He didn't know at the time that he was only going through the motions, but he often felt that he was missing something. Not living properly the way it looked like the people around him were living. He thought maybe that was how he was, and he just had to get on with it.

At the end of that session, Vivien told him she was holding a workshop in a few weeks' time that she thought he would find useful. Alex was doubtful: he had no idea what a workshop involved, but it didn't sound like his sort of thing at all. He visited her a few more times, but eventually Vivien put her foot down.

'I want you to come to the workshop, Alex. Unless you do, there's no point in coming to see me any more.'

'But I like talking to you.'

'So come to the workshop.'

Vivien's methods are more prescriptive than those used by many therapists. As she said recently to Alex, 'I go in with a pickaxe, love, not a toothpick.'

He dutifully took one of her leaflets home with him, but he hardly gave it any thought over the next few days. A workshop on 'inner child visioning' sounded altogether too weird for him. On the Friday before the workshop, Marcus asked him if he was coming to any of the parties they'd been invited to over the weekend. Alex found himself saying no.

He had no idea what he was letting himself in for, but he had decided he might as well give Vivien's workshop a try.

24

The Workshop: Saturday

Alex shifted uncomfortably on the plastic chair. He was sitting in a circle with about twenty other people in a hall in Putney. Apart from Vivien they were all strangers. He was on his own, he didn't know what was going to happen and he didn't know why he was there. It was just the kind of situation to trigger all his deepest fears. Several times he had to fight an overwhelming urge to get up and leave.

Everybody took turns to stand up and introduce themselves and say why they'd come. When it came to his turn, Alex rose to his feet and said, 'I'm Alex and I don't know why I've come.'

He sat down. He'd been expecting ridicule, but his statement was accepted without comment. In fact everyone seemed very nice. It was the first surprise of the morning. The second surprise was how normal everyone appeared to be. He'd been expecting a bunch of weirdos, but no. The other people taking part in the workshop were city workers, middle-aged housewives, even a couple of builders like him and Marcus. A mixed bag for sure, but all apparently normal, which was reassuring.

They stayed sitting on their plastic chairs and people started to talk about their childhoods. Most of them had traumas from way back, and Alex got the impression that these problems almost always centred on their parents.

Alex wanted to join in, but his childhood had been fairly normal and anyway he couldn't remember a single thing about it, so instead he spoke about his head injury and the memory loss. It was all he knew. The day progressed, with frequent breaks for tea and coffee, and so far as he could tell not a lot was happening. Just a bunch of people talking about events from their childhood, though he was surprised by how much crying was going on. That seemed odd. He thought to himself, *they've hardly said anything and yet people keep bursting out crying.*

It didn't really touch him at all.

By the end of that Saturday, he'd had enough. So that's what a workshop was. Well, in his opinion the whole business was perfectly pleasant but he couldn't for the life of him see where it was going. It was like he'd thought all along: workshops were not for him.

He went to get his coat and was intending to slip quietly away when Vivien intercepted him.

She said, 'You're not coming back tomorrow, are you?'

'No. Not my thing.'

She changed tack. 'A few of us are going for a drink. Why don't you come too?'

Alex didn't particularly want to, but felt it would be rude to refuse. 'All right,' he said.

Several other people joined them and they went across the road to an Indian restaurant. A drink turned into supper and soon Alex was wedged between a couple of others at the table and realised that it would be impossible to escape without making a fuss. Not that he was desperate to get away. He was sitting near the two builders, and conversation was easy. No one talked about childhood traumas or anything difficult.

He found he was almost enjoying himself.

Which is why, before he left, he heard himself agreeing to come back the following day and see what else the workshop had in store for him.

25

The Workshop: Sunday

Sunday morning began in pretty much the same way. Everyone sat in a large circle and talked, but Alex was feeling confused for some reason that he couldn't be sure of, and wasn't really following what anyone was saying.

It got worse. Vivien announced that the next part of the day was going to be a drawing session. All his dyslexic inhibitions about putting pen (or crayon) to paper and making a fool of himself came to the surface. He was going to fail, just as he always failed when a teacher asked him to write or draw. Vivien handed round huge sheets of paper, so he couldn't even draw a tiny picture that no one else could see. He became agitated. Vivien noticed his distress and tried to reassure him.

'Just draw a nice garden,' she said encouragingly.

He looked round. All the others were absorbed in the task, sketching elaborate gardens with fountains, trees and flowers. He had to try. He picked up a pencil and managed a box-shaped garden; he stuck in a circle for a pond, a couple of stick-like trees. He saw that the other people were using the crayons, so he picked up a brown one and a black one and put in a few more lines. He could tell it wasn't a very good drawing, just a few matchstick lines, but it was the best he could do.

Vivien was walking round the table and commenting on each person's drawing. When she got to Alex, he tensed, but all she said was, 'That's interesting, Alex. Why are there no gates or doors? There's no way to get in or out.'

'What do you mean?'

'Everyone's garden has a gate. How do you get in?' He didn't answer. It was just a drawing. Why did you have to get in? But she persisted: 'You need to put a gate there.'

Alex added a gate.

But Vivien still didn't seem satisfied. She said thoughtfully, 'It's a very bleak garden, isn't it? This is supposed to be a nice garden. Why don't you put in a nice statue, or a bench to sit on?'

Alex said, 'OK, I'll think about that.'

But he left his garden as it was. He didn't know how to draw a statue or a bench; it felt like he was failing some kind of test. His anxiety ratcheted up another notch.

Soon after that they split into two groups so they could talk about their gardens together. Alex listened while the people in his group explained why they'd put a shed in their garden, or what the wheelbarrow meant to them, or which flowers they'd chosen. He was baffled by all of it.

After a while, Vivien turned to Alex, who had so far said nothing. She asked, 'What do you think your garden means to you?'

'I don't know.' He was starting to feel shaky.

'Maybe that's your inner self. That's actually what we're drawing here.' And then she added, 'There's not much going on, is there?'

The feeling of shakiness increased. And then, out of nowhere, Alex found that tears were rolling down his face and he was crying. He didn't know why he felt such a rush of grief, but he was quite unable to stop. 'I was with a bunch of strangers, on a Sunday, in a place I didn't want to be. And I just started really, really crying. I had no idea why. I wasn't unhappy. But something had been triggered in me and it bothered me that I didn't know what it was.'

The other people in the group were kind. They weren't shocked or embarrassed. Instead they comforted him as best they could and gave him reassurance. For Alex, this was something new. In the first years after the accident he'd cried frequently and his friends had always been supportive in their way, as had Marcus, but on the whole they'd just waited till he got over it and then carried on as if nothing had happened. And that had all been a long time ago. With this group of complete strangers he got the feeling that his huge storm of grief was somehow respected, a positive release of strong emotions. Their kindness was almost as much of a shock as his outburst of inexplicable weeping.

Vivien said it was time for a tea break. Alex's crying had subsided and they all trooped into the coffee room. There weren't enough chairs, so Alex sat on the floor and leaned his back against the wall. A girl called Sarah came to sit beside him.

People were quietly chatting in groups, when suddenly, from nowhere, Alex burst out crying again. Crying and crying and getting himself into a terrible mess.

'And then,' says Alex, 'the weirdest thing happened, and I'll never forget this for the rest of my life. I was crying and crying, and Sarah was holding my hand and trying to comfort me. And then I just stopped.' Remembering, he snaps his fingers. 'Just like that. All of a sudden, literally in a second, I flopped against the wall. I passed out, left my body, and arrived on the other side of the room.'

From across the room he watched the drama that unfolded. He could see his body slumped against the wall.[8] He could tell that his heart-rate had dropped almost to nothing. Sarah and the others nearby were starting to panic. Someone rushed off to fetch Vivien. Alex remembers watching her come into the room. She looked down at his unmoving body and said, 'Right, now this is what we are going to do. Everybody get out of here except you, Sarah. You stay there.'

Alex was observing everything that happened. He saw that Sarah was still sitting beside him. She was desperately worried and glanced up with relief as Vivien took charge of the situation. Vivien sat on the floor, across his legs. She looked at him and put her hands on his chest, running them down his body in a sweeping gesture. She said firmly, 'You need to come back, and you need to come back NOW!'

And, says Alex, 'I whooshed straight back in. I remember the feeling.'

He opened his eyes and looked at her. His crying was all gone.

---

8 Like Alex's earlier experiences, this is a well-documented phenomenon, the result of extreme stress or head injury. Experiments have shown, however, that the subject can 'see' only what they would have been able to see from the position their body remained in.

'What the *hell* was that?' he demanded. What he had just undergone was quite unlike anything that had happened before. In the past he'd had sensations of spinning, and whizzing upwards or down through the floor, but this flying across the room and watching everything that was going on below was far more intense, and more visual.

'You've had an out-of-body experience,' said Vivien.

Alex was amazed: she didn't seem the least bit surprised.

Her next words shocked him to the core.

Carefully, she said, 'There's a lot more in your past that you don't know about. There's a dark side to your family, Alex, and that's what's coming out in your garden and in your subconscious.'

Alex said, 'Vivien, what are you talking about? There's nothing wrong with my family!'

Because, as far as he was concerned, there wasn't.

She was adamant. 'I'm telling you there is.' She hesitated just a moment before saying firmly, 'I think there's sexual abuse in your family.'

This was too much. Alex knew his family. OK, so he couldn't remember anything from the first eighteen years of his life, but Marcus had filled in the gaps and he knew his childhood had been pretty normal. A bit eccentric, maybe, but nothing really bad. Vivien's bald statement made him furious.

'You can't just sit there and say that!' he said.

But she stuck to her guns. She sat beside him and explained it all very calmly. All the work she'd done over the years meant that she could guess from his body language and the sessions they'd had together that there were serious emotional traumas buried in his unconscious. In her opinion, it was sexual abuse. And that was the cause of the outburst that afternoon, all the emotions coming out. He wasn't alone. Sarah, who was still sitting next to him, had had the same kind of bad experiences in her childhood.

This calmed him down. He began talking to Sarah, listening to her story. But still, he was in shock and was finding it impossible to take in what Vivien had told him.

The workshop drew to a close. It had been a long and very emotional day and everyone was shattered. People were saying their goodbyes, drifting back to their separate lives.

Alex was not yet in a state to go home, so he and Vivien had a cup of tea together, then talked for a while in the car park.

'I can't believe what you're telling me,' he said. 'Sexual abuse? How can that be?'

'You must ask your brothers,' said Vivien. 'See what they tell you. I think it's probably your mother.'

'Mummy? Is that possible?' Alex was in such shock that he barely registered what she was saying.

'Ask Marcus and Oliver.'

It was a long time before Alex was composed enough to drive across South London to his Brixton house, and his mind was in turmoil. For years he'd lived in a kind of limbo where nothing much seemed to touch him. All that had been blown away by what Vivien had said, but he still couldn't take it in. He was angry, confused, disbelieving, so full of conflicting emotions that he felt as though he might be going crazy. He wondered if perhaps she'd made the whole thing up, in which case his life could go back to normal. But why would anyone make something like that up?

He went into his little house and closed the door behind him. *Talk to Marcus*, she'd said, but right now he wasn't in a fit state to talk to anyone. It was just too huge to deal with. What was he supposed to say? How do you ask someone a question like that?

He went to bed, and lay all night without sleeping. He'd worked so hard to create a picture of his childhood and the years that had been wiped out. Was it possible he'd got it all wrong? What did it mean, that there'd been sexual abuse? How could Vivien just come out and say that to him? What if she was wrong?

Monday morning came and he was in no state to go to work. By now he knew this wasn't the kind of thing he could brush under the carpet, the way he and Marcus always dealt with anything too dark or difficult. Get on with your life, go out with your friends, work hard. It was what they'd always done, but that wasn't going to be possible, not with this.

By late afternoon he knew what he had to do. He got in his car and drove the short distance to the house in Clapham that Marcus shared with Oliver.

He had to know the truth.

26

Is It True?

Marcus hadn't long got back from work and was still in his work clothes. He was in the kitchen at the back of the house, with the door open onto the little garden, spring birdsong filtering in. He'd just made a cup of tea and was spreading a piece of toast with butter and jam.

'Hi Alex,' he said cheerfully. 'What's up?'

Alex had imagined a hundred different ways to ask the question, but now he blurted out, 'Vivien says there was sexual abuse in our family. That we were abused.' He hesitated. 'Was it Daddy?'

Marcus didn't speak. The smile died on his face and he turned pale. Alex pressed on. 'She thinks maybe it was Mummy.'

Marcus was still holding the mug of tea. He seemed frozen.

'Well?' asked Alex. 'Is it true?'

Marcus turned away, so Alex couldn't see his face. Still he didn't speak.

'Marky, talk to me! She was saying all this stuff and I don't know what to believe. I feel like I'm going crazy. What happened? Was it sexual abuse?'

Marcus's reply was almost inaudible. 'Yes,' he muttered.

'Yes? What happened? Tell me, Marky. I have to know the truth. It must have been Daddy.'

'No.'

'Not Mummy?'

'Yes.' Even fainter this time.

Alex went up to his brother and put his hand on his shoulder.

'I need to know.'

Marcus shrugged him off. 'No,' he said. 'Talk to Oliver. He'll tell you. Not me.'

'Oliver?'

'He's been in therapy. He's been remembering stuff.'

'But—'

'No!' insisted Marcus. He walked out into the garden. Though Alex had no way of knowing this, it was only three weeks since Oliver had confronted Marcus with the traumas that had been emerging in his therapy, and now here was Alex asking the same horrible questions. It was more than he could cope with.

Alex watched him for a moment, then turned and walked slowly up the stairs. There was music playing at the top of the house, where Oliver had a couple of rooms. He was back from university for the holidays.

Oliver looked up as Alex came into the room, pleased to see him as always. But when he saw the expression on his brother's face, his smile faded.

'Alex?'

'Oliver, I don't know what's going on. I've just been on a workshop with Vivien and she said . . . she said there was sexual abuse in our family. She told me to ask you and Marcus. Marky said it's true but he won't talk to me about it. What's going on?'

'Oh, Ali.' Oliver's eyes were brimming with tears.

'Is it true?'

He nodded.

'It was Mummy?'

'Yes.'

'Jesus! I can't believe it!'

Oliver crumpled, sobs shaking his whole body. Alex sat down beside him on the bed and put his arm around him and Oliver slumped hopelessly against him.

The horror of it was too much. Not just his own pain, but his baby brother's as well. Oliver was a strong young man who had always appeared supremely confident and sorted, and it was heart-rending to see him like this.

For years, Alex had been numb, cut off from his emotions. Not any more. Now he felt engulfed by a storm of grief that was going to tear him apart.

By the time he left the house a couple of hours later, Alex had no choice but to accept that Vivien's hunch, or visioning, had been correct. It was real: he and his brothers had been sexually abused, and their mother had been responsible.

One question had been answered, but a dozen more had sprung up in its place. Apart from confirming the fact of the abuse, Marcus refused to say anything more about it. Sexual abuse had taken place. Involving their mother. Over many years. But there were no details, nothing to guide him through this frightening new landscape that he'd stumbled into.

He wrote to Amanda in India and told her what had happened. Oliver wrote to her as well. A couple of weeks later Alex got a reply confirming that she'd always guessed that something like that had been going on.

In the fifteen years since his accident, Alex had built up a picture of the kind of childhood he'd had: family holidays, growing up, normal stuff. Of course, he had no memories of any of it, but the stories Marcus had given him had taken the place of memory. He'd trusted Marcus absolutely, right from day one. But if Marcus had left out something as huge as the fact that their mother had sexually abused them, how could he trust any of it? What else had Marcus decided not to tell him?

He had to find the answers. But now he was faced with the hardest challenge of all: how do you uncover your story and who you really are in a family where truth is a moveable feast? Where reality is obscured behind a smokescreen of silence and lies? It wasn't just his past he was searching for, but his present.

The task would consume him for years; it became fundamental to his survival.

With everything he had ever believed turned upside-down, Alex – once again – had no idea who he was.

27

Beginning Again

Years later, when he finally talked with his siblings about this period of his life, Alex spoke eloquently about the impact of the revelation.

'My life changed dramatically when I was thirty-two years old,' he told them. 'I think it was probably the biggest trauma of my entire life. Considering the appalling parenting, there have been a lot of traumas, but for me, that was way bigger. Bigger than the abuse, the accident, Mummy dying, Daddy dying, all of it fades into oblivion compared to that one day.'

In the weeks and months after the workshop, he struggled to absorb what he had learned. Sometimes he was angry that no one had told him anything before. He thought, 'Marcus has lied to me. My brother and sister haven't told me anything.' And he was bewildered. Inevitably he wondered how many other people knew about this. As he says, 'My mind was just going round and round, thinking, "What's happening here?" ' How had he got to be in his thirties without knowing or suspecting anything about it?

With the foundation of his life undermined, he questioned everything: what was real? What was false? Sometimes, in spite of what Oliver and Marcus had told him, he simply found it impossible to believe that the picture he'd created of his family and his life before he was eighteen was wrong. He still had no glimmerings of memory and was completely dependent on the information others chose to share with him. He no longer knew whose version to believe.

When he came round from the coma at the age of eighteen, Marcus had been at his side, ready to help him through every stage of the journey. Just at the age when in the normal course of events they would have started to grow apart and find their separate ways in the world, Alex had become totally dependent on his twin. Even when they were apart, that sense of dependency never went away. And in a strange way, Marcus had grown to depend on his brother's dependency. Sometimes he'd been impatient with him, as if he wanted to push him away, but the fundamental bond between them was unaffected.

The contrast now, fifteen years later, could not have been more stark. What Alex had to deal with now felt like going through the experience of the accident all over again, only this time it was much, much harder. Many of the after-effects of the motorcycle accident had been physical and he'd learned to deal with them in a practical way. Even the memory loss was a handicap he'd learned to manage. But this new challenge was horribly complex and he was at the mercy of violent waves of emotion.

All through his twenties he'd felt as though he was somehow detached from his experiences, but the traumatic events of the workshop had burst through the dam of numbness that had sheltered him. His feelings had been unleashed and now there was no stopping them.

Most significant of all, Marcus was no longer at his side to help.

According to Alex, Marcus 'went back into his shadow'. He had refused to talk about their childhood secrets when Alex first approached him, and he made it clear he had no intention of talking about them, ever. The subject was off-limits. Alex accepted this, the way he and Marcus always accepted the choices the other one made. He was not even aware of feeling resentful at his twin's way of coping.

Maybe he knew that at that time, Marcus didn't really have a choice. For Marcus, it was simple. He was neither ready nor able to explore the horrors that Alex had uncovered. He says, 'I'd done a good job of not remembering any of that stuff. The last thing I needed in my life was to go down that road.' His way of coping was to push it as far to the back of his mind as he could, where it could do less harm. All along he'd wanted to protect Alex from the toxic memories he had learned to forget, and he couldn't understand why Alex needed to dig out truths that would only bring pain.

Marcus was uneasy about Vivien's influence and the kind of therapy she practised, which he pooh-poohed as 'mumbo-jumbo'. He felt that Alex was going down a spiritual path he didn't understand and that was 'completely out of my realm'. It was one of the few times they found themselves in disagreement, and they avoided ever talking about the subject. There was never any actual falling-out – they still needed each other, and cared about each other in a way that no one else could understand – but their day-to-day dealings became practical and unemotional. They continued to work together and often socialised together as well, but Marcus kept himself firmly apart from the quest that was to absorb Alex over the years ahead.

Alex, trying to piece his life together for the second time, now found he had to do it without Marcus's help. He was on his own.

PART II

The Second Story

I

Egypt

Alex boarded the plane for Cairo and found a window seat. His stomach was knotted with tension. He had signed up for one of Vivien's spiritual pilgrimages. It had seemed like the logical next step after the workshop, but he had no idea what it was going to involve. The other people in the group all seemed to be old friends; they were sitting together, laughing and chatting, but Alex didn't know any of them.

The building side of Lewis Burton had finally been wound up the week before. In theory, Alex had the time to start discovering the truth about his childhood and his family, but right now that seemed an almost impossible task. Where could he start? How was he going to do it without Marcus's support? How was he supposed to know what was true and what was made up?

He had never felt so alone.

One of the last people to board the plane was a young woman who greeted some of the others in the group, then came down the gangway and saw the empty seat beside him.

'Can I sit here?'

'Sure.'

Alex noticed at once that she was attractive, with dark hair and a hippyish style. He moved his things off the seat and she sat down.

What happened next was, as Alex says, 'the weirdest thing'. Instead of the usual pleasantries – 'Hello, how are you? What do you do?' – they began talking together from that very first moment as though they were resuming a conversation they had been having earlier that day. *Anyway, as I was saying . . .*

Which is exactly how Marcus and Alex always feel when they see each other again after a separation, however long they have been apart. Alex had never experienced anything like it with anyone apart from Marcus. It wasn't, as he says, a sexual attraction back then, rather an instant and profound sense of connection.

Her name was Camilla.

They talked all the way to Cairo. He told her he was a twin, and about his memory loss, and she told him she had just come back from three months in North America.

The next ten days were extraordinary in many ways. Under Vivien's guidance, the group meditated in pyramids at the dead of night, with strange and visionary results. Camilla and Alex were together almost all the time, but their focus was on the spiritual journey they were taking together, and they both maintain they were unaware of the attraction growing between them. However, they remember a significant detail: neither of them spent much time by the hotel pool.

Both their rooms overlooked the pool. When Alex looked out of his window and saw that Camilla wasn't there, he decided there was no point going down on his own. Camilla, in her room, was peering down at the pool and, seeing no Alex, came to the same conclusion. They laugh now at the memory: 'We spent most of our time not going to the pool!'

Towards the end of their ten days, when they were sitting at opposite ends of the long dining table the group shared, a friend asked Camilla what she thought of Alex. She glanced over at him and said non-committally, 'Oh, he's really nice.' The friend was surprised, asked if she fancied him. It hadn't occurred to Camilla till then, but now she thought: 'Hmm . . . did I? Maybe, just a bit?'

They flew back to London, and Alex drove Camilla to the friend's house near the airport where she had left her car. As she had a long drive ahead of her, he suggested she come back with him to his Brixton house for the night and set off in the morning. She agreed and went with him to Brixton. She didn't leave the next morning. Or the one after that.

They have been together ever since.

2

Camilla

.

Camilla had known Vivien for about ten years, and had taken part in various workshops and trips with her. At the beginning of 1998, while Alex and Marcus were winding up the development side of their business, Camilla was in Washington State, working with a herbalist on a Native American reservation.

Her time there was nearly over when Vivien phoned her and said she was planning a trip to Egypt. Vivien added that she'd like the others in the group. She had mentioned Alex, and told Camilla she would 'really connect' with him, but apart from that all she knew when she boarded the plane was that he lived in London and was interested in photography.

That first conversation on the flight to Cairo was as much of a revelation to Camilla as it had been to Alex. 'It was like we had known each other all our lives,' she says now. They just started talking – *again*. Like Alex she had a sense that they were resuming a connection that had begun long before. She remembers Alex's astonishment when he said to her, 'I can talk to you like I can talk to my brother.'

And in fact, at this point in their lives, he could talk to Camilla about things that Marcus refused to discuss. Through all the false starts and conflicting discoveries that lay ahead, Camilla was the person who listened, commented, supported and encouraged Alex in his search.

When they got back, they only had three weeks together in London before Alex left to go trekking in Nepal with Marcus and Oliver. The trip had been planned well in advance and they were gone for six weeks. All three brothers remember this holiday as a bonding experience and, on the whole, a cheerful time. For Oliver it was a first experience of the positive benefits of extreme physical challenge, 'from feeling detached inside to alive and connected'. They talked about life at Duke's Cottage, what Jill and Jack had been like as parents, and Alex started to get a clearer picture of just how difficult life had been for them all as children.

The one topic that was never mentioned as they tramped through the spectacular mountain scenery was the sexual abuse. They might have felt that they were free of their mother's influence, but the habits she had drummed into them from an early age were hard to shift. Secrecy and denial had been inculcated in them from their earliest years, the secrecy and denial that is always necessary in an abusive family and which is so hard for people who have grown up in happier homes to understand. It was the secrecy and denial that had allowed the abuse to continue for so long, and which would seldom be broken for more than a decade.

While Alex was away, Camilla found a houseboat in Islington that they could share, and she prepared it for his return. They had known from the day they got back to England that this was a serious relationship. After six weeks apart she was eager to see him again.

During their time together before he left for Nepal, she had accepted Alex as he was, without delving too deeply into the emotional make-up of this man she wanted to be with. 'Alex was just what Alex *was*.'

It was only on his return that she began to realise what a relationship with him was going to be like.

'I missed you so much!' she told him, naturally expecting that he would respond by saying he'd missed her too. But he didn't. He seemed unable to express his feelings for her at all.

Although he had started to tap into strong emotions at Vivien's workshop, the normal expression of feelings was still alien to him. It wasn't that he was deliberately cold or dismissive – he simply had no language with which to reciprocate Camilla's words of affection.

Not surprisingly, she found his unresponsiveness difficult. The connection between them was so profound that she never doubted how much he loved her, but she would have liked to hear him put his deepest feelings into words.

And now, as Alex told her more about his family and the impact of his memory loss, she began to understand what a complex and unusual man she had fallen in love with. The word she uses to describe him at that time is 'haunted'. There was an emptiness inside him, a blank canvas where other people store their memories and their sense of self. Camilla wanted to help, but sometimes she found herself wondering who exactly she was helping. She gradually realised that there was an impossible disconnect between Alex's mind and his heart.

The situation was complicated by the fact that he was still enmeshed with his twin brother. It might have felt to Alex as though he and Marcus were beginning to grow apart from each other, but to Camilla the bond between them seemed at times like a merging of identities. It could be hard to know where Alex's personality ended and Marcus's began. Marcus had provided Alex's internal narrative for over ten years. So much of what Alex knew or felt about himself was based on what Marcus had told him. It was almost as if they were one person as if Marcus was both his feelings and his story.

It wasn't always easy. Marcus had recognised right away that Camilla was the right partner for Alex, but that didn't stop him from feeling ambivalent about her place in their lives. She says now, 'I felt that Marcus had the lion's share of his love,' and she needed him to be on side because he was her 'way in' to Alex. But Marcus blocked her as often as he helped her.

Although he was eager to strike out on his own, there remained a part of him that was terrified of letting go. The twins' absolute closeness had ensured their survival in the past; this Marcus knew in a way that Alex never would.

Camilla had become involved with someone who seemed to have no clearly defined identity, and time and again she found herself asking, 'Who is Alex?'

It was the question Alex himself would spend years trying to unravel.

Without Camilla's love and support, it is doubtful he would have ever come close to finding an answer.

3

Soul-Searching

Once Alex began to ask questions, his tenacity was extraordinary.

He was still finding it hard to accept that his early life was so different from the picture he'd created, but he had to learn the truth. The ideal solution would be if he could remember for himself what had happened. Had the memories been wiped out completely, or were they still locked away in some remote part of his brain, so that it was just a question of finding a way to access them? If that was the case, then he wouldn't have to rely on other people – because if he couldn't trust his own twin brother, how could he trust anyone? Even if he couldn't remember actual events and details, maybe there was a way he could unlock the feelings and sensations that had accompanied the events.

He tried everything. Therapy, meditation, workshops, hypnosis. He gathered documents and photographs; he talked to anyone who might be able to shed some light on those eighteen vanished years. The compulsion to know the truth was all-consuming.

Looking back now, he describes what it was like: 'I spent the next ten years soul-searching, trying to find out the real

Our mother had been a debutante. Lively and extrovert, she always had a full social life.

Our parents were married in Newbury in 1956, and she was determined to be a conventional 'home wife'.

Our mother's fun-loving instincts made her popular with children.

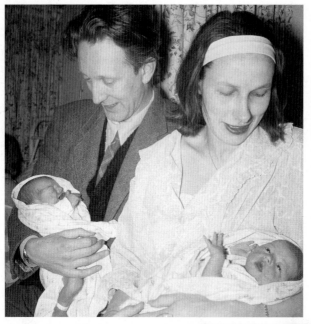

This is the only photograph of us with our father. He was killed a few days – maybe hours – after this picture was taken.

Left on her own, our mother literally had her hands full.

First steps, helped by our mother and grandmother.

'Marcus'n'Alex',
'AliandMarky' –
Because we were never
apart, people ran our
names together.

Our grandmother's
real love was her
Chihuahuas and
she sometimes had
50 in her house
at once. She is on
the right, our sister
Amanda in front.

We must have been
about 15 when this
picture was taken with
Oliver and Amanda,
three years before
Alex's accident.

Christmas was always a formal occasion. Our mother and Jack in a rare moment of tranquillity.

Alex as a steward on the *QE2* – real independence at last.

Duke's Cottage looked the rural idyll – but most of our teens were spent in an unheated shed, just visible on the right.

Marcus in the Hong
Kong movies – a flying
Ninja and a captured GI.

In New Zealand
we became
entrepreneurs
for the first time
and were always
referred to as
'The Hairband
Twins'.

Alex and Marcus relaxing on Lake Kashgar while travelling in Kashmir.

In 1988 we began working as painters and decorators
and called our company, 'Twin Decs'.

In Pemba almost all our workforce was from the local village. Marcus shared their life for 18 months while the hotel was built.

Ellis Flyte, Alex and Marcus relaxing on a dhow.

Fundu Lagoon is now recognised as one of the most romantic holiday destinations in Africa.

Oliver, Marcus, Alex
and Amanda finally
interred all four urns
in the family tomb.

Marcus and Vito were
married in Menorca.

It stops. We want our children's experiences to be different from ours.
A brighter future.

story. I had a puzzle in front of me, and everything was a lie, and then you've got to piece it together again and find out which bits are lies and which bits real. And who you really are.'

Always, at the core of his journey to learn the facts about his early life was this single overwhelming need: to know who he really was. Each discovery only led to more questions.

But what was obvious, as he started the search, was that their childhood had been anything but normal.

He learned from people who had visited, from friends and neighbours – and now, even from Marcus – that life at Duke's Cottage had been tough. Much tougher than he'd realised. The twins had to address their stepfather as 'Sir' at all times and stand up when he came into the room. There was never any physical affection: at bedtime, when they were still children, they'd shaken his hand formally when they said good night.

As soon as Jill had set up home in Sussex with her new husband, a strict routine of work had been imposed. 'We served them,' says Alex. 'That's what we were there for.' Alex learned they'd had to get up early to empty the bins, polish the shoes, wash up the dishes from their parents' evening meal. When they handed round drinks and canapés at the parties Jill and her society friends had in London, they were expected to do a professional job and clean up afterwards. In the evenings after school their play or homework was interrupted by frequent demands to prepare vegetables and do jobs around the house. If there was any lifting or carrying that needed to be done for their mother's antiques business, Alex and Marcus were the ones who did it.

This could sound like the typical complaints of teenage boys who resented having to help with the chores. Surely it wasn't that bad?

But, at the time, Alex and Marcus accepted the way things were because it was all they'd known; it was friends and visitors, people who were fundamentally well disposed to the Dudley parents, who observed that they were making excessive demands on the young boys. Many of them were uncomfortable with the situation, though they had no idea how bad it actually was.

Deirdre Brockway admitted to Alex that she'd been horrified by the way the twins were treated by her husband's old friend: 'It wasn't normal, the way you were exploited.' Like most people, she'd assumed that it was Jack who was mostly to blame.

Laura Hudson told Alex they had been treated 'like servants'. But like the rest of their social circle, she and her husband hadn't wanted to make things worse by interfering. She'd been aware of Jack's blistering comments and how people feared him; there seemed to be no way to change his behaviour. Instead, they'd offered the twins love and hospitality, hoping to compensate for what they guessed was often lacking at home.

As did Jenny Graham. She had just left school when she came to live with the family to look after Amanda, who was still a baby; Alex and Marcus were ten. Jenny stayed for eighteen months and enjoyed her time at Duke's Cottage. She was devoted to the whole family, stayed in close touch afterwards, and her memories were very positive. She described the atmosphere at Duke's Cottage as 'very free and easy and eccentric . . . I loved it.'

Her overriding impression of the twins at that time was that they were 'the sweetest boys. And happy, always happy.' She got on well with both parents. Yet, contradicting her claim that they were always happy, she added the proviso that if the twins had not had each other, she would have had to 'wrap them up and smuggle them out of the house' because of what she calls Jack's 'abusive' behaviour. He was always courteous to her, because he appreciated her close bond with Amanda, but she knew he was often 'horrible, horrible' with others, and could be 'very aggressive and loud'.

While Jenny was living in the house, she and the twins turned avoiding Jack's temper into a game. On their return from school they consumed vast quantities of toast and jam in the kitchen, and they'd imitate Jill and Jack, laughing uproariously at each other's impressions.

Her memories were full of laughter and fun, but underneath Alex realised there was something else going on. Because the moment they heard the latch on the door, as Jenny says, 'the laughter stopped' and the television was switched off; it was always better not to be caught larking about, especially if it was Jack coming in. She herself didn't fear him, but she feared him blowing up at the boys and did her best to protect them from his anger. It wasn't easy. Even though they spent a good proportion of their time at home doing chores, Jack accused them of laziness and, she says, 'would blast them for not doing it right'.

Another friend told Alex that she had once babysat for Oliver when he was small, and he had run off into the garden and disappeared. Jack had let rip in a rage, and she'd received a tongue-lashing she had never forgotten. She told him it was the most terrifying experience she could ever remember.

It was hard for people to assess the situation, because the twins always seemed so cheery. But Jenny told Alex she had always realised they weren't allowed to behave like normal ten-year-old boys. The garden at Duke's Cottage was huge, but it was Jack's pride and joy and football on the lawn was forbidden. They hardly ever ate with their parents.

She remembered that when she first went to Duke's Cottage the twins had slept in a little room next to the kitchen. In winter it was freezing, with black mould on the walls and condensation on the windows. Again, the twins assumed this was how all boys' bedrooms were, and it was family friends who noticed the contrast with the way Amanda and Oliver were treated: they both had warm bedrooms upstairs, though Oliver later spent many years in the chilly bedroom beyond the kitchen.

Alex knew that when they were about fourteen, they had moved out to what their parents called 'the annexe', and they called 'the shed'. In some ways they had approved of the change, since it gave them a degree of independence, but Marcus said that they'd been left in no doubt that they were moving out because they weren't welcome in the house. It was only when they began work, and were making a financial contribution to the house, that they were 'allowed' back. Marcus had always glossed over the problems in their childhood, and when he told Alex about their privations he found a way to make it sound like a joke. But the picture Alex was getting was bleak.

Jill's 'short arms' were legendary, and she never spent a penny more than she had to on clothes for herself or her children. Neighbours and people she worked with remember the twins always wore ill-fitting second-hand clothes and plimsolls without laces. Oliver and Amanda fared no better and were deeply embarrassed by their charity shop cast-offs.

Alex had assumed that his childhood included summer holidays and outings with his parents – after all, that was what 'normal' families did, and he'd found a batch of photographs showing the twins with their mother on a sandy beach, somewhere hot. The fact that there were no other holiday snaps was probably because they hadn't bothered to take a camera on the other holidays. But now he learned that seaside holiday had been a one-off, taken the year before she married Jack. Once they married and moved to Sussex there were no more holidays for the boys; at least, not with their mother.

The treats and holidays they enjoyed as children were entirely thanks to the close family friends who made such a difference in their childhood and beyond. As Alex says, 'By the grace of God, we've had all these angels dropping into our lives and looking after us.'

Jill and Jack had met Ian and Laura Hudson soon after their move to Rudgwick. The Hudsons were a generation younger and to begin with they were flattered and slightly overwhelmed by the attentions of this larger-than-life couple. Within weeks of getting to know them, Jill and Jack had asked the younger couple to act as guardians to all their children in the event of their deaths.

The Hudsons agreed. Jack was a friend of Ian's mother, and Ian was old-school enough to be respectful to his elders, and not to criticise them. By that time he and Laura had already opened their home to the twins and welcomed them with great generosity. They were unstinting with their energy and their love, and also with their money. When Alex and Marcus were about nine, the Hudsons included them in a family holiday to Portugal: they paid their fares and all their expenses, and though they felt a niggle of annoyance that Jill and Jack never made a financial contribution, they continued to invite the boys along for many years.

The results of their kindness are impossible to calculate. As Alex says now, 'I don't think we'd be sane without them.'

Perhaps at some level, Alex and Marcus knew even as small boys that they needed to reach out beyond their immediate family circle. A couple of high-spirited twin boys are not normally the easiest children to take on, but Jack's strict regime meant they had excellent manners. Besides which, they had grace and charm in abundance and many adults found them irresistible.

Laura remembers them as having been 'charismatic, and very good with adults.' They needed to be loved and they had learned from a young age how to inspire love in people beyond their immediate family circle. 'In a funny way,' says Alex, 'they must have read it in our persona, that we needed looking after.'

According to Marcus, this ability to forge an alliance with others has always been important. 'It's one of our only skills – our biggest skill. We connect with everyone.' And Alex adds ruefully, 'We had to.'

This skill won them valuable and lifelong friendships with the kind of people who would never abuse their trust.

But there were other adults, mostly friends of their mother's, who had a different agenda entirely. With these often shadowy figures, the twins' charm and their need to be loved made them horribly vulnerable.

4

Bad Education

The twins' schooling was another aspect of their early life that Marcus had glossed over after the accident. Alex knew their time at school had been 'quite hard' but now, as he pieced his story together anew, he wanted to find out more about it.

For Marcus their dyslexia was and remains the defining fact of their childhood. School presented them with a hopeless struggle. When they first moved to Sussex to live with Jack Dudley, they were sent to a prep school in the village. They were obviously of above average intelligence, but academic work proved almost impossible. When he was going through Jill's papers, Alex discovered two reports written by educational psychologists: one from when they were eight, the second written two years later. Alex was assessed as the more industrious of the two, and performed slightly better in the tests.

The first psychologist noted that he had 'a slight twitch of the shoulder and face which becomes more apparent in pressured situations, e.g. when reading.' He comments that 'there were, however, no indications of gross emotional difficulty.' What led to the psychologist even asking this question? Was the school aware that all was not well in the world of these little boys? Did some adults have their suspicions?

The records told Alex nothing more.

And he was left with the question: could anything have been done, back in the 1970s, if someone had bothered to look a little more deeply into what their home life was really like?

Probably not, not then. And they did not remain long at the little prep school; at the age of eleven they moved to the local comprehensive. Some of their parents' friends think this was a financial decision: Jack had taken out a bridging loan when they bought Duke's Cottage, and he was suddenly short of cash. Alex and Marcus believed it was because they weren't considered bright enough for their education to be worth any investment. Jack had no intention of 'wasting money' on them.

Whatever the reason, the comprehensive was a disaster. It wasn't a bad school, but as they were still unable to read or write properly, they were placed in the bottom stream, where their sense of themselves as academic lost causes was reinforced on a daily basis.

Marcus says that Jack never lost an opportunity to tell them how stupid they were. Deirdre Brockway remembers him introducing them to people as 'Jill's dim twins'. No doubt the boys grinned cheerfully; they had learned to hide their feelings under a mask of jollity. To her credit, Jill never accused them of stupidity, and even started claiming that she herself was dyslexic,[9] but she never made any effort to help with their

9 Her letters do not bear this out, and her self-diagnosis might have been an attempt at solidarity with her sons, or else a way of cashing in on their disability.

literacy and they had no specialist help of any kind during the rest of their schooldays.

Most people seem to have accepted that helping her sons with their schoolwork was quite simply beyond Jill's capabilities. As Jenny explained to Alex, 'Jill couldn't have helped. She wasn't that kind of person. She was great at being Jill, but she had her own agenda.' The very idea of her sitting down at the table to concentrate on their concerns was unthinkable. She was hardly ever still. To help her sons she 'would have had to clear all the clutter out of her mind, looked at the book, focussed – and that was too small a role for her.'

Their first couple of years at the comprehensive were tough. Not only were they in the bottom stream but they were different from their classmates. For once, their ability to connect with people let them down.

Marcus told Alex, 'We spoke with very poshy accents; they knew where we lived, and they hated it. They tried to get us to change our accents, so every day was abuse.' He's quick to explain that the comprehensive wasn't tough in the way an inner-city school might have been, and most days it was just verbal abuse, the odd thump or punch and having things thrown at them in class. But occasionally 'they'd all pile in and you'd end up with a black eye.'

Perhaps as a result of those experiences at the comprehensive, Alex and Marcus have remained acutely aware of social class. Unlike their mother, they are not in the least bit snobbish, but they learned the finer gradations of British class distinction at close quarters. From childhood, as Alex discovered, they had been dragooned by their mother to hand round the drinks at the London parties she threw with her society friends. They dressed smartly, were polite and charming, and knew how to get along with the great and the good.

Their comprehensive was light years away from those sophisticated gatherings, and in time the twins learned the chameleon skills of adaptability. After they left home, during their years of travelling, they mixed with people from all walks of life, and they evolved fairly neutral accents. As painters and decorators with Twin Decs, they considered themselves to be in working-class jobs. Now, Marcus says, 'all our working-class friends think we have a posh accent and all our posh friends think we don't. We're in the middle, aren't we?'

The daily threats and bullying at school continued for two or three years, until they made friends with a huge lad called Grant, who became their protector. From then on, they were at least left alone, but their education remained patchy at best. By the time they left, they could each write their name at the top of the exam paper, and not much more. Since Jack was continuously telling them they were stupid, they accepted that this was the reason for their lack of success. Then, one summer, they went on a special dyslexia course at Lyn Lewis holiday camp. They met other dyslexics. They met teachers who did not regard them as hopeless cases. They began to wonder if perhaps they weren't so stupid after all.

Alex had no idea what prompted this sudden attempt to tackle their dyslexia and Marcus couldn't remember. One or two of Jill's friends told him they had talked to her about solutions to their problem, so it's possible that social pressure prompted her and Jack to act.

If Marcus and Alex are bitter about anything in their upbringing, it's the fact that, apart from that one summer, they were never given the specialised help that would have made such a difference to the rest of their lives. Now, Alex has to some extent mastered his dyslexia: he can read well and writes fluently, though his spelling is erratic. Office work takes him twice as long as it would take a non-dyslexic, but he can get it done. Marcus still struggles: a form in a bank can reduce him to tears of frustration. He reckons that Alex is less handicapped nowadays because the memory of all those times Jack told them they were stupid was erased along with the other memories when he was eighteen. There's dyslexia, and there is awareness of dyslexia, and the memory of eighteen years of being told he was stupid is an extra burden for Marcus.

The misery of their first few years at the comprehensive was mitigated by the fact that they had each other. Whatever happened to them, at home or at school, couldn't touch them, because they were in their own world. Marcus told Alex, 'I think part of the reason the bullies gave up was because they couldn't really get to us. It got a bit dull.' As he says, from an early age, they had learned 'to suck it all up. We had each other.'

Their resilience was impressive. In their private twin world, they refused ever to see themselves as victims. Like many dyslexics, they had to work harder and be more enterprising than other people. When they were seeing the world, for instance, as Marcus says, 'Other travellers were working in offices, but because of our disability, we could either wash up in restaurants or be entrepreneurs. So you turn left and do off-the-wall stuff.'

The dyslexia that had blighted their schooling gave them one advantage: it forced them into adventures they might never have had otherwise. And Marcus was about to discover a haven where his dyslexia did not exist.

5

Escape

Marcus was growing uncomfortable with Alex's questions. He had developed his own strategies for coping, and they had always served him well. Now Alex's quest for answers and a clearer picture of his life before the accident was in danger of threatening his brother's hard-won equilibrium.

'You don't understand,' Alex told him. 'I *have* to do this!'

'Fine,' said Marcus. 'Just count me out.'

Marcus was already clear about the way he had always compartmentalised his life. He explains, 'You've got ten jars on the mantelpiece, and one of them's got a bad smell in it.' The solution is simple: don't open the jar and never ever peer inside. Occasionally you might lift the lid a fraction and take a sniff, but the smell is disgusting, so you put the lid straight back on again. Leave it alone.

He wanted to get on and enjoy life, not waste time talking about a childhood that was over and couldn't be changed. But Alex's compulsion to understand what had happened was in danger of blowing the lid off that poisonous jar. Marcus was ready to escape.

One warm summer evening he happened to be in the Groucho Club with Ellis Flyte, an old friend who was taking a break from her fashion company and was looking for a new project.

Over a couple of drinks, she mentioned that she'd always wanted to buy a beach in a faraway place.

'That sounds interesting,' said Marcus. 'Where would you go?'

They started to build castles in the air, describing the kind of beach they'd like to visit, thinking about their dream house. But as the evening wore on, a house didn't seem like enough of a draw: how about a guest house?

'Or a hotel,' said Ellis. 'Something really sexy!'

'Yes, a boutique hotel everyone would want to visit!'

Ellis mentioned that a friend of hers was looking to sell a stretch of beach in Zanzibar. That might fit the bill.

'Shall we go and look at it?' she asked.

'Why not?' said Marcus.

The next morning, Marcus told Alex about the scheme. Alex was not impressed. He thought it was just 'a bit of piss-talk in the pub,' and in no way realistic. So far as he was concerned it was the kind of crazy scheme you think up on a good night out, scribble down on the back of an envelope and then chuck in the bin the next day.

A week later, Marcus and Ellis headed off for Zanzibar.

Alex waved them off. 'Have a nice holiday!' he said sceptically.

But by the time they came back, even he was infected by their enthusiasm.

'The beaches are incredible!' Marcus told him. 'There's a great scene on the north of the island, and we've found the perfect place. You have to come and see it, Ali!'

Ellis was already drawing up serious plans with her father, who was an architect, but Marcus had made it clear that they couldn't close on the deal until Alex had agreed to it. He might be keen to distance himself from the quest that was driving his twin, but that didn't mean he was about to embark on an adventure like this without Alex being a part of it.

He and Ellis flew back to Zanzibar, their excitement growing all the time, and a few days later Alex flew out to join them. They took him to see the stretch of beach they were planning to buy.

'Isn't it great?' they demanded.

'I don't like it,' he said.

He and Marcus went for a walk along the sand, and he explained: 'There's sea urchins everywhere, so you can't walk barefoot. The tide goes out for miles and there's a hotel on each side. We'll be all in a row. You know what, Marky? This isn't *my* dream.'

It could have led to a row – except that Marcus and Alex almost never argue – but as soon as Alex listed the drawbacks, Marcus and Ellis realised he was right. They'd have to find somewhere better, and now, having seen Zanzibar for himself, Alex was on side. The hotel plan wasn't a pipe dream any more, but a potentially exciting project. He flew back to London, and they resumed their search for their dream location.

A few days later, they found it.

Someone had told them about the second largest island in the archipelago that makes up Zanzibar: Pemba. They splashed out on hiring a small plane and flew all over it, their amazement growing all the time. The beaches were stunning! Where were the hotels? Look, that beach there would be perfect!

Back on the main island, they hired a catamaran with a crew and headed north. It was an overnight sail, but during the night a sudden tropical storm blew up, a shrieking wind whipped the ocean to a fury and the skipper announced that his only chance of saving the boat was to drive it onto the beach. Exhausted, they fell asleep with the wind still crashing around them.

The next morning they went up on deck and looked around. The storm had vanished, the beach was strewn with rubbish thrown up by the waves, the sun was high in the sky.

The silence, the sheer beauty of the place, took their breath away. A long beach curved away on either side. Dense trees fringed the sand. No road, no jetty, nothing.

'It was incredible,' says Marcus. 'Just pristine. Raw Africa.'

They jumped down onto the sand and walked up and down, taking it all in. A few timid children began to emerge from the trees and stared at them from a distance. A handful of adults followed, and Marcus and Ellis asked to see the local Sheha:[10] They already knew this was the place where their dream could be made real.

---

10 In Zanzibar the real power in the community is held by the Sheha. They were more lucky than they realised: their Sheha was a man of absolute integrity and honesty, who wanted only what was best for his villages. Unfortunately this is not always the case.

Towards midday a dug-out canoe with outriggers appeared round the headland and a short, immensely dignified man came aboard and accepted their offer of a Coca-Cola.

'We want to buy this beach,' they told him.

He nodded, then asked through the interpreter, 'Are you Italian?'

Already the Italians were gaining a reputation as money-launderers in East Africa.

'No. We're British.'

In that case, he agreed to give them his blessing but only on condition that at all times half their staff must come from the local villages. They agreed.

'Now you must talk to Mr Rashid,' he told them. 'The land is his.'

Mr Rashid was sent for, and when he came the following day he said yes, he was prepared to sell.

'How much?' they asked him.

'That depends,' he said. To their surprise, Mr Rashid then went off and spent the next four days counting trees. The interpreter explained that in Zanzibar the land itself has no value, and what they were in effect buying was a few thousand trees. Marcus and Ellis were content to wait and luxuriate in this little corner of paradise.

Tree counting accomplished, they all sat down under a coconut palm and Mr Rashid named his price. It seemed very low. So they shook his hand and looked him in the eye. Deal done.

Now, looking back, it's their naivety that amazes them. It never occurred to them to ask why there were almost no hotels on Pemba, or why the land was so cheap. They soon found out.

As Marcus says, 'It's an opposition island, the government won't allow you to build, there's no road to this end, the people don't like foreigners, there's no infrastructure of any kind, no water or electricity, you can't buy anything, no shops, no aeroplanes land here . . . But apart from all that, it's a great place!'

Their first lesson came when, armed with an official-looking document in Swahili, they travelled by boat to the nearby town of Chukki Chukki to register their purchase. The government official looked at the contract and told them this piece of paper only meant they had compensated Mr Rashid for the trees; the land itself remained the property of the government, and they would have to lease it. Naturally, the lease would not be cheap. Their dream of building an idyllic boutique hotel on an African island on a budget crumbled to dust.

Welcome to Africa!

In spite of all the struggles with bureaucracy and the problems that lay ahead, they never regretted it for a moment. And once again, Marcus and Alex's lives were touched by the surreal. Ellis's husband just happened to be Brian Henson, who just happened to be the son of Jim Henson, creator of the Muppets. Brian has always been closely involved with the Muppet empire. The money for their project came partly from their mother's hoarding, partly from the hard work they'd done in their twenties, partly from Ellis's capital and partly from the zany world of the Muppets.

The story of the hotel that became famous as Fundu Lagoon, and was to earn a reputation as one of the top ten boutique hotels in the whole of Africa, ran in parallel to the story of Alex's search to discover the truth about himself and his family. And in a way, it was Fundu Lagoon that made his own journey possible.

That stretch of pristine beach in Zanzibar provided not just a perfect distraction for Marcus, but also the contrast that Alex needed as he probed into his family's story. The first time he visited the idyll that Marcus and Ellis had discovered, he was captivated by its exotic beauty and the utter simplicity of their days there. No matter the neglect that they had suffered or what had been done to them as children, they were still both resolute that they intended to get the most out of life. Marcus spent eighteen months almost entirely on Pemba. He lived with the locals and shared their food, a bottle of ketchup in his pocket his only concession to civilisation. Alex visited frequently. He came to love the remote beach almost as much as Marcus did, and in time, when the boat pulled in and he stepped ashore, he felt as if he was coming home.

Alex might have been determined to learn the truth about his childhood, but that did not mean he intended to be defined by the dark secrets he was uncovering. He and Marcus, together with Ellis, set out to construct one of the most beautiful hideaways on the planet. Not victims, not even survivors, but builders and makers.

6

Passing Around

The discovery of Fundu Lagoon and their project there came just in time. When Marcus came home for Christmas, something happened that meant he had to work harder than ever to keep the stench of bad memories sealed up in that jar.

Amanda was still in India, pursuing a different kind of dream, but Oliver was in London, pouring his physical energy into his passion for rugby and trying to deal with the memories he was finding the courage to speak about in therapy.

Memories that were not just about his mother.

'I keep having these fantasies,' he told his brothers. 'I want to get my own back on him. Sometimes I even imagine killing him for what he did to me.'

'Who?'

'Patrick. You remember. He had that stall near Mum's.'

'Why are you so angry with him?'

By now, Oliver was eager to talk about his ordeal.

Like the twins, he had often helped out on Jill's stall in Portobello Market. Like them he had got to know her circle of London friends: antique dealers, artists and the kind of people who used to be known as 'high society'. A couple of her gay friends had been especially generous towards him, and had invited him to visit them when he was about 9 or 10.

And his mother had dropped him off.

One of them, Patrick, had sexually assaulted him on several occasions. At the time he'd been so paralysed by shame and shock that he'd never talked about it with anyone[11], but now, the adult Oliver was at times overwhelmed with imagining revenge. His therapist encouraged him to write to his abuser, a letter which had been cathartic to send, and, when he was ready, to go to the police.

Each stage of the process was a massive challenge, but one morning Oliver summoned all his courage and walked into his local police station.

'I'm here to report an indecent assault,' he said.

A few days later the head of the county Child Protection Unit came to talk to him, but, after a long, and for Oliver extremely painful discussion, the officer said he would be unable to proceed with enquiries. For a prosecution to be successful, they'd need precise dates and places, and these Oliver was unable to supply.

When he was a child, he'd blurred over the details. The very mechanism that had enabled the child to survive now made it impossible for the adult to get justice.

Alex was appalled. He was still coming to terms with what their mother had done to them and now Oliver was talking about one of her friends.

---

11 This paralysed silence, so hard for people from families where everything can be talked about to understand, is normal for children from abusive homes.

Before Marcus went back to Pemba to start building the hotel, Alex said to him, 'Poor Oli. Why didn't he talk to Mummy?'

Marcus stared at him. 'What good would that have done?'

'But—'

'Ali, she knew. It's what she did.'

'What do you mean? She knew her friend was a paedophile?'

'Of course, Ali, same as she was. It was all part of her thing.'

'I don't understand.'

'She did it to us.'

'What?'

'She'd leave us at men's houses, pick us up in the morning.'

'For sex?'

Marcus looked away, a familiar expression on his face. Alex could tell the shutters were coming down again. 'Stuff happened,' he said. 'I don't remember.'

'But—'

'Leave it.'

'You mean, Mummy let her friends abuse us?'

A brief nod of assent. 'She passed us around.'

'She lent us out to paedophiles?'

Marcus shrugged. 'I guess so. I really can't remember.'

That was all Alex could get from him. Now he had the knowledge that not only had their mother sexually abused them herself, she'd also lent them out to her friends. It was beginning to sound like some kind of an organised ring, but Marcus refused to say any more about it. He just referred occasionally to 'passing around'.

Later, Marcus developed a new strategy for keeping the lid tightly closed on that particular jar of memories. Back in London again, he and Alex were having a drink with a friend and her mother in a pub. Alice, their friend's mother, had worked with victims of sexual abuse and said that abusers could be very cunning. Often, the abusive parent would single one child out for special treatment: that child alone would never be touched. So if the authorities ever investigated, the child who had been spared would tell a different story from their siblings, thus undermining their testimony. For Alex, it was a first glimpse into the devious ways of the habitual abuser.

But it gave Marcus a useful opt-out clause. Sometimes he claimed that he had been the child that was spared, and that Jill had never touched him. He was aware it had happened to Alex and Oliver, but not to him. This version of events contradicted much of what he had said earlier, but it stopped Alex from asking too many questions.

'I don't know. I can't remember,' he always said, and now sometimes he added, 'because it never happened to me.'

Alex knew Marcus almost better than he knew himself, but the unspoken communication between them was never infallible. He had no idea how much Marcus was holding back, or when he was bending the truth to protect his own secrets. What he did know was that the mother he'd got to know after his accident had been light years away from the mother who'd been capable of leaving them at the homes of her friends for their sexual gratification.

Was that possible? Sometimes Alex found it hard to believe, despite everything that had been said.

Jill was as far from the popular picture of a paedophile as you could imagine. From the little Alex had seen on TV and in the papers, he'd always assumed that people who abused children were different from normal parents. And anyway, she was a woman and it was fathers and stepfathers who were usually to blame, surely. Not a mother.

Paedophiles were oddballs and losers, everyone knew that. Abuse happened in overcrowded homes with inadequate parents. Their mother had been an attractive young woman, born into a conventional and affluent family. She'd been a debutante. She'd had a wide circle of friends and a successful career in antiques. What could have happened to make her deviate so radically from the path laid out by her upbringing?

Marcus was now completely absorbed in building the hotel, so if Alex was going to find out the truth, he'd have to find another source of information. He remembered the huge box of papers they'd kept from Duke's Cottage; he hauled it down from the loft above their office and rifled through the letters and documents that were jumbled together inside.

He started to look more closely at the life of the woman he had learned to call Mummy, but who for some reason he had never felt completely at ease with. Jill Wakefield / Lewis / Dudley. A mystery.

7

A Conventional Girl

Jill Wakefield was born in 1931 into an affluent, and apparently stable, family. Their home was a large house called Sillwood, now pulled down, in Wash Common. She grew up in a typical village in Southern England, the sort of place whose privilege and childhood comforts are evoked by John Betjeman:[12]

> In among the silver birches
> Winding ways of tarmac wander
> And the signs to Bussock Bottom,
> Tussock Wood and Windy Break,
> Gabled lodges, tile-hung churches
> Catch the light of our Lagonda
> As we drive to Wendy's party,
> Lemon curd and Christmas cake.

Her father, Harold Wakefield, had been a captain in the First World War and had won the Military Cross for bravery in the Salonika Campaign. He was invalided out of the army

12 'Indoor Games Near Newbury'. *Collected Poems*. 1948. John Murray.

before the war ended, and suffered with ulcers for the rest of his life. In the 1920s he worked as a tax inspector, but he retained a keen interest in military history, and every Remembrance Day he marched proudly past the cenotaph with his comrades.

Jill's mother Rosalind was born an Attlee. Alex and Marcus have a family tree drawn up in the 1930s which causes them much merriment: it traces their lineage back, somewhat improbably, to 1132 and 'Sir Richard Atlee, a friend of Robin Hood'.

Her brother William was three years older than her. He was sent away to boarding school when he was nine, and from there he went on to Shrewsbury, a public school that gave him a solid education. He studied at London University.

Jill was a day-girl at the Convent of St Gabriel's in Newbury throughout her schooling. Her parents were traditional Anglicans, so presumably they chose this school because it turned out well-behaved young ladies who were not going to spoil their chances on the marriage market by being too brainy. Along the way she absorbed a fair quantity of Catholic guilt, and she continued to write out pages of confessions to Father Dawkins when she was eighteen, a few of which survive. The list of 'faults' are those of any teenage girl of the time. Beginning with 'I have neglected God,' she went on to list every minor transgression, such as 'I have been depressed and worried unnecessarily about the future' and, more specifically, 'I have been silly in my conversation' and 'I have cheated the bus companies'. 'Impure thoughts and conversations' are also mentioned. After leaving school she kept in touch with the nuns and with her many friends, but in later life she was resentful that her brother's education had been so much better than hers.

The many letters she wrote in her teens and early twenties are neatly written, properly spelt and as formulaic as those of any schoolgirl in the 1940s and 50s. She seems to have been without any intellectual curiosity, or to have enjoyed books particularly, or the arts – but in that she was very much a product of her era and social group. In a typically brief letter, a friend reminds her, 'We are counting on you for netball!' As she matured into a tall and attractive young woman, her days and evenings were taken up with tennis parties, meetings with friends, voluntary work and occasional jobs. She campaigned loyally for the South Berks Conservative Association at elections, and was responsible for the Wash Common collection for Poppy Day each year.

In 1949, when she was eighteen, she came out, though perhaps for financial reasons, or perhaps because neither of her parents was able to organise the necessary social events, she seems to have done the economy version of a debutante's season.[13] She was presented at Court but did not attend Queen Charlotte's Ball, nor did she have her own coming out party. She and her brother William were invited to frequent dances and balls. As William says of her at this time, she 'was never particularly shy or retiring'. She was enjoying herself and her confidence blossomed: she became very much a party girl.

13 Fiona MacCarthy in *Last Curtsey* (2006) writes that in 1958 1441 debutantes were presented at court, but only a hard core of about 230 stayed on in London to do the full season.

In between trips to town and meetings with friends, the parties and the sports, she had to make a little money. Her mother sent her an advertisement for a job that might be suitable: Derry & Toms, the now vanished department store on Kensington High Street, were looking for 'a young lady of good appearance and keen business ability as First Sales in their handbag department'. Being a shop assistant was all right so long as it was the right kind of shop: lots of well-bred young men and women were to be found working in Harrods during the sales, or in Fortnum & Mason. Jill also did the occasional stint at the Earls Court Exhibition Centre. But mostly she got temporary work living in as a mother's help; it was customary then for new mothers who could afford it to have someone living in during the first few weeks after childbirth. She seems to have impressed her employers as conscientious and hard working, and Poppy, one of her employers, quickly became a close friend. When her next child was born, she asked Jill to be her godmother.

At Sillwood, the problems were getting worse.

Her father Harold was anxious and often unwell, legacy perhaps of his service in the Great War. Rosalind was domineering, 'a very forceful personality' as William explained to Alex. After his retirement, Harold retreated into himself. He slept till lunchtime and stayed in his study reading his books on military history and making notes till four in the morning. Because his wife was not keen on socialising, he turned to various local ladies, mostly widows, to accompany him to dances and functions. He was a hoarder and collector, a trait that both his children inherited.

Rosalind found solace with her dogs. All fifty of them. Her first passion was for dachshunds, which she bred and exhibited widely, but she later switched to the Chihuahuas Alex remembered. As she grew older and more bitter, her dogs made up for the shortcomings of her family. After a row with William, she wrote to Jill, 'Thank God for my dogs and my many dog friends. Without them I could not go on.'

Rosalind tended to get involved in bitter feuds, and she could be vindictive. When William was about ten, he had started to collect postcards which he kept in a toy Royal Mail van. He returned home one day to find that his mother had cut them all up and thrown them away, perhaps to punish him. His father had retrieved them and was trying to repair the least damaged with Sellotape. He was remonstrating with his wife: 'Why did you do that?'

Perhaps she didn't know herself.

Her rages grew worse as she got older. Increasingly she turned against her son, and Jill became her ally and her confidante.

8

A Suitable Marriage

The box of papers from the attic was a rich source of information. Gradually, as Alex – with Camilla helping from time to time – sorted them by date and topic, a picture of his mother as a young woman was starting to emerge.

The only thing that set Jill apart from her friends, during the years that she was being an outwardly typical upper-class young lady, was her height: she was six foot tall with huge feet and hands. Otherwise, she seems to have been in every way conventional, and her sole trajectory once she had left school was to marry, settle down in a pleasant home and produce a family.

There were occasional boyfriends, but no one serious until in 1953 she met an attractive, but not very confident young man called John Lewis. He was taller than she was (important for a woman of her height) and three years older than her, and they made a striking couple. John worked in London as a salesman for a wool company and lived at home with his widowed mother and his sister Isabel.

Their cottage in Beenham Hill was about halfway between Newbury and Reading. His father had been a barrister. John had been a day-boy at the Merchant Taylors' School in North

London, and seems to have worried that he had missed the character-building benefits that boarding school would have brought. Like all young men after the war, he had done National Service for two years.

John had a kindly, open face, but was often anxious and rather solemn. William told Alex that he had been 'a gentle man, as well as a gentleman. Very straight, but also unworldly.' His idea of a thoroughly enjoyable weekend, as he described it in a letter to Jill, was to visit a friend who lived not far away. After a game of darts at the local pub, they went back to his house for 'a very good lunch that Mrs Hall had left of cold pork, potatoes in their jackets and spinach followed by apple tart' and 'then we started on the stamps – swopped 150 each way!'

He quickly fell under Jill's spell. In May 1955, when he was twenty-six, he wrote her a letter that shows he was still in many ways a gauche and adoring schoolboy:

> *My darling,*
> *. . . It is exactly two years to the day since I first kissed you. Looking back on those two years I'm jolly glad that I did kiss you. In those days, and even now, I was not a very courageous person, or very good at taking the initiative in anything, but what would have happened to me if I hadn't taken the initiative then? You were terrifically attractive, and as far as I could tell, a nice sort of girl, and it was even possible that if I did kiss you you would respond quite readily (I thought that from the Swedish dance). So with the lights out, and William and Susan Cooil in the corner, I thought I would try it. I came*

close to you, so that your hair was in my face, then I kissed
you on your cheek, and you didn't mind, so I did it again,
and again. Then I dared to do something I had never done
before, and I kissed you on your lips. Jolly clumsily – I admit,
but the wonder was that I realised then that that was what you
had been wanting me to do!

I am feeling very dreamy now thinking of all that resulted
from that one action of mine, all these past two years. I mean,
how I've come to know you, and honour you, and respect you
and love you. What times we've had! I look forward with
great happiness and confidence to our partnership together as
husband and wife, and mother and father . . .

Jill's letters are livelier and more direct, neat pages full of news
and warmth and good intentions for the future. She was twenty-
two when they first kissed, but in spite of the occasional 'impure
thoughts' she'd confessed to Father Dawkins, she was still an
innocent by today's standards. While she was working for a
family friend as a mother's help, she met a woman called Sibyl.
She wrote to John that one evening, she and Sibyl 'had a very
interesting talk about — and I have learned quite a lot from it.
Nothing like talking to a married woman.'

A few months after she and John had met, she went to
Leiden to live in with a Dutch family who became good
friends and kept in touch for many years. One letter begins:

My darling, darling John
I am 'Cinderella' tonight, sitting on the floor writing this, in
front of a lovely wood fire. I have been staring into the fire for

such ages, letting my vivid imagination run away with me, as
it always does, and I often feel that I think too much . . .

Clearly marriage had already been discussed, but John was cautious and did not feel able to think about starting married life until he was earning enough to give her a decent home; one of his letters contained a pamphlet about the benefits of saving through 3½ per cent Defence Bonds. In the early 1950s, living together before marriage was not an option. Jill tries to be sensible about it, but one senses that she feels depressed at the prospect of a long wait.

> *Living in the clouds and making wonderful plans is great*
> *fun – then down to earth with a bang. You speak of the 'not*
> *too distant future', but that I know means a long way into the*
> *future and we are now living in 1953 and not, shall we say*
> *– perhaps 1958.*
> *Where are we? Tomorrow for you – up to London for your*
> *day's work, then the weekends and so the days pass by, year*
> *by year. Tomorrow for me brings just the same days, now here*
> *in Holland and afterwards somewhere else . . . We shall, I feel*
> *sure, have a lovely time at Christmas together – probably lots*
> *of parties and dances, which are all great fun, but that's not*
> *being together and really knowing each other, is it?*

She ruminates about marriage, the impossibility of starting married life without a proper home, her feeling that she wants to be a 'home wife', not a 'career wife', except perhaps at the beginning 'to help things out a little'. She recognises the need to be patient, though she adds a warning, 'I only hope you are not taking too much for granted' and by the end she has got into such a cobble, she even thinks about tearing the letter up and starting again, but instead encloses a leaflet for the Dutch flood appeal because she approves of its motto, 'I struggle and emerge'.

In the end she did not have to wait till 1958. Their engagement was announced in the autumn of 1954 and their wedding was fixed for summer 1956. John said he was glad they were having a long engagement because 'the best things in life are those that progress slowly – but surely.' He felt he had grown to know her intimately, and saw her as 'a born looker-after' and 'most successful at looking after children'. He was also anxious to improve his character. A few months before their engagement was announced, he wrote hopefully, 'I'm much better for knowing you. What do you think I'm like as compared with when you first knew me? Hasn't there been an improvement? I'm certainly less nervy and jumpy, tho' I've a long way to go yet.' His nerves contributed to the trouble he had passing his driving test, but he writes, 'please remember what I always remember myself: I am a perfectly normal person, I do NOT go around in a state of nervous tension all the time.'

There were other indications that did not bode well. He wrote during their engagement that, 'I think sometimes you feel that I am so serious that I tend to be dull. Well, I don't feel that being serious is a fault, rather the opposite, because the great thing to me is to be sound and reliable.' Whether this was Jill's opinion at the time, one can't tell, but there are hints that she was suppressing her more flamboyant side in order to fit the image of the dutiful fiancée. She writes conventionally that 'I feel the privilege of falling in love is not given to everybody, and the inestimable privilege of falling deeply in love is given to few.' But alcohol brought out a different side of her character.

It's a measure of John's naivety that on the one occasion she got drunk in his company, he writes forgivingly that when he found her she was 'giggly in a hysterical sort of way, and floppy . . . to me it was perfectly clear you were ill.' Now he feels he has seen her at her worst, and it had only proved to him how unshakeable his love for her was. Jill had written in a ferment of remorse: 'Please forgive me for everything I said and did to you yesterday. It certainly was not the Jill you know and next time you see her it will be your own Jill again.'

That other, less reliable Jill was kept firmly in check and the engagement proceeded along the traditional lines, through 'trousseau time' and the endless minutiae of the wedding list – friends gave everything that was necessary to equip a home, all meticulously catalogued, with a tick beside the name to show the 'thankyou' letter had been sent – all 200 of them. A Mrs Bellamy contributed 'tea set, asparagus rack, coffee cups, cocktail tray' while the Buckinghams sent a leather-covered blotter. They were married on 5 May at the parish church of St Nicolas, Newbury. After their honeymoon in Sicily, they bought a flat in Stanhope Gardens in South Kensington where they spent the week. She still did occasional bits of work, and they often returned to Sillwood and her Newbury friends at weekends.

Jill had married a man who was in many respects a younger

version of her own father, a man she could dominate as her mother had always dominated Harold. Not a recipe for great marital happiness, perhaps, but there was no reason to suppose the marriage would not endure.

On the surface at least, she was fitting into the role of proper 'home wife'.

9

'The New Jill'

In May 1958, almost two years after the wedding, Jill's mother sat down and wrote John what must be one of the oddest letters a woman ever sent to her son-in-law.

John had taken a new and better paid job in Italy earlier that year. He was working as a leather salesman, based in Genoa, and had gone ahead a few months earlier to get settled in his work and find them somewhere to live. Jill had remained in London to prepare their Stanhope Gardens flat for tenants. John was looking forward to seeing his wife again after a separation of some months. What he must have felt when he received the following, one can only imagine. Rosalind wrote:

My dear John,

. . . Time is flying by so fast, and I shall feel very sad when Jill has gone. Much more so now she is so changed. I wonder how you will like the new Jill. I prefer the old. Perhaps you will be blind like Fa always is and see no difference . . . But her new personality is a bit dangerous I warn you, tho' you'll just say to yourself, Silly old Mama. She has turned from a domesticated home loving and thrifty girl to an extremely attractive and pleasure loving young woman. She has

discovered what extraordinary power she has to attract older
men and even the B— man is quite absurd over her, to say
nothing of the postman who won't stop ringing the bell even if
he has only a letter which should go into the box with no ring
of bell! Naturally she is all out to attract now she has found
this out and I daren't think what will become of her in Italy!
So don't be glad she has been got out of her rut and much
loved little home where she was happy and settled and would I
hope have produced a family ere long . . .

It's an extraordinary letter, but perhaps it wasn't quite so unexpected after all. The letters Jill had been sending her husband
during their long separation also reflect a singular change in
tone and content. Gone are the conventional clichés of the
dutiful schoolgirl and the bride-to-be.

She was furious with him for the hard work she'd had to do
to get their flat ready and to find tenants, and she reproaches
him for not having done more before he left for Italy. She
complains bitterly about being exhausted and having too much
to do. One weekend she writes from a friend's house, where
she has gone for a rest, which was necessary because she's been
working 'SO hard like slaves in that flat that I thought I would
pass out.'

Most striking of all, her handwriting has changed
dramatically: no longer neat and schoolgirlish, it bursts in an
extravagant scrawl onto the page, as though written at great
speed and without bothering too much. Or under the influence of alcohol, or maybe the amphetamines that would have
enabled her to clear the flat by day and party every night.

The underlying reasons for this transformation can only be guessed at. Long after his death, Jill hinted to friends that there had been sexual problems with John; his chronic anxiety and lack of confidence and social skills might well have prevented him from being a satisfying lover. It's likely that whatever happened in the spring of 1958, an affair and the discovery of sexual pleasure was a part of it. Alcohol too, as well as uppers and downers – perhaps to drown out the inner voice of Catholic guilt and inhibition.

Whatever it was, it spelled disaster for their marriage. Even when their London flat was ready for tenants, Jill delayed her departure for Italy as long as she could. When she did finally arrive in Genoa, she never settled. As a salesman, John had to be away for long periods of time. Jill was bored and unhappy and yearned for England and her friends. As Christmas approached, John generously agreed that she should go back to Newbury for the holidays, though he had to remain behind on his own in Italy. The festive season passed, church bells ushered in 1959, but still she did not return to her husband. She procrastinated for as long as she could, and when she could put it off no longer, she sat down and wrote to tell him she wasn't coming back.

Alone in Genoa, John was devastated. It seemed to him like 'the blackest of black treachery'. When he had got over the first shock he sat down and wrote out, in his meticulous way, a two-sided document headed 'THE SITUATION'. It begins:

1. *John loves Jill.*
2. *Jill doesn't love John, though she is fond of him.*

3. John is happy in Italy, though he would be happier still if Jill could share his life in Italy with him.

4. Jill is unhappy in Italy, though she would be less unhappy if she really loved John.

5. Jill and John have characters which are opposite to each other in many important respects.

6. Though, in London, the opposition of character combined to make a very happy marriage, in Italy the circumstances are so changed for John and Jill individually that the same opposition of character works so as to pull the marriage apart.

After several more statements of fact, John reaches the sad conclusion that a legal separation is inevitable and 'time alone can provide the final answer.'

10

Fundu Escape

He'd read enough.

Alex returned the papers to the huge cardboard box and shoved it out of sight; he put his passport and plane ticket in a carry-on bag, filled a money belt with cash and flew out to mainland Tanzania. From there he got the ferry to Mkoani, the port in the middle of Pemba where Marcus had arranged for him to be picked up in a little fibreglass Duck boat with an outboard motor. As he came round the headland, he was blown away by the astonishing beauty of the place, its isolation and unspoiled serenity. Fundu was everything Marcus had led him to expect, and more.

He and Marcus greeted each other, the way they always did – which is to say, with a total absence of fuss. It hardly mattered that they'd been involved in such different tasks and living half a world apart: they connected the moment they saw each other, or rather they resumed at once the connection they both felt was always present. On the flight, Alex had been wondering if he'd be able to talk to Marcus about the discoveries he was making, but as soon as he stepped ashore he realised that Marcus was even more caught up in the excitement of his project than he was with his quest, and no wonder. Fundu was a massive undertaking.

And as he started to relax into this different world, Alex could see there were advantages to Marcus's immersion in his African adventure. On his first visit, and every time he visited Fundu over the years, he was able to leave his dark soul-searching behind, unwind and throw himself into a very different kind of project. It was like coming up for air; a chance to breathe deeply for the first time in a long while.

Right at the beginning, Marcus and Ellis had had a stroke of luck. It had happened on their very first visit. While Mr Rashid had been busily counting trees, they'd passed the time sketching plans for their perfect hotel, and from time to time the skipper's girlfriend, Emma Garstein, would bring them a meal or a drink. She'd glance at what they were doing, then disappear down below again.

After a couple of days she said casually, 'Would you like me to draw something for you?'

'Why?' they asked.

'I'm an architect. I'm just here with my boyfriend.'

'OK, let's see what you can do.'

She squatted next to them on the deck and started to draw. They were stunned. As Marcus says, 'She'd had three days of watching us do shitty little drawings and biting her tongue. She could draw whatever we described.'

Marcus and Ellis asked her if she'd stay and help them, and she agreed to stretch her year out into two.

One of the first buildings to be put up on the site was the office where Emma designed and drafted the detailed architectural plans which took shape on a daily basis as they got to know the area through the changing seasons. Ellis was responsible for the overall vision and spent a good deal of time travelling round Africa and India to find furnishings for the interior.

Marcus showed Alex round the site. He showed him the well they had dug in the traditional manner, and, now that a generator had been installed, just big enough to run a fridge and three light bulbs, Marcus proudly showed him the fridge full of cold beer.

Marcus introduced Alex to his team. As well as Emma, this now comprised a manager, Abdi Hajji Ussi, who spoke good English, two foremen, Patrick and Abbas and 300 staff from the local village. When the sun began to sink over the horizon, Marcus took Alex back to the old concrete boat they'd got hold of: it wasn't much to look at, but it meant they had a place to retreat to when the day's work was done.

'We're running this our way now,' Marcus told him, as they relaxed with a drink.

Emma nodded in agreement. 'When we started, everyone told us we mustn't trust the locals.'

'They said, "Run a hard site and let the workers know who's boss," ' said Marcus. 'We tried it for a couple of weeks but, you know what? It didn't work.'

'So we had to figure out how to do it our way,' said Emma.

'The next day I called Abdi and the two foremen and told them, "As of today, I'm not your boss." They were upset. "Who is?" they wanted to know. I told them, "You are. From now on, this is a black site and you have to take the responsibility. If you're fed up with a guy because you've found him sleeping under a tree, fire him. If he comes to see me, I'll tell him you've got the same power I have." '

'Did it work?' asked Alex.

'It took a couple of weeks for them to realise I meant it, then it was great. And also, I told them there was one more rule: if they thought I was making a mistake, they had to tell me. I said, "I want you to say No to me. If you mean No, say No. And those are the only two rules." '

'And that wasn't all,' said Emma with a grin. 'I discovered it's the women who do all the work, but they were only getting half the wages of the men. So I said they all had to be paid the same. There was uproar to begin with and they all went on strike!'

'So what happened?'

'I explained they'd all be better off,' said Marcus. 'It's a Muslim village and some of the men have two or even three wives. Once they did the maths, and figured how much more cash would be coming into their home, they could see that equal pay worked for them too.'

The beach, with its fringe of trees, was sinking into darkness. Alex thought of asking Marcus about their mother, the things he'd been finding out, but the bay was working its magic on him, and he decided to let it go. This was a different world. Sitting on the boat under the dazzling African stars, it seemed hard even to believe that their mother and father's 1950s world of deb dances, wedding lists and 9–5 jobs had ever existed.

Not only that, but Marcus himself was different here: more confident, more purposeful. He was a man who had found a place where he belonged, the task he should be doing, and Alex couldn't bring himself to shatter that serenity. Not in this enchanted place.

Soon afterwards, Alex returned to England. He had a good idea of what the project entailed, and he was to source the materials and equipment that Marcus couldn't get locally, as well as carrying on with the administration of the Lewis Burton properties. And in Fundu Marcus and Emma soon discovered that there was a different, and more complex, magic at work in their remote idyll.

Pemba was far more complicated than they had imagined: it was a black African island, run on English law, while the government business was carried out in Swahili. And the population was 90% Muslim.

His workers came to him. 'You must build us a mosque.'

Marcus was taken aback. 'I'm building a hotel,' he said, 'Why would I want to build a mosque?'

But soon he realised how important it was, and duly put up a small, mud-brick mosque. Everyone was delighted. When Ramadan started, Marcus shared the fast with his workforce, which gained him respect locally.

Marcus was so busy that it was a couple of months before he realised the identity of the stocky man who had been hanging round the edge of the site. Hajji al Hajji was the local witch doctor and had been employed as a security guard. Pemba might be a Muslim island, but voodoo[14] remains fundamental to the lives of the inhabitants. As Marcus says, voodoo is not a

14 Evelyn Waugh in the 1930s: 'Zanzibar and Pemba are the chief centres of black art on the whole coast, and novices come from as far as the Great Lakes to graduate here. Even from Haiti, it is said, witch doctors will occasionally come to probe the deepest mysteries of voodoo.'

way of seeing the world, 'it is the world' and it controls every aspect of their lives. In the small village community there would be a chief and a few elders, but the man who really wielded the power was the witch doctor.

Marcus first became aware of Hajji when his workers went to see him when they were ill. If his treatment didn't work, they'd come to see Marcus and Emma, who would take them to the hospital in their boat; by then it was often too late.

Marcus is ambivalent about the witch doctor's powers. After months of living on the boat, he and Emma were relieved when they were able to move into the first of the bungalows which would make up the hotel. They had no way of knowing that the site they'd chosen just happened to be a 'bad' place to build. Nor had it been blessed. The first signs came when things started to go wrong: first the electricity failed, then people got sick, others were possessed and started to have fits. A few even ran into the sea and tried to drown themselves. Finally a new and very expensive catamaran someone had donated to the hotel burst into flames and sank on its mooring.

The insurance company said it was an electrical fault.

The local people had a different explanation: they had built their first bungalow on a site already occupied by a devil bushbaby. Apparently the witch doctor's father had killed a devil on that very spot, but just before he died, the devil's spirit leaped into a bushbaby, with the result that everyone was terrified of this no-go area. Marcus went to see Hajji al Hajji, who duly went into a trance and told him he had been discourteous to build on the site without asking permission, and that he had to cleanse the site by killing a cow in the bungalow.

Marcus was not impressed. He said, 'The bungalows been decorated with nice white sheets and fluffy pillows and killing cows with a knife in the neck isn't really what I'm after.'

Still in his trance, the witch doctor said that in that case $100 should see the problem sorted.

And it did.

Marcus might be cynical, but he never underestimated the power voodoo had over his workforce. He enjoyed the first voodoo ceremony he took part in, but after a while it became 'a bit of a chore'. Ellis and Alex refused ever to join in, leaving Marcus to quaff cows' blood and haggle with white-painted witch doctors. From time to time Hajji al Hajji got cross and put voodoo on him, but it never worked. The local explanation for this varied; either the Europeans smoke too much marijuana, which inhibits the voodoo, or simply that they don't believe in it.

'Always excuses,' says Marcus. Yet he is the first to acknowledge that it's 'the most powerful mind religion' he's ever seen.

Marcus and Alex were learning that the human mind is infinitely mysterious and there is much that we have yet to understand. About how a religion like voodoo works, about how we create memories and how we forget, about how people are shaped by the world they grow up in and how they make their own choices and decide on their path in life.

Sometimes, contemplating Alex and Marcus's story, a witch doctor on a faraway island seems easier to understand than an apparently conventional woman who ends up lending her sons out to be abused by her paedophile friends. At least Hajji al Hajji's motivation is not so hard to figure out: money, a good meal for his fellow villagers, a bit of prestige, a sense of empowerment in the face of random events.

But Jill? A woman who apparently loved her children. Who was not mad, or alcoholic, or in thrall to an abusive partner. What could possibly have driven her to act the way she did?

Back in England, Alex was still struggling to piece together his mother's journey.

II

Hombres

At the beginning of 1959, Jill had found a temporary escape from the boredom and loneliness of her unsatisfactory marriage, but if she had thought life on her own would be easy, she was quickly disillusioned. The bundles of letters in the huge cardboard box gave Alex a detailed picture of her struggles to find happiness and John's despairing efforts to win her back. She was hampered by the fact that she had no independent means and was compelled to take on the kind of menial jobs that marriage to John was supposed to have rescued her from. Once again she was back working at the Ideal Home Exhibition, applying for temporary jobs in Fortnum & Mason, even taking jobs as a mother's help for friends of friends – which must have been a humiliating climb-down. After three years of marriage, she should have been the one doing the hiring.

But, it is clear from her letters, Jill had discovered the power of sex, and was on the hunt for a man who could provide not only security, but sexual satisfaction as well. Unfortunately, finding both in the same man proved difficult.

She plunged into a passionate affair with a young officer in the 1st Battalion, Royal Sussex Regiment. Alan was twenty-three, five years younger than her, and called himself an 'hombre'. In their correspondence, he was Olé and she 'Bubbles'. His letters show him to have been intelligent and charming, in love perhaps for the first time, and intoxicated with the idea of romance.

Those who knew him then said he had bags of charm but was extremely immature and, according to William, 'absolutely useless'. He was incapable of living within his income, and soon after their relationship started, he was facing court martial for bouncing cheques.

He wrote an abject letter listing the implications. He would be cashiered, have to resign from all his clubs and would become, in effect, a social outcast. But he maintains that his only real regret is the realisation that because of him, her name may be 'besmirched'. The prospect, he writes, 'torments me and makes my very limbs ache so that I feel I am languishing in some furious torture house . . . If only I had not fallen so in love with you! It is what people will say about you that gnaws with relentless agony at my conscience and tears my very heartstrings to shreds.' However, the shredded heartstrings did not stop him from borrowing money from Jill a few weeks later.

Her Italian friends were horrified. An elderly neighbour wrote Olé an almost incomprehensible tirade, saying that he regarded Jill as a daughter, and blaming him for corrupting her. One of the more coherent sentences concludes, 'The J was always one adorable housewife, to know you, to fall, to decay moral . . .' (Though a couple of years later, when Jill had returned to Italy, this fatherly neighbour was himself involved in a sexual relationship with 'the J'.)

In the autumn, John came over from Genoa to try to patch up his marriage, and Olé decided, in a ferment of self-sacrifice and undying love, that it was time to bring the relationship to an end. He wrote, revealingly:

You see, darling, the more I think of it, the more I realise that
I can never provide the sort of security that you require.
Looking back on us, I see that when I met you there was a
large vacuum in your life which needed to be filled – you
needed someone to love you, and I filled that vacuum. But you
have said yourself that you will marry the first man who can
give you a home and security, and that first man will not be
me . . .

In the end, after nearly two years' separation, Jill discovered that the only man who could offer her the home and security she craved was her husband. A letter survives from a Harley Street doctor written in March 1960 in which he says, 'I have had a talk with your husband and I think it might help if I could see you too.' Whether this consultation was to do with the sexual difficulties between them, Alex had no way of knowing, but by the summer his parents' marriage had been patched up.

As John so painfully knew, she was 'fond' of him, and this fondness lingered long after his death. Years later, when she had been married to Jack for some time, she spoke to a solemn little boy called Freddy, the son of close friends, who was shy and quite incapable of subterfuge. She never talked to Alex and Marcus about their real father, and all the photographs of him had been hidden away, but: 'You remind me so much of my John,' she used to tell Freddy gently.

But fidelity was no longer a part of the bargain, at least not so far as she was concerned. As Alex and Marcus had discovered when they were emptying Duke's Cottage, from then on until John's death three years later, she had as many lovers as she wanted or could get. There's no way of knowing how much John knew about his wife's affairs. Like so many people whose lives she touched, he seems to have been mesmerised by her larger-than-life persona.

And the need for frequent sex was now a central part of that persona.

12

'Good Old Jill!'

'Everything was about sex with her.'

Alex was talking to people, asking questions, listening to memories and anecdotes, then going home and sifting through her piles of papers. What he was learning about Jill's behaviour after her marriage hit the rocks tallied with the memories of friends and colleagues. When he mentioned the sexual abuse to the people who had known her, their reaction was usually shock to begin with – but on reflection, several people said they were not altogether surprised. It fitted with much of what they remembered about her.

She was flamboyant and she was outrageous and she got away with behaviour that no one else could have got away with, just through the sheer force of her personality.

Jenny Graham was sixteen when she went to Duke's Cottage to look after Amanda, who was then still a baby. Jenny loved the family and remained close to Jill until her death. To her, the atmosphere of the house seemed free and easy compared to her more formal upbringing, and the fact that she was left in no doubt that Jill had 'a voracious sexual appetite' was all part of the openness she discovered there. But sometimes, even she found Jill's behaviour disconcerting.

Jill and Jack used to spend the evening in the drawing-room next to Jack's study; both were rooms where the twins were not admitted. Jenny's bedroom was just above Jack's study – all part of the rabbit warren of the old house – and she had to pass through it to get to the kitchen. She used to hear their laughter and their talk, and was aware of the strong bond between husband and wife, in spite of their frequent rows.

But at the same time, as she told Alex, 'I almost felt I had to keep all my clothes around me to get through there to make a cup of tea.' On one occasion, when Jenny was wearing a zip-up cardigan with nothing much underneath, Jill lunged towards her and unzipped it from top to bottom with a whoop of delight. With the elderly Jack watching, Jenny was mortified. 'Sober,' said Jenny, 'she probably wouldn't have done it.' But after a few drinks, all boundaries were blurred.

She was distressed when Alex told her that Jill had abused them, and found it hard to understand. Her opinion had always been that Jill was devoted to her children: she had known Jack was harsh, but Jill had lavished affection on them all. But Jenny did remember being surprised by some of Jill's behaviour, in particular her fascination with her sons' genitals. More than once, when the twins, age ten or eleven, were having a bath together, Jill wandered into the bathroom and called out excitedly, 'Jenny, Jenny! Come here and look at their willies!' And when Jenny was looking after Oliver as a baby, Jill showed the same almost childish fixation with her little son's penis. But as with everything about Jill, it was done with such high spirits and openness that it seemed harmless.

The impression Alex was getting was that visitors were often struck by the aura of sexuality at Duke's Cottage. So far as he and Marcus were concerned, their home was 'normal': like all children they accepted their family as standard issue. Now he was discovering a different perspective.

The daughters of one of Jill's closest friends, who were roughly the same age as the twins, remembered visits to Duke's Cottage. One summer, when they were about ten or twelve, tents were put up in the garden and the children all slept outside. Jill came out to investigate and tried to persuade the boys and girls to get into sleeping bags together 'because it would be more fun!' On another occasion when they stayed the night, she encouraged the boys and girls to share beds. Even then, the sisters thought it was weird – but Jill was an adult, their mother's friend, so they never mentioned it to their parents.

As Jill got older, her behaviour grew ever more uninhibited. Her favourite topic of conversation was sex: 'Life is about sex and everyone's at it all the time,' was a frequent mantra. She often misjudged the company. Laura and Ian were frequent visitors at Duke's Cottage for years. One evening, when they were enjoying one of Jack's famous gourmet dinners, Jill startled them by saying, 'Jack and I are having the most terrific sex these days. We've found a wonderful book which has pictures and masses of great ideas.'

Laura and Ian were embarrassed, especially as Jack was now well into his seventies, but Jill didn't seem to notice.

'I know what!' she said. 'I'll go up and get it for you. It will help you and Ian when you're having sex. Liven things up like anything – there's lots to try out!'

Ian was so horrified he began to get up to leave, and for once Jack realised his wife had gone too far.

'Stop talking like that!' he said fiercely. 'You're embarrassing them.'

Jill did as she was told and the conversation moved to other topics, but Laura and Ian were careful in future only to accept invitations if others were going to be present.

Though Jack was increasingly critical of his wife, he shared her overt sexuality. He had a habit of donning loose and very short shorts as soon as the weather warmed up, shorts which revealed more than most of his guests ever wanted to see. 'He fancied himself as a ladies' man,' a friend told Alex. 'But his shorts were gross!'

It's a fine line between being uninhibited and being 'inappropriate,' and few people ever challenged them. Those who were put off by Jill and Jack's behaviour simply steered clear, and besides, when everyone is having a good time and the alcohol is flowing, no one wants to be the prude, the kill-joy, the party pooper.

And there was a safety valve: friends would talk to Jill with a kind of brutal honesty they'd never risk with anyone else. Even Ian, brought up to be courteous at all times, would occasionally exclaim, 'Oh, shut up, Jill!' when she was getting out of hand.

Laura told Alex, 'You'd talk to Jill in a way that would completely humiliate anyone else.' But she appeared to lap up the rudeness, and if someone roared, 'Jill! Stop being so ridiculous!' it only spurred her on. She had turned herself into a kind of caricature: a woman who was apparently so impervious to criticism she made herself virtually untouchable.

Her uninhibited sexuality was combined with what one friend called her 'bravura philistinism'. She had no interest at all in books or current events, history or the arts, but she was always keenly aware of social interaction.

It was a long way from the earnest schoolgirl who confessed to Father Dawkins that she had been 'silly in her conversation' or the conventional bride dutifully ticking off each wedding gift when the thankyou note had been written.

The middle-aged Jill had turned herself into a force of nature. Alex knew, from what Marcus had told him and from his own memories of life after his accident, that there had been advantages to having such an unusual mother. She might not cook for their friends, but she enjoyed having handsome young men around her and made sure the alcohol and cigarettes were freely available. Duke's Cottage became known as a place where anything was allowed; not surprisingly, their teenage friends thought it was terrific.

Making your sons available to paedophile friends was definitely a step too far. Alex was still finding that almost impossible to take in, especially as he had no way of knowing what exactly had been involved. Once again, Marcus would only give him the headline fact; the detail was left to Alex's imagination. And in his darker moments, Alex's imagination painted a truly horrific picture.

Were it not for Camilla's support, and the frequent trips to Fundu, Alex might well have been overwhelmed by the unfolding tale of his mother and his childhood.

When Marcus was asked recently how he had coped with the early traumas in his life, he laughed and said, 'I just stick my head in the sand!'[15] Not many people can do this quite as literally as he did. In Fundu, he had found a spectacular stretch of sand in which to evade the unpleasant truths Alex was so keen to uncover.

And that wasn't the only advantage of his African adventure.

15 Most psychologists and therapists now endorse Marcus's strategy: it used to be thought important to excavate negative memories. The present view is that the brain buries traumas for a good reason, and horrors should be left buried, at least until a person is ready to explore them.

13

An Island Hotel

'In Africa, I'm not dyslexic,' says Marcus.

Once they started to build the hotel in January 1999, Marcus had to learn a whole new way of working, and he quickly discovered it was one that suited him perfectly. He spent eighteen months operating in a society where hardly anyone could read or write and a deal was made with a simple handshake. He and Emma spent all their time outside, sharing the simple diet of the villagers, cut off from newspapers, phones and TV. For the first time his dyslexia was an irrelevance: his confidence soared, and even today friends notice how he changes as soon as he sets foot on the shore of the lagoon.

Shopping Pemba-style was a revelation. The guest rooms were built using traditional building methods, and many of the materials were sourced on the island: they needed mountains of stones, thousands of mangrove poles, thousands of the layered palm leaves called *makuti* that formed the roofs.

The economic unit for the provision of mangrove poles was the family. Patrick, the foreman, was put in charge of supplies and each family was allotted a section of beach on which to stack their poles. The system was simple: a family would set off in the morning in their dugout canoe and paddle down the coast to a

remote bay; the following day they'd walk far into the government sustainable forest, chop the mangrove trees down by hand
and then haul the poles back to the boat, one at a time. When
they had enough, they'd tow them back one at a time to Fundu
behind the canoe. Each expedition took three or four days.
Once their haul of poles was stacked up on the beach, Patrick
examined the pile, checking each pole for size and straightness,
and gave them a price.

Larger items like timber and cement were brought in on
traditional dhows or the larger *jahazis* and unloaded at low
tide. Marcus came to love the beauty of the traditional boats:
construction methods had remained unchanged for gener-
ations and their creation was a spiritual event, never to be
rushed. Marcus was an experienced builder, but learning the
Pemba way of doing things was a whole new adventure. As he
says, 'We're talking biblical methods: hand saws, hand drills,
everything by hand. Lathes with string.' He was constantly
amazed at what could be achieved with so little.

By Christmas 1999, the work was complete. They had been
advised to begin with a 'soft opening'. Between the three of
them they invited about forty close friends and family to visit
Fundu. Everyone paid their own fares, but food and drink,
diving and all extras were free. All the guests had to do in
return was fill out a questionnaire at the end of their visit.

No one knew what to expect. His friends hadn't seen
Marcus in eighteen months, and though they'd been hearing
about the project, the scale of their achievement took everyone by surprise. The journey itself was epic. Everyone flew to
Dar es Salaam, where two twenty-seater planes were waiting

to take them to the airport on Pemba. From there they were driven to the port at Mkoani and three fast boats took them and their luggage on the final stage of their journey to Fundu Lagoon.

Among the friends on the three boats were Oliver and their sister Amanda, who had travelled from India.

It was an extraordinary moment.

The boats rounded the headland, and the long white beach was revealed with its backdrop of dense trees. And there at one end was the long jetty and the buildings made from long poles and thatch, everything magically blending into the idyllic landscape.

Alex, Marcus and Ellis were standing at the end of the pier to welcome them. As the boats approached, they could make out the faces of their friends; they saw the astonishment light up their faces. A hundred yards away, as the boats slowed down to dock, all their friends broke into spontaneous applause. A few of them were crying. The twins were laughing through their tears; it was one of the most emotional occasions of their lives.

For Alex and Marcus that was the moment when they felt their friends started to take them seriously. 'You have to remember, most of our friends were university educated, doctors, lawyers, scientists, in high-end jobs,' Alex points out. 'Except for me and Marcus. They'd seen us throw elaborate parties, but this was different.' At last, they felt they had something to be really proud of. Something that helped them forget all those years of being introduced as 'Jill's dim twins' and dismissed as unteachable.

★　　★　　★

It's now more than a decade since Fundu Lagoon first opened and its success has surpassed all their expectations. The pipe dream that began with what Alex had dismissed as 'a bit of piss-talk in the pub' has gone on to become an internationally recognised hotel, winning the Good Safari Guide's award for best beach hotel in Africa for three years in a row. And Wamba, which had been one of the poorest villages on the island when they first showed up, has now become the richest.

The story of Fundu is integral to Alex and Marcus's journey. However bleak the events of their childhood were – and as the revelations continued, so the horrors would mount – they held fast to their refusal to be defined by what they had suffered as children.

Alex and Marcus aren't victims and they aren't even, as the current jargon has it, survivors. They are dyslexics who became successful entrepreneurs as many dyslexics do. They are men with a wide circle of friends, many of whom they've known for decades. They have enjoyed the opportunities that came along and made the most of them.

When they were children they reached out to good and decent people who showed them that families could exist in a supportive and caring way. As adults they chose to create something magical and to give back to the community from which it sprang.

Their childhood affected them but they refused to let it dictate the course of their lives. This is perhaps their greatest achievement.

And one expression of that is Fundu Lagoon.

14

Secrets on Top of Secrets

Marcus continued to spend a good proportion of his time in Fundu, maintaining the hotel and adding new features each year, but in 2000 he came back to London for a major trade show at his mother's old haunt, the Earls Court Exhibition Centre.

Alex and Marcus were working flat out on their stand when a familiar, but wholly unexpected figure emerged from the crowd.

'Hello,' said a sonorous voice they recognised at once. 'I thought I'd find you here.'

It was William, their mother's older brother, whom they had not seen since her funeral more than five years before. Marcus turned away at once and busied himself with a group of tour operators who were asking about Fundu, but Alex saw William as a potential source of information, and agreed to meet him for a drink. Alex explained to his uncle that he was trying to get an idea of the kind of woman his mother had been. William said, with an expression of regret, that Jill had become very promiscuous after the problems in her marriage.

'Yes, I know,' said Alex.

William looked at him steadily. 'Do you also know that John was not your father?' he asked.

'What?'

'It was that Italian chap. Aste. She was having an affair with him in 1963, at the time you and Marcus were conceived. He's your real father.'

Something in William's voice made Alex suspicious, but then he remembered the piles of letters they'd found in the attic when they were clearing out Duke's Cottage. At the time, doubts about his paternity had worried away at him and William's blunt assertion revived all those suspicions.

He needed to know, but how?

DNA, that's how you get proof of paternity. With Oliver's help, Alex tracked down some organisations that offered DNA tests. Could they help him find out who his father was?

Each time he contacted a firm, their first question was the same.

Is the person still alive?

No.

Were they buried?

Cremated.

At that point Alex would be told that there was nothing they could do to help.

Alex phoned every possible organisation, but always with the same result. He was on the point of giving up when a friend suggested he try the police forensic scientists, which he did. The forensic scientist told him that, after forty years, this was an almost impossible request, however there was one route that might just work.

'What is it? I'm prepared to try anything.'

'Stamps.'

The scientist explained. In 1963, you had to lick a stamp in order to fix it to the envelope, so the back of each stamp should contain a complete set of DNA. But they couldn't be just any stamp. 'What I need from you,' he explained, 'is letters in their envelopes. But they have to be love letters.' He wasn't interested in any other kind. His reasoning was that even a man with a secretary would himself take care to put the stamp on the envelope that contained a love letter.

Here Jill's inability to throw anything away turned out to be an advantage. She had not only kept almost every letter she'd ever received, but many of them were still in their envelopes. In the papers they'd salvaged from Duke's Cottage, Alex had found envelopes containing John Lewis's love letters, a few of Jill's replies and Aste's love letters as well as letters from other lovers. As Alex comments wryly, 'There was a lot happening in 1963.'

Extracting the DNA from such a difficult source was a long and complicated process. And, it seemed, a costly one: a cool £5,000 per stamp. As they needed to use more than one stamp for each person, they were looking at a figure in the region of £30–40,000. It was much more than Alex could possibly afford.

By now, however, the scientist had become mesmerised by Alex's story. He persuaded his superiors to let him classify this as a research project. He wanted to try out their new technology on Alex's case, since they'd never extracted DNA from a forty-year-old sample of saliva before. It proved extremely difficult to get any DNA from the stamps after such a long time, but by the end of the process the scientist said the balance of probability tipped towards John Lewis being their biological father.

Marcus felt entirely vindicated. Once again, he couldn't understand why Alex even wanted to know about the affair with Aste, let alone spend time and money uncovering the truth about their genetic make-up. As far as he was concerned, the unknown John Lewis was just about perfect.

When Alex had asked him to contribute to the cost of the DNA process, he said, 'No. Why bother? We've already got the best father in the world.'

'How do you work that out?'

'Think about it, Ali. John's never done anything wrong to us. He's never told us off. He's never done anything at all. He lives in this little box of whatever we want him to be.'

But for Alex, the truth was crucial.

'You don't understand, Marky. I *have* to do this for myself.'

Fine, Marcus had said. Just count me out.

When Alex told his twin that John Lewis was, in all probability, their father after all, Marcus was jubilant. 'There, you see. You spent all that time and money and effort and our dad was our dad all along.'

By then, Marcus had turned the whole saga into an entertaining story for his friends, and Alex joined in. It became part of their repertoire of funny tales about their eccentric family.

'I was Italian for a year,' said Marcus with a grin.

15

Vendetta

This wasn't the end of their paternity saga, however. A year later, Alex finally discovered the reason for his mother's long feud with her brother. Her undying hostility towards William had always troubled him, right up to her insistence that he be banned from her funeral.

Alex knew that she had always blamed William for John's death. To the twins that had always seemed to be a part of her illogical way of interpreting events: just because the fatal accident happened on the way home from a visit to William's house, it could hardly be seen as his fault.

The collision had taken place on 20 February 1964, the day John collected Jill and three-week-old Alex from Charing Cross Hospital in Hammersmith. (Baby Marcus remained in the hospital with a chest infection.) At that time William was newly married and living in Wimbledon; he expressed a desire to see the newborn, and persuaded the proud parents to visit him for lunch before returning to their Kensington flat. When lunch was over, he asked them to drop a friend off at her home in Clapham.

It was a lot to ask of a young couple who were bringing their newborn infant home – the thoughtlessness, perhaps, of someone who hasn't yet discovered how demanding new parenthood is.

After this brief detour to Clapham, they were travelling north on Bolingbroke Drive when they crashed into a car at the junction with Battersea Rise. If they hadn't made the detour to Wimbledon and then gone home via Clapham, they would have been safely back in Stanhope Gardens at the time of the crash.

Alex had the papers relating to the accident because the insurance claim was not settled for more than a year after John's death. Alex and Marcus could understand how their mother might have blamed William in the first onslaught of grief, but to hold onto the grievance for the rest of her life, and even after death, seemed extreme, even for her.

William is an intelligent but eccentric man. Like Jill, he's a compulsive hoarder. He believes they both inherited this trait from their father; his home is piled so high with possessions that no one can enter it but him, and he has a troubled relationship with all four of his surviving sons.

A couple of years after the DNA saga, William again visited Alex at the trade show, and once again they met for a drink in the evening and talked about John's death. William's account of what happened on that February day changed the picture entirely. Matter-of-factly, he explained to an astonished Alex that at some stage during lunch at his home in Wimbledon, just as John was about to take the first of his precious babies home from hospital, William had dropped his bombshell and calmly told John that he was not, after all, the twins' biological father. Their real father was Jill's Italian lover.

Less than an hour later, John crashed his car.

No one will ever know what took place on that final journey. Presumably William had told John when none of the
other lunch guests were listening. Did John keep this poisonous news to himself? What passed between husband and wife
in the few minutes before the fatal crash? Did his doubt and
rage finally explode?

John was an anxious, highly strung man who had never
been a confident driver: it had taken him a number of attempts
to pass his driving test. There had been problems in their
marriage, but the twins had been long awaited and much
wanted. And now, on the day he was bringing the first of his
little sons home, he was callously informed that the boys
weren't his. The malice is astonishing. At the very least, John
must have questioned Jill. One imagines raised voices and
reproach, a full-blown row perhaps. He must have been in
turmoil as he headed towards their Kensington home.

The inquest and the investigation by the insurance company
did not apportion blame. There had been a problem with the
traffic lights at that particular junction on Battersea Rise. A
policeman had been directing traffic for most of the day, but
the flow of traffic had been slight. Shortly before the accident,
a police inspector decided it was no longer necessary for the
crossroads to be manned and the sergeant on duty had left.
Officially, at least, it was an accident.

There's a codicil to this dark episode. There is a family tradition that the driver of the other car, who was only slightly injured
in the collision, had been educated at the Merchant Taylors'
School. This just happened to be John's old school. Not only that,

but they had been classmates. Two years later, for whatever reason, Alex was told that this unfortunate man took his own life. Whatever the truth about this double tragedy, if William really did tell John that the twins were not his sons on the day of the accident, it explains Jill's undying enmity towards her brother.

16

Children Without a Father

The extraordinary conversation with William gave a new urgency to Alex's search. He flew out to Fundu, and told Marcus about this remarkable confession. Marcus was dismissive.

'He's probably making it up,' he said.

'Why would he do that?'

Marcus shrugged. 'Does it matter?'

For Alex it did. Once he was back in London again, he began to wonder how his mother had coped once she found herself a widow, with two infant sons to support. The letters and other documents he had kept continued to give a vivid picture of her life during this period.

John had no life insurance, and the claim following the accident took nearly two years to be settled: money was a continuous worry. All her life, Jill struggled with anything administrative – finances and legal matters. When John died, she owned two flats in Stanhope Gardens, one of which they had been renting out, but which she was now persuaded to sell. From time to time she took the kind of temporary jobs she'd done in the past: she worked on the Express Dairy stand at the Boat Show at Olympia and for a short time she gave evening demonstrations for the caviar importers, W.G. White.

Around this time she started dealing seriously in antiques. A magazine article that was published in 1966, when the twins were two, quotes her as saying she'd first had a stall five years before, when her husband was still alive. She had 'only sold junk. But it was fun, and when I was expecting the babies, profits went into a nappy fund.' After John's death, the article says, 'a nightmare of despair and financial disaster followed.' She told the interviewer 'everyone was unbelievably kind but at the time this meant nothing to me.'

A few months after the accident, some of her dealer friends persuaded her to meet them at Bermondsey market one Friday. Then 'the most moving and wonderful thing happened,' she told the magazine. 'Two of the dealers closed their stalls and went round the market collecting for me. At lunchtime, I was presented with a box full of money – on the strict understanding that I used it to buy stock and set myself up in business again.'

After that she never looked back, and by the time the article was written in 1966 she had worked her way up to the 'better end' of the market trade and was specialising in the tiny objects that became her signature items: fine-quality scent bottles, collectors' thimbles and sewing accessories, *papier-mâché* and miniatures.

One of her god-daughters went to stay with her for a few days soon after John's death. For a twelve-year-old-girl from the provinces, a few days of the high life with Jill was an unforgettable experience. Sasha helped out on the stalls: hard work, but with lashings of laughter and fun.(Strangely, Sasha has no memory of the twins being around during this visit.)

In all these accounts, the young widow comes over as courageous, energetic and enterprising, and she needed all those qualities. Convention required that she cut a tragic figure, and so she did, sometimes to get help, or sympathy, or simply cheaper deals – and sometimes, one assumes, because she did grieve for John. Her strength in adversity was much admired.

In early 1966, when the twins were two years old, she took part in a discussion on the Home Service for a programme entitled 'Children Without Fathers', and a couple of months later she received 12 guineas for recording a talk for the World Service entitled 'Think On These Things'.

It's unlikely that she mentioned this on the World Service, but at this time, apart from her antique business the 'things' she was thinking mostly of were her lovers. Jill was on the lookout for a suitable husband to take John's place, and meanwhile she appeared to be enjoying herself. With her two closest friends, Poppy and Cynthia, she became a formidable part of the London social scene, an 'It' girl, as Alex says, with lovers who were wealthy and sometimes well known. Cynthia's husband was descended from Nell Gwyn and the three friends joked that they were running 'a high-class whore house'.

Their anything-goes lifestyle was in tune with the times: it was the sixties and free love was suddenly fashionable. London was the 'swinging' capital of the world and Jill and her friends were at the centre of the party culture.

When the twins were still babies, Poppy wrote to Jill asking about 'the hombres? How's Wiley Willie? . . . unless he starts paying for dinner, or at least changing nappies—? John W? Ted—?' It was accepted by her friends that Jill had a whole string of boyfriends, all with odd nicknames – the hombres. It was a huge joke, and lots of fun. A couple of years later, the same friend wrote: 'Your Dover-soul still sounds A1 – straight out of a F. Sagan novel – and the perfect lover – so long as you never let yourself love him! Don't work too hard and stay happy with your hombres.'

How happy Jill was with her hombres, it's impossible to know. She appeared to be having a good time, revelling in this new world where the old rules no longer applied, but in some ways she remained the conventional, convent-educated girl, as well as the fun seeker. What she wanted was marriage and respectability and a father for her sons. In 1967 she signed up with the Marriage Bureau in New Bond Street, but they wrote regretting that they were unable to find her anyone suitable.

Marcus and Alex got to know many of her lovers well and some of them continued to be friends of the family for years; in their opinion most of them were distinctly 'wet'. She attracted a particular sort of public-school-educated man with limited experience of the opposite sex. Gentle men, kindly men, men like her late husband and like her father; men whom she could enthral and dominate. And who weren't too possessive.

One particularly loyal lover, whom she and the boys always referred to as 'Wok', wrote to her when he was going to be abroad for some weeks:

Jill, my darling – I don't want to hold you to anything about making love – I know how you have the urge my sweetheart

and if you really feel you must have it I don't feel I have any
right to ask you not to, as I cannot be there myself darling to
satisfy you. So I just leave it to you my own darling to do as
you think best . . . I shall make every effort to keep myself for
you my brown eyes so you may rest assured.

Many of her lovers, like Wok, were from prominent families,
but they never quite matched up to her requirements – often
because they were already married. London might be swinging
but getting a divorce was still a complicated and uncertain
business.

Vivien, who was to play such a crucial part in the family's
story when she persuaded Alex to go on the workshop
thirty years later, first encountered Jill at about this time.
They were both guests at a lunch party and Jill swept in on
the arm of a high-profile, but very definitely married man.
She made an instant impression: a big character in every
way.

Alex and Marcus were fitted in around her social life and
her work. Most of the time they were in a local day nursery,
or with a nanny, though when necessary Jill took them with
her to visit friends or her family.

In October 1968 her father died. Jill's mother Rosalind
was devastated to discover he'd been having an affair not just
with a neighbour she had regarded as a friend, but also with
the paid companion who lived with them at Sillwood.
Consumed with rage, she heaped up all his possessions on the
lawn, including his entire library, and set fire to them.
Rosalind had already fallen out with William by this time,

and turned to Jill more and more for support. She wrote affectionate letters to her little grandsons, even when they were still babies, and they visited Sillwood from time to time all through their childhood.

17

A New Father

In June 1968 Jill met Jack Dudley, a man who could not have been a greater contrast to her usual admirers. He was tall and striking, a man who immediately took command of any situation. The letters he wrote to her before their marriage show that the chemistry between them was immediate and intense. As he trawled through his mother's papers, Alex started to get a more rounded picture of the man who had so dominated their childhood.

Jack was more than twenty years Jill's senior, and had been reared with the Victorian values of toughness and self-reliance. At King's College, Cambridge he had read first Mathematics and then Economics, and he had rowed for his college. He had gone on to be articled to a firm of chartered accountants and in 1937 he was initiated into the Empire Lodge of Freemasons, the beginning of an association with the Masons that would endure his whole life. During the war he was a lieutenant in the Intelligence Corps. He was anything but 'wet'.

To begin with, his devotion to Jill encompassed her four-year-old twin sons as well. Two weeks after their first meeting he wrote, 'Thank you, darling, for giving me such a happy evening – and for allowing me to meet Marcus and Alexander

– I hope not for the last time.' A fortnight later he went round to her flat in Stanhope Gardens, even though he knew she was away at an antiques fair in Brighton. He reported that he had been greeted with 'positive yells of joy from the Boys.' He goes on, 'They were very good and I left them my old canvas bag to play with, as I had no pressies for them, one handle for Marcus and one for Alexander – so they each have a bit! No tears this time [on a previous occasion, Marcus had wept when Jack left] but expressions of great sweetness and happiness.'

Even at the age of four, the little boys had learned to be demonstrative with the random adults who wandered in and out of their lives.

Within a month of their first meeting, Jill had given him the assurances he wanted. Jack was anxious about the age gap between them. He longed to take care of her and relieve her of the burdens she had been struggling with as a widow, but, like so many of the men she had been involved with, he was not free and not sure if he ever would be.

Nora, his wife, was wealthy. When they married in 1949, her father put 'Of Independent Means' in the box marked 'Rank or profession of father'. Their marriage had been unhappy for many years. Within a few weeks of meeting Jill, Jack wrote to Nora to tell her he had met someone with whom he hoped to rebuild his life. He told her that between them it was obvious that 'everything is dead and finished'.

In 1968, the death of a marriage did not guarantee its termination. The 'innocent' party could and often did refuse to grant a divorce to their 'guilty' spouse, so it was possible that Jack would never be free to offer marriage to Jill. And 'living in sin' was still a phrase that carried a good deal of social stigma. If the worst came to the worst, Jack wrote, 'I would still want to be with you for ever. It is possible always to change names by deed poll and no one except your special friends would ever know we weren't in fact married – nor need the twins.' Such were the necessary subterfuges before the divorce law was changed.

A year later, Jill was in Ibiza with the twins and a male friend who appears in the photographs with them, but whose name Alex and Marcus have forgotten. Jack wrote that he missed her 'desperately – and the twins too.' He had bought a cottage in the Sussex village of Rudgwick where he hoped they might all live. He was also hopeful that the Divorce Bill currently going through parliament might yet offer them the solution they longed for, and in fact, his divorce from Nora must have been one of the first under the new act.

Jill married Jack Dudley in February 1972, and she moved down to Rudgwick and joined him in Lavender Cottage. At the time of their wedding he was sixty-two and she was forty. It seemed like a new beginning for both of them: Jill after years of struggling (and a good deal of fun) in London; Jack after a long, unhappy marriage. His letters give the impression that Jill entered his life at a time when he had given up hope of finding happiness: she brought him love and affection and a new burst of energy.

There's no reason to doubt that he was sincere in wanting to be a good and devoted father to Alex and Marcus, but it didn't work out that way. Jack Dudley's powerful personality was to have an enduring impact on their lives.

18

Lucinda

Being a father to two lively little boys was much more challenging than Jack had bargained for. In a rare moment of self-reflection he had written that 'I was brought up in an atmosphere of quarrelling parents, which has left its mark on me.' Lavender Cottage was not large, and in the little rooms of their new home, his earlier delight in Alex and Marcus soon gave way to a more or less continuous irritation.

Six months after their wedding, when Jill was forty-one, she gave birth to a daughter in St Luke's Hospital in Guildford. This was the little girl she had always longed for. The walls of her house were hung with pictures of little girls in old-fashioned dresses, all part of her fascination with the miniature and the feminine. She and Jack were overjoyed: Baby Lucinda was a new beginning indeed.

Marcus remembers what then followed.

Lucinda was six weeks old and taking her afternoon nap in her cot. Jill asked him to check the baby in her room on the half landing. Marcus tiptoed in, but his little sister wasn't moving. He gave her a shake, but she still didn't wake. Something was horribly wrong.

He ran downstairs. 'I don't think she's breathing!' he cried.

Jill shrieked and tore up the stairs. The house was in uproar. An ambulance came, swiftly followed by the police. Alex and Marcus hung back and together peeped through the crack in the door as the police interviewed the grieving parents in the kitchen for hours. 'That must have been hard,' says Marcus now. 'You lose a baby and they decide you've killed it.' Through the crack in the doorway, the twins saw that Jack was crying uncontrollably. The image stayed with Marcus for the rest of his life – Jack just wasn't the kind of man who showed emotion.

He did now. Their stepfather was utterly devastated. He cried and cried for weeks. And when the first onslaught of grief passed, he emerged a different man. Marcus believes that after that tragedy, 'he went a little bit hard'. The death of Lucinda, a random, heartbreaking cot death, made him more bitter and cold than before.

Jill was nothing if not courageous. Just over a year later she gave birth to another daughter, Amanda, and early in 1974 the growing family moved to a larger house, Duke's Cottage in the same village.

Having lost one precious daughter, the new parents were thrilled all over again, but this time their delight was shot through with anxiety: they could deny the baby nothing and were in a constant state of fear that she might come to harm. It was at this stage that Jenny Graham came to work as a live-in nanny. She brought order and shape to Amanda's life and remained devoted to her from then on. She loved the whole household, but was concerned at Jack's harsh treatment of the twins.

She was not alone in her concern.

Oliver was born in Spring 1976. When he was still a baby, Jack's mysterious daughter Molly came to visit for a few days with her mixed-race son, who was just a bit older than Oliver. She was so troubled by the way Jack treated his stepsons that she wrote him a long letter. She refers to his 'frightening insensitivity to the needs of others', and says that he gives the impression that people 'are things to be manipulated in order to serve you'. It may be a mistake to read too much into what is written in the heat of a family quarrel, but her words have the ring of truth:

'Jill . . . has four children at home,' she wrote, 'you have two. You married Jill *and* the twins – yet you so often forget the twins. They notice and are quietly hurt. They chose to call you "Daddy". A beautiful compliment to you. Are they "sons" to you?'

It was a good question and the answer, so far as Alex and Marcus could see, was a resounding 'No.' They craved his approval, but more and more they were told that they were useless and stupid. A highly academic man, Jack found their inability to do well at school completely baffling and he made no secret of his contempt. For him, dyslexia was just a posh word for stupid.

An elderly man of fixed habits may well have found family life challenging under any circumstances, but Jill's behaviour only made the situation worse. Some observers reckon she felt bad about inflicting another man's sons on Jack; others think she saw his rejection of the twins as in some way a rejection of her, and tried to appease him, usually with the opposite result.

Marcus is convinced that she orchestrated the situation to prevent any possibility of closeness: Jack was cast as the bogey-man, the cause of all the unpleasantness in the household, and her sons were encouraged to rally round and support her. Sometimes she would sympathise with them, and appear in the role of their champion, albeit an ineffectual one, because she too claimed to be afraid of him.

Her 'fear' of him seems to have been mostly play-acting and sometimes it could be comical. Often she seemed to try to make herself smaller and literally cringe before his onslaughts. Other times she would run into a room and crouch down behind the sofa in apparent terror, calling to her sons to protect her.

But there was no hint of play-acting for Marcus and Alex. They were terrified of Jack, and no matter what they did, it was always wrong. A frequent visitor to the house says, 'We knew they were scared of him.' The couples' friends responded by taking the boys off for weekends and holidays away, an arrangement that suited everyone.

Besides, however badly he treated them, they remained cheerful and loving, at least on the surface.

They had something no one could take away: they had each other.

No matter what was going on around them, they existed in their own private twin world. They did everything together. At almost every moment of their childhood, whether they were being bullied at school, being terrorised by Jack or carted around by their mother, getting up early to clean the shoes and clear away the dishes from the night before or retreating to their icy-cold room away from the rest of the family, their fellow twin was a constant presence, a companion and a refuge, a cheerful reflection and a source of complete acceptance and approval.

In some essential way, everything that happened outside their private bond was an irrelevance. 'When we were little, no one could touch us,' Marcus told Alex. 'We were in our own little bubble world. Always together.'

If their lives had followed a more normal path, they would have begun to separate in their teens. Alex had begun the process when he got the job at Bramley Grange Hotel and left Marcus behind at Duke's Cottage. But his accident, and his total dependence on his twin, interrupted their efforts to separate. In their twenties there was a constant push–pull between them: Marcus encouraged Alex to join him in Australia, but then went off on his travels and left him to fend for himself. And Alex's determination to uncover the truth about his childhood drove another wedge between them.

Both of them knew instinctively they had to forge separate identities, separate lives. But the task, though essential, was to prove extraordinarily painful.

19

First Wedding

A lex had been talking to Marcus for some time about his wish to marry Camilla. He'd got it into his head that he wanted to propose to her before his thirty-fifth birthday, which fell on 31 January 1999.

Marcus was in Fundu, starting the build. He was far away, not just geographically, but also psychologically. During this period it was Camilla who was supporting Alex in his quest to learn the truth. It was time to celebrate the bond between them.

One the eve of his birthday, Alex booked a table at a restaurant near their home in Brixton, but when he and Camilla got there the place seemed too noisy and crowded for an intimate proposal. By the time they got back home it was nearly midnight and time was running out.

Alex says, 'I thought I'd better ask now!' So he proposed just before midnight struck, and Camilla accepted.

A lot of the family jewellery was stored in a bank, so rather than produce a ring right away, Alex whipped out a photograph of one of his grandmother's rings. In his words, the sequence went: 'Will you marry me? And here's what the ring looks like!' Camilla thought the whole thing was funny and sweet. In the end they had one of Rosalind's brooches broken up and reset to their own design.

They were married two years later, in the summer of 2001, and their wedding was very much stamped with their own personalities. Vivien had opened a healing centre at Alliblasters, a country house near Rudgwick. With plenty of rooms and lawns surrounded by idyllic Sussex countryside, it was the perfect spot for a wedding.

Amanda flew over from Sri Lanka. The highlight of the church service was a gospel choir about twenty strong they'd shipped in from Brixton. Ian and Laura Hudson acted as stand-in parental witnesses, sealing their informal role as adoptive parents.

At Alliblasters, Marcus took charge of all the arrangements. A large marquee was put up on the lawn. When the florists pulled out at the last minute, Amanda stepped in to take over. She went to Covent Garden at dawn and filled one of Lewis Burton's white vans with tropical flowers and spent two days creating huge displays and covering all the poles with flowers. For her it was the perfect commission, an outlet for her creativity. She even decorated the large four-poster which had been set up in the middle of the marquee.

Camilla had been suffering for some time with a bad back, the result of a manipulation that had gone wrong. She was in a lot of pain and could only stand up for short periods; sitting down was torture. A few weeks before the wedding, flat on her back in bed, she had said to a friend, 'How am I going to manage this wedding?'

The friend thought for a bit, then said, 'Why don't you take the bed? Then you won't have to keep going back to the house to lie down all the time.'

It took Alex a couple of days to get his head around the idea, but in the end it turned out well. Amanda smothered the bed in flowers, so it looked as beautiful as Titania's bower in *A Midsummer Night's Dream*. Everyone took a turn sitting beside Camilla on the bed with their champagne, and she was able to enjoy the whole day.

Then it came to the speeches. The best man gave a speech, then one or two of the couple's closest friends spoke up as well. And then, all unprepared, Marcus stood up on his chair and began to speak. He started off conventionally enough, with a toast to Alex and Camilla. Then he went on,

'But I wanted to say, this is a very *sad* day for me.' With the word 'sad' he gained the total attention of all 120 guests sitting in the marquee. Absolute silence. Marcus said simply, 'This is a marriage . . . and a divorce. All in one day.' At which point he started crying and sat down.

The mood had changed in a moment, and half the guests had tears in their eyes. Alex was stunned. Up to that point, it had been a typically happy wedding celebration, but Marcus's impromptu speech cast a shadow that was hard to lift.

Alex says now, 'It was the most extraordinary moment. Nobody will ever forget the power of what he said. *He's* gaining a wife. And *I'm* losing a twin. Right now. And that is how I feel.'

In spite of the amazing gospel choir during the service, the stunning flower arrangements and all the effort that had gone into creating a memorable wedding, the part that no one will ever forget was the spontaneous outburst from Marcus.

Alex might have been perplexed by his twin's behaviour at the time, but when Marcus married seven years later, it was his turn to act out of character.

20

Vito

Marcus was nervous. He was on his way to an unusual kind of blind date. Unusual, because it wasn't really a date, as he was simply meeting up with a bunch of friends for a meal, but he knew that among the group would be a young Spanish woman he'd never met. And it wasn't really 'blind' either, as he knew exactly what Vito looked like: he'd met her identical twin sister, Ana, who had spent her honeymoon at Fundu Lagoon a few months before. He also knew that Vito was an architect and had played hockey for the Spanish team.

Ana had done a bit of scheming. Her sister was over for the weekend from Barcelona, where she was a partner in a busy architects' practice, and had no idea what lay in store. She couldn't understand why Ana was paying such attention to what clothes she intended to wear for the evening.

'You might want to get prettier,' Ana said looking at her critically.

'Why?' asked Vito, who as usual had dressed for comfort.

'Oh, you might meet someone.'

Ana's fussing made Vito feel anxious.

They all met up at St Martin's Hotel, but Vito and Marcus only had half an hour together that evening, as Marcus had to drive to Heathrow to pick up a friend, ('Sounded like a girl-friend,' said Vito. 'It was,' said Marcus. 'I broke up with her that night.') Their first encounter was not a total success.

Marcus was attracted to Vito right away, overexcited and aware that he was trying too hard but unable to stop himself. Vito thought he was handsome, but she didn't like the way he was showing off: in the space of that half hour he'd been name-dropping for England, had told her about meeting Mother Teresa and the Dalai Lama and had generally been working flat out to make an impression.

When Vito went back to her sister's flat that evening she wasn't sure if she liked Marcus all that much, but she had a strong feeling – *I've just met someone very important in my life* – without knowing why. For Marcus, the connection had been instant, but their path to happiness was not at all smooth.

For a start, Ana had lost her phone and he was unable to contact either of them. When he did finally get in touch with Vito she was back in Barcelona. They talked for half an hour, chatting like old friends about everything and nothing, and when they hung up, he said he'd get in touch again in a day or two.

But he didn't.

One week went by, then another, then a third. Vito couldn't make it out. He'd seemed so keen, and now – nothing. What was going on?

After nearly a month, she got his number from a friend and phoned. Again, they talked like old friends. Again, when they hung up he said he'd be in touch in a day or so.

Here we go again, she thought.

But this time he phoned back the next day. They talked every day on the phone and just before Christmas, Marcus flew out to Barcelona. Vito was to meet him at the airport. Both were anxious they wouldn't recognise each other.

The drive into Barcelona was acutely embarrassing. They made awkward small talk to begin with, but conversation eased on a detour to view the city from Tibidabo Mountain.

Vito pulled up in front of a city hotel. Marcus looked at her in dismay.

'I'm not staying at your place?'

She shook her head. 'I'll pick you up in an hour,' she said, and drove off into the traffic.

Marcus was thinking he'd made a terrible mistake as he went up to his room and had a shower. But that evening, over drinks and a meal, they were getting on really well. Later, they went dancing.

And later still, Vito drove him back to his hotel. A peck on the cheek and she said she'd come round for him in the morning.

This is not going so well, thought Marcus, letting himself into his solitary room. He ended up spending another two nights in the hotel before Vito invited him to go with her to the Costa Brava for a couple of days to visit her childhood haunts.

Next it was her turn to visit London. She was appalled by the way Marcus and Oliver lived in their shared house. Not just that it was a typical bachelor pad, with dishes piling up in the sink and food lying around everywhere, but it sometimes seemed to her as if half of South London had the key to the front door. In fact, it was only key workers from Lewis Burton, and a few friends, but Vito never got used to the total lack of privacy. ('It was a boys' flat,' says Marcus. 'What did you expect?' 'It was *impossible*,' says Vito firmly.)

Vito was teaching architecture in Barcelona, but got a day's work each week at a London firm, so spent Friday to Monday with Marcus. However, conditions in his house were not conducive to making her feel at home. One morning she was woken soon after Marcus had gone to work by the arrival of a huge Afro-Caribbean man in the bedroom.

'Hi, I'm Everton,' he said. 'I do boiler repairs for Marcus.'

'The boiler is not in here,' she told him crossly.

'Just checking the radiators.'

She told Marcus their relationship was in serious danger unless they got a place of their own.

In the summer of 2005, Vito spent three months in Fundu with Marcus. Since the hotel had opened Alex and Marcus continued to work together on their enterprises in Brixton and in Zanzibar. The properties still had to be maintained: Alex did most of the administration and Marcus looked after repairs and decoration. And in Fundu, Marcus was constantly upgrading the hotel: one year a swimming pool was added, another year several more units for guests. Alex flew out at least twice a year to negotiate VAT and ensure the bookkeeping was up to date. They remained close, though without ever discussing the topic that so absorbed Alex. Their conversations were practical: to do with friends and the logistics of running their businesses.

In Fundu, Marcus didn't just improve the hotel, he worked to improve the lives of the villagers whose world had given him so much. They had more than fulfilled their original promise to the Sheha that half the workforce should always been drawn from his village. Right from the start, they had also encouraged local entrepreneurs to set up small businesses.

They had provided the funds for a well for the village with an electric pump, and now they were going to finance a school with money that had been raised from the hotel guests and from fundraising events in London and Barcelona. Marcus, whose own education had been such a disaster, was determined to provide a better one for the children of the village.

Vito was puzzled by her lack of energy. The island was beautiful, the pace of life relaxed, she was normally full of vitality and she was used to heat. What was wrong?

The local women smiled. 'You're pregnant,' they told her.

On her birthday on 7th July, which is a national holiday in Tanzania, they invited her to a special women's event, a traditional celebration for a young woman before she gets married. Vito was flattered: just to be invited to take part in this secretive women's ceremony was a great privilege. But when the dancing began, her pleasure turned to amazement.

The women in Pemba are Muslim and famously modest. They walk with downcast eyes and hardly ever put themselves forward. But during this African equivalent of a hen night, the women performed a dance that was uninhibitedly erotic, a danced simulation of sexual intercourse intended, presumably, to prepare a bride for what lay ahead.

Lola was born the following year, but it wasn't until they went skiing together over New Year that Marcus decided it was time to propose. His plan seemed like a good one, and highly romantic.

He and Vito were going to ski down a notoriously difficult slope, and as they travelled up in the ski lift together, he checked that the ring he'd bought was still in his pocket. Vito, a strong sportswoman, set off ahead and he sped after her. His intention was to pull to a halt next to her at a spot where the view was unparalleled and whisk the ring dramatically out of his pocket while he proposed, surrounded by crisp mountain air, pure snow and ravishing scenery. It would be perfect!

At the last moment, just as he was catching up with her, he lost control of his skis, failed to stop in time, was unable to steer and ploughed into her at full speed. Vito crashed to the ground with a cry of pain.

'Are you all right?' This was not what he had planned at all.

'My leg!' she wailed. 'I can't stand up. Oh, it hurts!'

'I've got something that will make it better,' said Marcus.

'Oh good. A painkiller?'

Marcus went down on his knees beside the crumpled figure lying in the snow. 'Something better,' he said and pulled the ring out of his pocket. 'Will you marry me?'

Vito burst out laughing, her painful leg forgotten. 'Yes, yes, yes! But you'll have to help me up first.'

21

A Second Wedding

Vito and Marcus were married in September 2008 in the whitewashed fishing village in Menorca where her family had had a villa for years. There were 200 guests, and most of their British friends came out for the whole week. They laid a carpet from the villa to the church, which overlooked the sea. The service was all in Catalan so Marcus had to keep asking Vito if they were married yet.

Everything was idyllic: their friends drank champagne beside the water, the celebrations moved to a nearby restaurant where they enjoyed the local lobster dish, then danced through the night while the warm September rain fell outside.

Marcus and Vito could not have been happier.

But Alex was distraught.

He had travelled out with Camilla and their son, who was now three, a year older than little Lola. Marcus had asked him to be his witness. Being a twin, he had two best men, Rob and Jules, to do the speech together, one in English and one in bad Spanish. But apart from the occasional wedding rehearsal, there was not much for him to do, and even though it was a lovely place for a holiday, he felt excluded. Vito's family were, quite naturally, organising everything – but Alex's Spanish was non-existent and most of the time he didn't have a clue what was going on.

As the week went on, Alex's unhappiness increased. Even though he had a family of his own now, a part of him didn't want Marcus to get married. He wasn't ready to lose him, any more than Marcus had been ready to let go of him when he and Camilla married.

The evening before the wedding, in his hotel room, Alex collapsed. Camilla did what she could to comfort him, but for him, the next twenty-four hours passed in a blur. He got through it, and played his part in the ceremony, but only just.

Unaware of Alex's misery, Vito and Marcus headed off on their honeymoon while Lola stayed in Barcelona with her grandmother. Marcus had planned it all, without saying a word to Vito, and he had called in favours from all their friends in the travel business. They stayed near Cape Town and flew out to see the whales; they went on the luxurious Rovos Rail train ride from the Cape to Johannesburg, a four-day trip through stunning scenery; they flew over the Victoria Falls in a microlight and went on safari in Zambia at the famous Sausage Tree Lodge.

Alex returned to London in turmoil. He hadn't understood why Marcus had acted so out of character when he and Camilla got married. Now he understood only too well. Deep down, he knew that it was right for them to go their different ways, but he found the pain of the separation almost too much to bear. The closeness that had enabled them to endure so much when they were children, and which had supported him after his accident, the closeness which had always been a fundamental part of who they were, still felt essential to his survival.

He knew it was wrong, but he was angry with Vito, and blamed her for the agony he was in now. A few weeks after they got back from their honeymoon, Alex put all Marcus's paperwork into a box in the back of his car and drove over to their home. He handed it all to Vito, all the bank statements and tax forms and bills he'd always dealt with for his twin.

'This is your job now,' he told her. 'You married him. You do it.'

His action was childish and out of character, and even now he finds it hard to understand what made him act in such a hostile way. Perhaps he was fortunate that Vito was herself an identical twin, and even though her relationship with Ana had not been forged in such adversity, she was more forgiving than most new wives would have been in such a situation.

22

Going Public

In 2009 Oliver was involved in raising money for Kids Company, a charity started by the charismatic Camila Batmanghelidjh to provide positive experiences for children in deprived situations – a cause closer to Oliver's heart than many who knew of his 'privileged' background can have ever imagined.

One aspect of Kids Company's fundraising work is the Plate Pledge – to raise money to give meals to children who would otherwise be hungry. Oliver invited Alex to come with him to a fundraising evening. Each guest was given a paper plate and asked to draw a favourite childhood memory on the back. Needless to say, this was not a task that appealed to Alex and it revived all the anxieties that Vivien's instruction to draw a garden had generated ten years before.

A friend of Oliver's was making a video of the evening. She came to where Alex was sitting, his plate still unmarked, and asked him to tell her about his favourite memory from childhood.

'I don't have one,' said Alex.

She was intrigued and wanted to know more. Alex told her about the memory loss, and how his twin had become his memory. But when the story was passed to a *Guardian* journalist for the Personal Experience page in the Saturday magazine, Alex decided to tell the whole story, not just the simpler version that had entertained viewers of *That's Life!* and Carol Vorderman's *Mysteries*.

For the first time he spoke publicly about the revelation that had turned his world upside down when he was thirty-two. He said that after the accident, Marcus had become his memory. 'But,' he told the interviewer, 'what he didn't tell me was that our mother had sexually abused my brothers and me from an early age until we were in our teens. I couldn't have known it at the time, but I am sure this is why I felt so frozen emotionally. There was a crucial piece of the jigsaw that was missing.'

He says in the article that he is sure Marcus acted 'out of love' because he wanted Alex to have a fresh start. But it wasn't until he learned the truth that his emotional responses came flooding back, 'good as well as bad: anger, relief, sadness'. He goes on, 'you could argue he denied me my past, but I feel he saved me – I didn't have the capacity to deal with the memory[16] of abuse straight after my accident.'

He ends on a positive note: 'I'm forty-six now, and feel I'm in the third stage of my life. I know all there is to know, and I wouldn't want it any other way.'

Perhaps at the time Alex really did believe he knew all there was to know. And maybe for him it was better that the real

16 As always when he talks about his 'memories' Alex is referring to the memories that Marcus has told him about.

truth about his childhood was to be revealed gradually. But his quest was by no means over, as the events of the next two years were to show.

The *Guardian* article appeared in June 2010. It was picked up by a radio journalist and the next time Alex told his story it was in a recorded interview for *Saturday Live*, which was broadcast later that year. The interviewer, Mishal Husain, was sensitive in her questioning. Hesitantly, Alex went over the familiar ground. Once again, he emphasised the positives. People had asked him if he was cross with Marcus for not telling him the truth, but no, he said. 'I think he did a wonderful thing in not telling me. I don't think I was mature enough at that age. I couldn't have coped with that information.' And again Alex stressed that Marcus acted 'out of love', adding, 'the other way round, I would have done it myself.'

Why?

'Well,' replied Alex, 'why would you want to tell a young man *that*?'

When questioned about their desire for justice, whether they wanted to name their abusers and see them punished, Alex said, 'I think, no. It's too long ago. We've dealt with it, and I just think it would be too difficult to open that book.'

As for forgiving their mother, Alex thought for a moment before saying, 'I think forgiveness is an easy word to say. I don't think she'll ever be forgiven, no. Never. No. I've started again.'

Alex's sincerity and the simple power of the story he was telling had a profound impact. Messages of support poured in from people who had heard him speak but also from his friends.

For Alex, the experience was transformative. Challenging certainly, because at heart he's a shy person, who finds it difficult to stand up in public. But more than anything, he says, 'I felt good about it' because 'I wanted to get my story across.' It seemed that finally someone out there was listening to him. He'd been trying to hunt out the truth for more than ten years, with very few people able to help him and to understand what it meant to him. Now, suddenly, friends were getting in touch; they were shocked and moved by what he had said; their admiration for his courage in speaking out, and their compassion for what the siblings had suffered was almost overwhelming. Their old friends, the ones who had known them since the Duke's Cottage days, were appalled, but their response was unequivocal. As Alex says, with typical sincerity, 'They were genuinely very upset. Basically, they just gave us their love.'

And Marcus also found himself engulfed in the wave of support. The response was completely unexpected. Friends and colleagues got in touch, telling him how brave he was, even though it hadn't been him on the radio. He was overwhelmed. The shameful secret that he'd worked so hard to keep hidden all these years wasn't driving friends away; it was making his connections closer and more genuine. He had always assumed you had to be positive and upbeat with your friends at all times, turn the horrors and the sadness into funny stories. Now he learned that friends were there to support each other, as well as to be entertained.

Going public was to be a turning-point for them both.

PART III

The Third Story

I

October 2011

By the autumn of 2011, both Alex and Marcus seemed to have established solid and rewarding lives. Both were married, with two small children apiece. Marcus and Vito lived in North London, Alex and Camilla near the south coast.

They continued to work together. In London, Lewis Burton ran a small portfolio of properties, which demanded constant attention: Alex dealt with the administration and Marcus with practical repairs and upkeep, while James Burton continued to oversee the whole enterprise. On Pemba, their hotel in Fundu Lagoon had gone from strength to strength and continued to absorb a lot of their time and energy, with frequent visits to improve the facilities and deal with the day-to-day management, as well as trade shows and publicity in Europe. All profits were ploughed back into the hotel, but for Marcus especially it was a source of great pride, and he revelled in his visits to the place where his dyslexia always vanished the moment he stepped onto African soil.

For Alex, the situation was more complicated. It was more than ten years since Vivien's life-changing workshop. Since then he had been dogged in his determination to track anyone down who could help him piece together an accurate picture of events, but even so, the search felt far from complete.

So many versions were piled on top of each other in his mind, and often it was hard to know which one was 'right', or even the most recent. There were the stories he'd absorbed in the years after the accident, the images that had taken the place of memories, most of which he'd got from Marcus. These had been thrown into doubt, but sometimes he found it hard to remember which of them were still good, and which he should discard. And now he had all the recollections and descriptions he'd got from everyone else to sift through – and they might prove just as unreliable.

The empty inner world that Alex inhabited when he came round from the coma was now filled with a cacophony of different voices and images, a jumble of events and stories, sometimes overlapping or out of sequence, sometimes contradictory, often interspersed with huge gaps. In some ways he had made a lot of progress, but in other ways it often felt as though he had made hardly any at all.

Questions continued to haunt him. What had he been like before the accident that robbed him of his memory? How much had he changed afterwards? Was he a totally different Alex Lewis in 2011 from the confident-seeming young man who had driven away from the summer wedding that warm July night almost twenty years before? And what did his amnesia really mean? Were the memories deleted entirely from his brain, or had they simply become inaccessible? Were the events of those first eighteen years still shaping the person he was now, even though he couldn't remember them?

Most troubling of all was the idea that there might be another, more real, Alex Lewis buried deep in his subconscious, forever out of reach.

It didn't help that he still had no real details of the horrors Marcus, Oliver and Amanda had confirmed. He knew their mother had sexually abused them over many years, that they had been passed around among her friends. But that was all. He only had his imagination to fill in the details. It was like seeing a headline in a newspaper – *Twin Boys Sexually Abused By Mother!* – but with no article underneath to explain what it all meant.

What had happened? When stories emerged in the media about children being abused, Alex always wondered: is that what happened to us? Is that what it was like? Sometimes the stories were very dark, involving satanic ritual and all manner of cruelty, and those images were piled into the ragbag of possible scenarios.

He was beginning to wonder if he was doomed to carry this not-knowingness for the rest of his life. It was a bleak prospect, though he continued to put a cheerful gloss on it whenever he could.

Then, as a direct result of the Radio 4 interview, a new opportunity suddenly came his way: the offer to turn his story into a book. He would need to involve Marcus: their journeys had been so intertwined there was no way one could be described without the other. It would be a chance, once and for all, to sift through all the conflicting narratives and create a solid history.

When he talked about it with Marcus, his twin was no more

enthusiastic than he had been all through Alex's searches. They were close, as they had always been, but for some years now almost all their interactions were to do with their businesses or their friends. So far as Marcus was concerned, their childhood and their family background were irrelevant, consigned to the past. But he could see now how important this next stage was going to be and he had no wish to stand in his brother's way. Because for Alex, it wasn't just his story he wanted to write, it was his whole sense of self.

As Alex said when he committed himself to this new enterprise, 'I want to write this book because I want to know who I am.'

2

A Family Together

Autumn sunlight was pouring in through the windows, and children's voices rose up from the playground below. Marcus and Alex had met up to start thinking about the book, and they had invited Amanda and Oliver to join them. After all, this book was going to be about their family too.

By great good fortune, Amanda was spending a few months in London, longer than she'd ever been in the UK since her mother's funeral. Tall and attractive, she'd spent the years since Duke's Cottage was sold in self-discovery and exploration. She had lived for many years in India, and had recently moved to Australia. In her teens she had shown artistic promise, but had turned down a place at art school in order to travel, as her older brothers had done. Recently she'd picked up the threads of her creative life and was currently studying to be a milliner.

Oliver enjoyed extreme physical challenges, pushing himself to his limits, whether breaking the world record for rowing across the Atlantic or running seven ultra marathons in seven continents in eight days.

Just being together, the four of them, had already turned this into a special occasion. Since they left Rudgwick they'd hardly ever been in the same continent, let alone the same room. Amanda and Oliver were both feeling understandably cautious about this new project. They too grew up in Duke's Cottage and had to find their own ways of coming to terms with the legacy of their childhood.

Important questions needed to be answered.

To begin with, the solution seemed to be obvious: stick to the unvarnished truth, and you won't go far wrong. As Oliver said, 'My only opinion about it is that if it's the truth and factually correct, then fine.'

Amanda agreed: 'It needs to be truthful if it's in there.'

'No twisted truth,' said Oliver. 'No sensationalism.'

Which was fine, so far as it went. But it quickly became apparent that pinning down a single, absolute truth about something as complex as a family was going to be just about impossible.

Marcus told a story that illustrated the slippery nature of truth, even when people are recounting quite recent events. A few years ago, he and a group of friends had been walking through Brixton when they were mugged. They went to the police to report the crime: they said a group of youths had set on them. Six of the muggers were black and one was white. The police interviewed them separately, and later, when they went over events in the pub, Marcus and his friends realised it had been the other way round: six of their attackers were white and only one black. As Marcus explained, 'because we were in Brixton, a black area, we were in shock, our minds told us what we expected to see.'

He applied this to their family history: more than ten years separate him and Alex from their younger siblings. Inevitably, Oliver and Amanda's experience of their childhood would be very different from his and Alex's, partly because Jill and Jack were older when they were children, and partly because Jack was their real father, rather than a reluctant stepfather. 'In that sense,' Marcus said, 'there is no truth. We can only tell the story the way we see it.'

Amanda suggested instead the notion of 'personal truth' which, for the time being, seemed like a helpful concept to hold on to.

Oliver was curious to know what Alex and Marcus's motivations were for working on a book. He saw this as the essential question, what he called the 'Why of the book'. More important to him, perhaps, than to people from a more ordinary family because, in his memorable phrase, 'We lived in a household of ill-truths.' Alex tried to explain to his siblings why he was doing this. 'It's thirteen years since I learned the truth about my family,' he told them. 'And I've spent the last thirteen years searching for the truth. So for this to suddenly come up, for me it's a way for me to learn a lot more about our family. I've taken photographs, I've researched, I've got the passports and the documents, I've done the best I can. It's like a journey for all of us to put all the myths to bed and put down what really happened. And in a funny sort of way to move forward in our lives. Almost getting it out, if you like, after holding it in for so many years.'

His siblings listened to him in silence. They were attentive and respectful, relieved to be talking, perhaps for the first time, about so much that had always been hidden in their family. It was impressive that in spite of their anxieties they were all so determined to make this a positive experience.

'I just think, as a family,' Alex went on, 'it would be nice to get it out. And maybe it would help in our future life that we've done this journey together.'

There was a moment of silence. They could sympathise with his hope, but there was a sense of wariness that his gain might be at their expense. They had so many reasons to be suspicious of each other, to question motives and to be fearful that their interests would be ignored. But Alex's three siblings were aware of the burden of his memory loss, especially when he spelled out exactly what it meant to him, even now.

'I can honestly say,' he said, 'I probably only know 30%. A lot of detail is missing still, it really is.'

The mood shifted, and they chatted together, sharing memories of family life. Some of them were funny – like Alex and Marcus, Amanda and Oliver have a keen sense of the absurd – but there was pain behind a lot of their stories. And while they talked over old times, it was obvious that Alex could only join in the discussion by proxy. He contributed some of the anecdotes he'd been told but with no way of knowing how accurate his story was. Each of his siblings had their key memories, the incidents that for them seemed to epitomise their early years. Their revelations came as a shock.

For Amanda, the memory that stuck out most was the way she felt when she heard that Marcus and Alex were not coming back from Australia. The morning they'd sat on the swings in that empty playground in Sydney, and Marcus had persuaded Alex that the moment had come to ignore their parents' demand to come back and look after them, they'd had no way of knowing how their decision would impact on their sister. At the time, she had been thirteen and alone in the house with her parents. Oliver was already at boarding school. Alex and Marcus were horrified to learn that when she was much younger, Janet, one of her childminders had been sadistic and violent. When their mother noticed bruises on her body, she fired the woman at once, but significantly, the police were never involved. All the time the twins were away, Amanda had been holding on for the moment they would come back, her big brothers whom she relied on and adored. When the letter came confirming their intention to stay on in Australia, her parents were furious, but Amanda was plunged into despair. At the time it had felt to her as if suicide might be the best way out of her misery.

Marcus admitted that he had always felt guilty about that aspect of his decision. He had known that their mother was impossible, and that Amanda was suffering at Duke's Cottage. And still he had not come back.

For Amanda, even though she was young when the elder two left home, her brothers have always been the most significant figures in her world: all that was good about family.

'I never trusted my parents,' she explained. 'I hated them. So I only have my brothers.' It was poignant that Amanda, the adored and pampered replacement daughter who arrived so soon after Lucinda's death, the child who was refused nothing, is the one who is least ambivalent about her parents. Quite simply, she loathed them, and couldn't wait to get away. It was not ingratitude, nor even what her brothers consider to be her feminine intuition. So far as her brothers could see, she was indulged as they never were, but even so, she never felt safe. Nor did she ever feel truly loved. At Duke's Cottage she was always lonely. She listened at doors, but never found any answers to her unease. Trying to put her finger on what she'd experienced, she said, 'I was not feeling right the whole time.'

Amanda's account of her childhood is an important corrective to the way sexual abuse distorts our vision. The moment it becomes known that there has been sexual abuse by a family member, it inevitably comes to seem like the most significant trauma, even when the details have not been established. But it only takes place in a context of other, less obvious but potentially just as damaging, parental malfunction. At Duke's Cottage it seems that the parents could only ever relate to their children as objects – albeit in Amanda's case a loved object. That was the core of their inadequacy. Jill and Jack might have appeared to be smothering her with affection, but they were quite incapable of giving her what she needed: security and a kind of harmony with the world. It was a troubled and unhappy household for all the children who grew up there, but Amanda had never really understood why.

This chimed with what Alex had been told by a friend and neighbour in Rudgwick. She had liked Jill, but had been struck by the way neither she nor Jack ever did anything just for the sake of their children. There were no picnics, or outings. No treats. The children seemed to exist only as adjuncts of their parents' lives, and there was no sense that they had needs, or even identities, of their own. Marcus and Alex were treated like servants, but Amanda and Oliver were treated like ornaments, or accessories, and though the ill-treatment was less obvious, it was just as hard for the child to make sense of.

One of the most heartbreaking images of life at Duke's Cottage is that of Amanda crouched outside her mother's bedroom door, listening, listening, never understanding, and feeling rejected and excluded from whatever it was her mother and brother were doing together in the room. She said, 'I knew something not right was going on, but I didn't realise it was sexual. I just had a feeling of being left out, that they were doing something in there that I'm not involved in. Looking back now, I think, *thank God*. But you don't think that as a kid. You think: what are they doing in there that's so special and I'm not doing it?'

On this October afternoon, she generously supported Alex in his enterprise. 'I know,' she said, 'that hole in your life, you want something filled in there.'

'I have done for years,' said Alex. 'I've been searching for this moment.'

'So it will be great to put this picture together,' she said.

They continued to share the familiar stories: the feud with William, Jack Dudley's harshness, the rules by which the house was governed. As always, when they got together to talk about the past, they came back to the character of their mother, her 'eccentricity', her chronic meanness, the power she exerted over people, and what drove her. The question of responsibility was one they'd return to time and again. She was sick, certainly, but did that mean she was unable to act in any other way? That she couldn't be held to account for what she did?

The question of forgiveness arose, as it would again from time to time. Was it necessary for them to forgive their parents so they could break free of the past and move on? For Alex, who had no memory of the traumas, forgiveness did not at that moment seem an impossible ask. For Marcus, it was simply irrelevant.

There was no shortage of horrifying stories, of reasons why forgiveness might be impossible.

One of Oliver's defining memories from childhood occurred when he was still quite small, and it stemmed from Jill's inability to throw anything away – that hoarding instinct William believed they had both inherited from their father. Oliver said, 'She was having a clear-out of all the medicine bottles that lived in the kitchen. She couldn't physically throw away the bottle unless the contents had been used, so she gave me the contents of *all* the medicines, so then she was able to throw the bottles away.'

The little boy obediently swallowed pills and syrups, as the empty bottles piled up in the rubbish, until he could swallow no more. Then he vomited.

Remembering, Oliver commented calmly, 'It's a great insight into her mindset. I was violently ill. I don't believe she was doing it to be cruel, but her sickness was so extreme she couldn't understand the knock-on effects of doing that to that child – just so she could throw away the bottles.'

Oliver gave his account with little apparent emotion, apart from the slight incredulity that anyone could act that way; it was a chilling story, and the others were all subdued as they listened. But there did seem to be some comfort in sharing the memory, talking openly in a way that had never been possible when they were children. The conversation continued to roam over reminiscences from their early years, how to interpret all that had happened, all they had been through. There was laughter and compassion in spite of the remembered horrors and the tears. The sexual abuse was alluded to on several occasions during this rare moment of sibling togetherness, but it was never spoken about explicitly. This reticence would cause problems in the future.

But today, it felt as if some kind of start had been made on this journey to construct an honest shared family narrative free from the deceptions that had permeated their childhood. For Oliver this was a continuation of the discussion he had first initiated with Marcus thirteen years before. And it was Alex, with a blank where his memories should be, who was driving this stage of their endeavour.

In the 'household of ill-truths' it was the child with no memory who was now starting to loosen the lies and secrets that had kept them bound for so long.

3

The Night Life Changed

Amonth after their meeting with Oliver and Amanda, Marcus and Alex decided the time had come to start setting down their narrative.

The first problem was where to begin.

For Alex, it was obvious: the start of his conscious life was the moment he woke in the hospital in 1982 and recognised his twin sitting beside his bed.

But Marcus disagreed. For him, the crucial start point was the summer's night when Alex had his accident. He had described his premonition in detail on the Carol Vorderman show, but that had been filmed fourteen years before, neither Alex nor Marcus had a copy, and when he started to talk about the accident now, they had both forgotten exactly what he'd said on that programme.

Marcus began confidently. 'It started with me waking up at 3 o' clock in the morning, phoning my mother and telling her something awful had happened to Alex.'

How did he know?

Marcus said simply, 'I woke up and had the accident.'

This is one of those examples of twin communication that some people accept without question, while others are convinced that it's either a coincidence or a subsequent glossing of events. No one is more aware of the sceptics' response than Marcus, but he held to the truth as he remembered it.

'It was like a very vivid dream,' he said. 'I had a dread, something very powerful struck me. I woke up in a sweat, in a panic. I just knew something very bad had happened to Alex. To the point where I did something I've never done before or since: I phoned my mother at three in the morning. It wasn't like I saw the accident in a dream or anything like that. I don't really want to call it a dream because it sounds airy-fairy.'

'A premonition?' asked Alex.

'No, not a premonition,' said Marcus. 'Just waking up with the knowledge. And sweating.'

Where was he?

'I was in Scotland.'

He was remembering the house of Gordon Richardson, the cabinetmaker who had invited Marcus to go with him and his wife Gill to Dumfries and Galloway, the couple who to this day are regarded as grandparents by Marcus's children. So far all this was familiar ground for them both, the stories they have told so many times they have become formulaic. Individually they are both great entertainers, and as a double act they are unbeatable. But now, in order to create the narrative they were looking for, more detail was required: for instance, a description of the house and the room where he had woken suddenly that night.

Marcus began to describe his room in the Richardsons' house, 'It was a little bedroom on the left as you came up the stairs. Quite basic, just floorboards and a bed in the corner. I remember waking up and going downstairs to the kitchen and phoning. It was still a bit of a building site. So I rang my mother and she was pretty pissed off.

'"What's this about?" she asked. "I'm fast asleep."'

Marcus went on, 'I'm imagining at this stage that Mum and Dad weren't in the same bed because he was in the next-door room. I can't be certain of that. I was panicking and explained that something terrible had happened to Alex and she said, "You've been having a nightmare."'

'I said, "No, it's serious, I know it is. I can feel it."'

'And she said, "Go back to bed; it will be fine." And then maybe an hour later the hospital phoned her—'

He broke off and turned to Alex. 'What time did you have your accident?'

'About half past one.'

For some reason this information seemed to carry particular significance for Marcus and he fell silent; it looked as though he was struggling to reassemble the sequence of events. Alex took up the story.

'I'd been to a friend's wedding in Ewhurst,' he said, narrating the story he'd pieced together from talking to people over the years. 'I was eighteen, there was loads of champagne. I wasn't drunk, but I'd probably had a bit too much. I had my Mini. The drive from Ewhurst back to Bramley Grange Hotel where I was living and working wasn't all that far, but I ran out of petrol. So I parked the car at the side of the road and hitched a lift back to Bramley. I got the chef out of bed and asked him to give me a lift back to my car, a mile and a half down the road. Only five minutes. He had a motorbike and he said,

"Yes, sure." We filled a can at the garage opposite. So I'm sitting on the back of the motorbike, holding a can of petrol, with a half-face helmet on which I haven't bothered to do up because it's only two minutes down the road . . .

'We were two corners away from the car and I think he took the corner too fast, but I'll never know. It wasn't a horrendous accident or anything. We just went round the corner and slipped and went down. I think the heavy petrol can sent me off balance. His reactions must have been quicker. He was thrown into the ditch and I was trapped under the bike. The half-face helmet came straight off so I smashed my head on the road, the petrol can broke, sparks from the bike hitting the road went in the petrol and – *boomf!* – the whole thing went up.

'I was burned. Not too badly. My understanding is he got out of the ditch and pulled me clear before the next car came along and I was run over. And I was screaming my head off. With blood everywhere. And I can imagine the scene—' Alex had been talking with increasing animation, but suddenly he broke off and became thoughtful. 'Well,' he said quietly. 'I can't really imagine the scene because I can't remember it. But that's sort of how I've put it together over the years.'

So many of his stories were like this, a patchwork of other people's memories with his imagination filling in the gaps as best he could. The only person who could have accurately told Alex what had happened was the chef. He had been at Godalming College with Alex and was about the same age, but Alex hadn't seen him since the accident, and so had no memory of him. He might have felt guilty, but Marcus thought he blamed Alex for the accident and the damage to his bike.

Marcus came back into the conversation and asked, 'You were unconscious from that point?'

'No,' said Alex. 'I screamed all the way from Bramley to the Accident & Emergency in Guildford, and then down into the corridors. Screaming and screaming and screaming. I was in such pain. I'd broken both my arms, I'd fractured my wrist in seventeen places, I'd fractured my skull severely. I had burns on my back. I'd damaged my neck. A whole host of horrendous injuries, and I was just screaming.'

'When did you go into a coma then?' asked Marcus. Something about the story being narrated was puzzling him.

Alex said, 'They had to get me to the hospital, splint my arms up and my wrists. And they had to give me a lot of blood. It was quite a lengthy process. It would have taken them a couple of hours to get me stable. And then I fell into a coma.'

'That's strange,' said Marcus. 'I thought you fell into a coma straight away.'

'I was in a semi-coma,' said Alex. 'If you go into a permanent coma, there's no telling how long you will be there. It could be weeks or months – years, more like, if you go into a deep coma.'

What did Jill tell Marcus when she phoned him at 3.30 a.m. after the accident?

'She didn't ring then. She phoned me back in the morning.'

'Which is an extraordinary thing in itself,' said Alex.

'She just phoned and said Alex had had an accident. As if I'd never phoned her. Which I always thought was very strange. So then obviously I drove straight down and arrived the next day.'

From Scotland to Guildford in a little Mini is quite a journey, especially for someone who finds road signs so difficult to follow. Alex commented, 'It must have taken a while to get everything together, get in your little Mini, drive all the way down . . .'

Marcus was thoughtful, but didn't respond.

What had his mother said to him on the phone?

'She just said he'd had an accident and was in hospital.'

'She didn't tell you what had happened?'

Marcus considered this carefully. 'No. She didn't.'

How had he felt when he got the news?

Again Marcus paused, then he said, 'Surprisingly calm. Because I knew it was all right. Mum had confirmed that he was alive, that he was in hospital. But she didn't mention that he was in a coma. Maybe he wasn't at that stage.' Once again, Marcus seemed uncharacteristically subdued as he thought back. 'I don't know,' he said, a note of uncertainty creeping in. 'It's all a bit hazy for me.'

The conversation drifted to their mother, that powerful, charismatic, and ultimately damaging woman. As Marcus remembered it now, she hadn't seemed to be anxious at all.

'Though she must have been! You never knew with my mother!' Marcus said, and he added with a laugh, 'She wasn't that bad! I'm sure she was anxious.' As so often, each negative statement Marcus made about his mother was swiftly followed by one that revealed the opposite side of the coin: however dysfunctional she was, she wasn't all bad. Marcus refused to take the easy route and caricature their mother as a monster: she had good qualities as well as bad.

Did she not show her emotions?

'Mother was a games player,' said Marcus firmly. 'Everything was done for a reason.'

Alex said, 'Give her a small incident and she'd create a scene and be melodramatic. You give her a real-life drama, cool as a cucumber.'

A good person in a crisis, then?

Marcus and Alex burst out laughing at the very idea. 'No!' said Marcus. 'A good person in a crisis would know what to do. I'm just saying she was quite a calm person. You wouldn't want to be the last person on a boat with her! She wouldn't know what to do. Or she'd push you off!'

They both roared with laughter again, genuine bubbling laughter. The laughter that was always near the surface with them, which made them such engaging companions. The laughter which must have seen them through many traumas, and which often broke the tension caused by talking about their mother.

But even if Jill hadn't been panicking, seeing Alex for the first time after the accident must have been a huge shock.

'D'you know, it was all very strange . . . I was never in shock, never. It was just . . .' Marcus struggled to explain, '. . . what it was. And they all kept running round and saying he was in a coma. Days went past and I went to see him all the time, and the doctors said we had to be prepared . . . because they didn't know what damage had been done.'

'Because,' said Alex, picking up the story, 'this was my second time with multiple head injuries.'

The conversation veered off once more, this time to the accident that had taken the life of their father just three weeks after they were born.

Marcus remembered talking to his mother about what happened after the accident in 1964. Jill told him that John himself had made the decision not to continue with life even though he was unconscious. 'Apparently,' Marcus explained, 'and this is not a scientific fact, you have people who are in that vegetative state who fight, and people who don't. The nurses say that if you fight, you can come out of it, but if you decide you're going to go, then everything starts shutting down.'

Alex took up the story: 'So basically he stopped fighting and everything started shutting down. In the end there was nothing left.' He ended with one of his devastating verdicts: 'And then Mummy shut *him* down.'

They described the disaster that had taken their father's life with a combination of certainty and doubt. Had he gone through the windscreen or been thrown through the driver's door? Had he been impaled on railings, or had another car smashed into the back of his, which then went over him? 'These are all just family stories,' said Marcus, 'and we never know . . .'

The conversation returned to Marcus's total certainty that Alex would not emerge a vegetable.

'I knew he'd be all right. All the way through. And again, this is one of those airy-fairy things, but I was talking and communicating with him while he was in his coma. So I knew, 100%, that he wasn't brain-damaged and he was going to be absolutely fine when he came out of it. Now, whether that was blind belief, or whether it was an actual knowledge, nobody can ever know. But I knew in a very strange way. I didn't know otherwise, if you see what I mean. It was an absolute truth.'

This led to what was, for Alex, the starting point for everything. It has become for him a kind of foundation myth, the single truth from which all other truths flow, and he returned to it time and again.

'The opening memory of my life,' said Alex, 'is waking up and opening my eyes. I saw Marcus sitting beside the bed. "Hello, Marcus," I said. And I have this vivid, vivid memory of this hysterical woman who was going mad running round the bed, making a lot of noise and getting very overexcited. And she disturbed me greatly. I didn't like that. So I said to Marcus, "You have to get her to stop, get her out of the room." And he said, "Don't you know who she is?" And I said, "No." He said, "That's your mother." '

'She was faffing about because he didn't know who she was,' Marcus said. 'She kept saying, "Hello, darling! Hello, hello, *hello!*" She was shouting at the doctors, "This is my son! Of course he knows who I am!" She never once admitted that Alex didn't know her.'

'I had to have her removed,' said Alex. 'I couldn't cope with her. The doctors said she'd have to leave and she was extremely upset about that.'

At this point, Marcus began to make a connection that had not occurred to him when he was eighteen. He speculated that his mother might have thought Alex was deliberately blanking her because of what he called 'the whole child abuse thing'. 'She's thinking to herself, *he's lying in bed and he's woken up and he's decided to forget me.* I didn't put two and two together. For me,' Marcus said, 'it was like the whole child abuse thing was completely wiped from my brain. It hadn't happened.' He paused, then added thoughtfully, 'Alex lost it legitimately and I lost it voluntarily.'

Having brought up the child abuse issue, he quickly dropped it. 'We're diverging,' he said firmly, and they moved on to talk about the weeks after Alex came round, the time he spent in hospital learning to perform basic tasks like walking up and down stairs, feeding himself. Much of those first two years after the accident was still fuzzy for Alex, but he did remember it all being very traumatic. His mind was affected: in his words, he had 'a low mental age' but he made good progress.[17]

They talked about the months after his return from hospital; some of the time he'd spent back at the hotel with Mrs Taylor and Gail. Marcus had returned to Scotland and the Richardsons; once Alex was out of danger, he would have had to go back to work.

'My whole life was about survival,' said Alex. Jack had been told not to shout at him, because the slightest upset reduced him to tears.

---

17 Alex's medical notes for this crucial year have vanished. They were available in 1997 as the makers of the Carol Vorderman programme seem to have had access to them, but his GP does not now have them. It is possible they have been mislaid somewhere in the NHS bureaucracy, but it does mean that a real assessment of his medical progress is impossible.

With Marcus in Scotland, and no proper care provided at Duke's Cottage, Alex must have been on his own a good deal of the time.

'I'm just trying to work that out now,' said Marcus. He was silent for a bit before saying, 'I can't remember what happened.'

No one spoke. Silences are rare with Alex and Marcus. The conversation flows back and forth between them as they echo each other, repeat, modify, disagree, piece the story together. Often both talk at once. Now, more than an hour after they started talking, they are uncharacteristically quiet while the silence grew.

And grew.

Something about the story was troubling them both.

4

Scotland

It was Alex who finally broke the silence. He said, very quietly, 'I don't think you were in Scotland.'

And Marcus echoed, 'I'm not sure I was in Scotland.'

'Because I hadn't even gone to work at—' Alex was trying to create a sequence.

'So I couldn't have been in Scotland.' There was incredulity in Marcus's voice.

Were they referring to the time immediately after Alex came out of hospital?

'No, before.' They both spoke at once.

'We've got the dates wrong,' said Alex.

Suddenly the whole tone of the discussion shifted into a different gear. Up to this point they had been on familiar territory: from now on it was uncharted. Marcus was struggling to picture where he could have been on the night of Alex's accident.

'Maybe I was at a friend's house.' He was casting around. 'No. Because it's an absolute blur now.'

His familiar narrative was crumbling, and he had no way of knowing what was going to take its place.

Alex prompted him, 'You were working in Haslemere . . .'

'I worked there for years. So I couldn't have been in Scotland.'

'You couldn't have been,' said Alex.

'I've been telling myself I was in Scotland for the last fifteen years.' There was silence, then, 'Jesus!' Marcus let out a lungful of air. 'I've been a bit quiet for the last ten minutes because I've just been studying the whole thing, about waking up. And I wasn't in Scotland. When you said, "Think about the room," that's what got me going.'

So where was he?

'Not in that room. And when I said the telephone was downstairs, I didn't use that telephone either . . . Jesus Christ! I've had this memory of being in Scotland forever. Planted in there.'

Marcus fell silent again.

So, if he hadn't been in Scotland . . .?

'I was—' Marcus broke off with a gasp.

'Where are you?' Alex asked quietly.

There was a long silence, and when Marcus finally spoke, he was disbelieving. 'I was—' he paused again. 'In the bedroom. At home. I was in the bed in the corner.'

'What?' Alex was amazed.

'I was in the bed in the corner. I remember the condensation on the window . . . Oh my God! How weird!'

'So you didn't phone Mummy up?'

'I must have gone upstairs. And woken her.'

It was a lot to take in. Alex said again, 'You weren't in Scotland in 1982.'

'No. I'm just trying to work out where I was. I wasn't in

Scotland, because I could be with you at any time. And the other thing that got me thinking was when you said, "You must have gone back." Because going up to Scotland for me was a big fucking deal in the car. Driving up and down in the car, I didn't do that.'

'So *you* would have been looking after me. That's how I survived.'

'I was looking after you, in the house. You know what is so strange? We were so in our little world that we didn't let anybody come and get involved.' He was still thinking back to that momentous night. 'I've got a very strong memory of waking up with condensation on that bloody window. Because we were allowed back in the house when we got a job. That room at the back.'

Alex still couldn't quite believe it. 'You really were at home?'

'Yes. So then I *didn't* ring up.' He was silent again, then, 'I think I must have—' He lets out another huge breath. 'Phouah! I'm a bit . . . This has really done my head in,' but he and Alex were both smiling in disbelief.

'So *you* looked after me?'

'That's the funny thing. I definitely brought you home.'

'And you were in the house,' said Alex. 'I kept thinking, you couldn't have gone to Scotland because you were always around. How could you have had that much time off?'

'I remember you crying a lot, always crying.'

'Every day,' Alex agreed.

'Not like an adult sort of crying. More like a child. It switches off, then on.' Again he exhaled loudly, 'I've been—' Marcus broke off and slammed his fist down with a thump on the table as the last of his doubts vanished. 'I woke up in that bed! And then I went upstairs.'

'No telephone involved,' said Alex.

'You know why the telephone's involved? Because I was in Scotland, so I put the telephone in. Because for the last fifteen[18] years I've been convinced I was in Scotland – '

'So you thought you had to telephone,' said Alex.

Marcus agreed. 'I went up to her room, and as we go through it, I'll remember.'

They both recognised that suddenly their narrative was shifting into a deeper kind of truth. The well-rehearsed stories were giving way to something altogether less predictable. Now, as Marcus said, 'We're talking hard-edged memory.'

He continued to speak, as the pictures that had remained hidden began to emerge.

He woke up in the back bedroom at Duke's Cottage. 'In the corner of the room. Two beds in the room. Condensation on the window because there was no heating in the room. And I was always in the right-hand bed. And I woke up in that corner. And I remember – Oh my God!' As the memories took hold, he got up and like a sleepwalker crossed to the

18 The fact that Marcus says '15 years' here is significant. When he was talking, it was closer to 30 years since the accident, but nearly 15 since Vivien's workshop. In 1997, before the revelation of sexual abuse, Marcus had felt able to tell the researchers on the Carol Vorderman programme that he had been at home when Alex came off the bike. The shift to Scotland only became necessary when he had to distance himself from his mother. But in some part of his brain the maths remained accurate: hence the '15 years'.

corner of the room. He leant his back against the wall and slid down in the corner until he was crouching. He said, 'I remember sitting up in bed like this for ages! Shaking!' For a moment he was eighteen years old again, experiencing every sensation, then suddenly he burst out, 'It's like going to hypnosis!' and they both let out a roar of laughter, cutting through the tension. 'I remember it! Fucking hell!'

As he returned to his chair, he said with a kind of triumph, 'I remember! I was shaking. Panic.' Then suddenly he was uncertain again. 'I don't know how long it lasted but I guess I must have gone upstairs and woken my mother up.'

He paused, as the memories shimmered on the periphery of his inner vision, then coalesced and became solid.

'I think I do remember it!' He was still amazed. 'I remember going up and knocking on her door.' Now he thumped the table loudly, another memory nailed and certain. 'I knocked on her door and she told me to go back to bed.'

'Where was Daddy then?' asked Alex.

'They weren't sleeping together. He wasn't in the room. That's why I knew! She told me I was having a nightmare and to go back to bed. She was quite pissed off at me waking her up. And I went back downstairs. And then the phone rang – that's the phone! – the phone rang in the middle of the night!'

'That was the hospital,' said Alex.

'I heard it from my room. I know exactly now. Jesus Christ!' Marcus and Alex were laughing with a mixture of shock and a kind of euphoria of discovery.

Had he been able to overhear Jill's conversation with the hospital?

'No. She would have taken the call on the phone by her bed, but the phone rings through the house. I know when the phone rang I got out of bed. And I went upstairs – Oh my God, it's all coming in now – and then I caught her having the end of the conversation with the doctor. Fuck! That's *exactly* what happened. By the time I got to the top of the stairs she was at the end of the conversation. And it was an hour later. That bit I do know.'

'You just remembered all that?' asked Alex.

'Yes.' Marcus paused, then said, 'The problem with a lot of this stuff is that Alex and I have been doing dinner-party stories for years. And because we're not very good on dates, you think, oh I was in Scotland, because I lived in Scotland for years. So then you just start chucking stuff in willy-nilly and by the time you've told the story ten times, I was *in* Scotland. But that is exactly what happened. I remember knocking at the door.' Marcus was getting agitated again, as he returned to the start of his story and remembered the first time he went up the stairs to wake his mother up. 'I remember the door; it was a wooden door, with slats on. An old-fashioned wooden door.'

'You pull a piece of string,' said Alex.

'And the latch went up. It made a click when you did it. And I remember standing outside for ages, and then I pulled the string and it went *click* like that.'

He was knocking and she didn't answer?

'No. I didn't knock. I was waiting to pull the string. I was very, very nervous, because I was going to wake her up. But I had a very strong conviction that I had to do it.' He paused, then, 'Fuck! That is a memory that has just come flooding into my brain.' He went on, 'She had a big double bed as you come in. A chest of drawers on the left, dressing table here, and then windows that looked out into the garden. And,' Marcus's voice gained in confidence all the time, 'and she slept on the left-hand side of the bed next to the telephone. I woke her up. She sat up in bed and I explained the whole story. And she said, "You're having a nightmare, go back to bed." I went back to my room, but I couldn't sleep. I remember it like it was yesterday. How bizarre! And then I remember being in bed, and then – *ring, ring* – that phone, it went right through the house.'

'The old-fashioned phone,' said Alex.

'There's one downstairs in the study, one in the hall, and one by the bed. And she picked the phone up. Because she'd barely been asleep again. It was an hour later. She picked the phone up on the second ring. And I was so awake. And then I remember—' He gasped. 'I remember spending a few minutes thinking, Fuck, *fuck*! What is that, what is that? And then I eventually crept up the stairs, because you had to come through the kitchen—'

'And through the breakfast room,' said Alex, who was now living every moment with him.

'Through the breakfast room, into the hall, and then you come up the stairs and around, and then the door's on the right. And then I remember standing outside the door, listening to her. I couldn't hear what she was saying, obviously, and then I pulled the cord and went in and she was still on the phone.'

He paused, then, 'Her voice was calm. And she was saying, "Yes, yes, yes." And then she put the phone down, and she looked at me and said, "Alex is in hospital." ' He let out a long breath. Tears were flowing down his cheeks.

'Well,' said Alex gently. 'Well done.'

Why the weeping? Was it the shock of remembering his twin in the hospital?

'No. It's the shock of remembering my mother. Because I can see her. I try not to think about my mother.'

This was puzzling, since he and Alex had never shown any inhibition before about discussing their mother. Whenever they talked about their childhood and growing up, the conversation always came back to Jill. But Marcus explained there was a crucial difference between the woman they had joked about, and the reality they'd grown up with:

'*Actually* talking about her, that's very different from the character that I've built up, and the dinner-party stories, and laughing. We did tend to make it all a bit of a joke.' They had turned their mother into an almost harmless figure, a pantomime villain who might be a little bit frightening, but had no power over them. Remembering the reality was altogether more sinister.

'And then,' Marcus's voice was getting stronger again, 'she spent *two fucking hours* before she went to the hospital!'

'Why?' Alex asked.

'I've no idea! I can't remember what she was doing – faffing about. Jesus!' He was weeping again. 'I don't even remember Dad waking up. Never saw him! I don't think the fucker even woke up. Jesus Christ!'

He fell silent for a while, clearly distressed by his parents' callousness.

Alex took over and described as best he could the weeks he spent at the hotel with Mrs Taylor and her daughter, Gail. But his memory of those months after his accident was still fuzzy. 'We just used to hang out together,' he said.

He asked Marcus about Mrs Taylor, but he was still consumed by the freshly recovered memories from the night of Alex's accident.

He said, 'I'm remembering Mummy's bedroom and her bed.' Tears were still flowing freely. 'I've got lots of other horrible feelings . . .'

His voice trailed off and there was a long silence.

Then he said, 'About her bedroom and her bed.'

Alex waited. Marcus's face was wet with tears. His twin was gazing at him with sympathy and a kind of amazed fascination. 'That *fucking* bed,' said Marcus, at last. There was another long silence, then he said in a low voice, 'I haven't thought about it for years. She used to make us touch each other in that bed, Alex.' He broke down completely. 'I remember! I just remembered that. She really was a horrible woman!'

'I didn't know that,' said Alex quietly.

'That's why I don't remember anything. Because I don't fucking *want* to remember anything! Much nicer that I was in Scotland.'

'Once it's remembered,' said Alex, 'it can be let go. I'm a great believer in that. I think you did really well, Marcus.'

'No!' insisted Marcus. 'For me it's never going to be about getting rid of it. It's about telling the story.'

He continued, thoughtful now: 'I spoke to Vito about it last night and she said, "Why do you want to do this book?" And now I am absolutely convinced. I wasn't half an hour ago. Look what's happening in the Church!' He was growing angry. 'They had paedophiles in that Church for forty years and nobody spoke up, they all protected those fuckers. 98% of the Church is not paedophiles, there's only 2% of the bastards. They all protected those 2% because silence is so powerful; better to sweep it under the carpet. But I'm not going to do that. I'm not prepared to do that. This is what powers them all; this is what they thrive on. This is what Mother *did*!'

'Secrecy,' said Alex. 'Don't tell anyone.'

'Don't rock the boat, let's be quiet, let's not talk about it. It's a terrible thing! This is what goes on all the bloody time, and it's why kids will keep getting abused. That's why I'm writing the book. I never realised until that moment: it really *did* happen to me!'

At this admission from Marcus, Alex began to cry, as he remembered the way Marcus had distanced himself from his search to find out the truth, the lonely path he'd been on. 'All those years,' he said, 'all those years you said no to me.'

'I had to,' said Marcus. 'Had to. It was the only way to survive. But we knew it happened.'

Not remembering had been Marcus's way of dealing with it all ever since he was a boy, and it had gone on for so long that he had always been afraid of the consequences if he allowed himself to peep into that jar with the bad smell. It was why he had avoided therapy and why, sometimes, he had gone so far as to claim that nothing all that bad had happened to him. But now he had begun to share with Alex some of the horror of those early years, and far from destroying them both, the revelation seemed to have had some beneficial consequences.

Alex put his hands behind his head and looked up at the ceiling. He was still trying to take it all in. But already he was looking lighter.

'It's just good to finally have you on board, Marcus, and not to have to think, why just me? Because I don't remember. Maybe I too will remember if we talk about it enough.'

'I was remembering waking up in Mother's bed,' said Marcus. 'I can remember the colour of the sheets, everything. We spent years in that fucking bed! I've just seen it.'

Alex was laughing through his tears. 'That's changed everything for me, to have you finally on board, Marcus.'

'I've always been on board, Ali.'

'You always said it happened to—'

'I've always been on board,' Marcus repeated. 'I've never denied it.'

'Marcus, what are you talking about?' Alex protested. 'You always said that it happened to the rest of us, but not to you. You were the child who was left out.'

'Not that. I meant the other stuff, the passing about. I only have one memory. And I didn't let him do anything.'

'That happened a lot,' said Alex, who had heard about it from Marcus, but had never known any details. 'The passing about.'

'The passing about happened a lot,' echoed Marcus. 'I remember being in a famous painter's house, in his four-poster bed. And there's probably lots more I don't remember.' Marcus was puzzling over the slippery nature of memory, the way myths and facts get jumbled up together so it becomes impossible to tell which is what. He said, 'There's a certain amount of fantasy world I had to create to protect you, Alex. Which never really went away.'

'Which then became your fantasy,' said Alex.

Marcus corrected him. 'No. It became a reality. Like the Scotland thing. I would've gone to my grave telling you that's what I did.'

The conversation drifted into a calmer path. After two hours of intense discussion and reminiscence, they were both exhausted and ready to call it a day, but in a strange way, they felt exhilarated too. They had wanted the journey of the book to be a challenging one, and so it was proving. Already new vistas were opening up. For Marcus, the realisation that he had created such a blatantly inaccurate memory of a key episode in their shared life was unsettling.

Once he had decided on the core fiction, that their childhood had been 'normal' and happy, all the other fictions had to follow. And most probably, that original untruth had been such a fundamental element of growing up that lying had become second nature: a whole inverted pyramid of falsehood erected to maintain the first lie: *the twins had always been such happy boys, with a wonderful, if eccentric, mother.*

It was like Marcus had said, when he was trying to explain what had happened to their memories of the childhood traumas: 'Alex lost it legitimately, and I lost it voluntarily.'

5

Ripples

In the weeks that followed, the ripples from that conversation continued to spread.

For Alex, there were several fundamental changes: firstly, Marcus was now at his side once more and no longer distancing himself from his search for their shared past.

Also, he now knew once and for all that the abuse he'd been told about by Vivien in the workshop really had taken place. With no memory, and little information apart from the bald fact that yes, they had been abused, there had always been flickering doubts. As he said, 'In the back of my mind I always thought, maybe it never did happen. Maybe we just blew it all up. Maybe something happened to one of us and the whole thing got blown up out of proportion. Maybe she wasn't that bad a person.' But once he had seen Marcus living out the acute distress he had learned to suppress when he was a child, it was impossible for Alex ever to slip back into the comfort of half-believing. The sexual abuse was a reality, not just an imagined story – sometimes Alex had wondered if maybe it had only happened once or twice, perhaps in a fleeting moment of experimentation . . . but no. 'She obviously knew she was a paedophile, and that was the bit I was struggling with.'

From then on Alex referred to that conversation as 'the time when Marcus was ten years old again'. For him, even though much of the conversation had centred on the events of 1982, the crucial moments had been when his twin remembered being in their mother's bed. Horrifying though the information was, the fact of knowing, and at last having Marcus alongside, felt like progress.

The painful experience of regression was not something Marcus intended to repeat, if he could help it. Luckily he had efficient strategies for recovery. As he said a week later, 'I haven't taken the lid off the jar and put my nose quite so close to it for many, many years, but by the time I got outside, the lid was back on.'

It would be many months before Marcus remembered more of the abuse, in a powerful unleashing of memories that was to have a devastating impact on both him and his brothers.

That autumn afternoon in 2011 was the first occasion Alex had ever seen Marcus's armour dented. Always upbeat, always insisting the glass is half full and that anyway, the dyslexia impacted much more on his life than the childhood abuse had done, Marcus had devised a multitude of ways to keep the memories safely locked out of sight. His strategies had enabled him to develop a full and interesting life and never fall into victim mode.

He had said he couldn't remember, or that it hadn't happened to him, or that it wasn't such a big deal. Later, Marcus explained how this habit of denial had begun. In order to survive in any meaningful way, the abused child has to learn to compartmentalise their life. No matter what happens behind closed doors or in the parental bed, that child still has to cope in the everyday world. They have to get up in the morning, have breakfast and head off to school. They have to act normal, as though nothing has happened, and the only way they can do that, in Marcus's opinion, is to tell themselves that nothing *has* happened and, in his words, 'you just shut it down'. To the point where, eventually, he had almost persuaded himself that nothing *had* happened.

As a child, Marcus had needed to hold on to a positive image of his mother: she was his only real parental figure and he clung to any loving gesture she made, each friendly word or action. In spite of her failings she was energetic and fun-loving, an entertaining companion. He didn't have to fabricate her few good points, just make a joke of it and mentally erase the bad ones.

When Alex first told his story, he said it was a brother's love that made Marcus omit telling him about all the darkness in their childhood. This is only partly true; the full picture is more complex. In the first months after Alex emerged from the coma, all he needed to know was the basics: where is my bedroom? Who are these people who say they are my friends and who claim to know me? What is this TV programme about? How long have we lived here? Who are Oliver and Amanda? And then, after a year had passed and the topic had never come up – and why would it? – Marcus himself had stopped thinking about it. He had suppressed the dark memories – so far as that was possible – the same way he'd suppressed all the other bad things that had happened in their childhood. He never actually told Alex they'd been on holidays together as a family, but then he never corrected his twin's false assumptions either. Somewhere deep down he realised he'd have to talk about it eventually, but then again, he thought maybe it was better for Alex not to know. And so the half-truths endured.

When Alex confronted him after Vivien's workshop, Marcus was shocked, but at that point in his life he was simply unable to deal with those memories. In protecting Alex, he had been protecting himself as well, and by then the habit of silence was impossible to break.

The ripple effect continued over the following weeks. Camilla noticed a change in Marcus from the time that he first talked to Alex about what had gone on in their mother's bedroom. Marcus had always recognised that she was the perfect partner for his twin, but until now she'd had the feeling that he was in some way shutting her out. After he had started to admit how the abuse had affected him, it was as though that blockage had been removed. Her relationship with her brother-in-law shifted into a different, and easier, space.

As Marcus and Alex continued to work on the book, the topic of what they call 'passing about' cropped up from time to time. Marcus admitted that their mother had left them, often overnight, and always singly, with various of her paedophile[19] friends, often people from the London antiques world. Unspeakable things had happened over and over again until it

19 Paedophile, but not necessarily gay. It turned out later that several of the men who regularly abused them were happily married, with children of their own, respected and apparently 'straight' members of society.

all became a blur in a child's mind. But the only occasion Marcus was prepared to access in any kind of detail at this stage was the moment when he was able to bring it to an end. He had been in the house of one of her painter friends, in his four-poster bed. The man had his hand on Marcus's thigh. Marcus said 'No, I don't want this. Please stop.' He kept going and began to get very aggressive. It was then that Marcus had had enough. He very quietly got up, stopped him from doing anything more, and left the house. He thought he was probably about twelve at the time, though it is possible he was older: he might have backdated the event in his mind to bring the memories of the abuse to an end sooner. Whatever the timing, he was certain that the 'passing about' stopped for him on that day.

He explained how it had worked. Jill had been hauling them about with her since they were babies, leaving them in places without warning and collecting them again in a random way. She had never shared her plans with them, never told them what to expect when they set off from home.

'Come on, boysies! Coats on. We're off to London!' And the friends she left them with now weren't strangers; they were people the twins had got to know when they helped her on her stall in Portobello Road, or when they'd been handing round drinks at her London parties or just as family friends. Sometimes just one son went with her. On the way home, she might stop off for a drink at someone's house, someone they knew, and then after a while she'd announce that she had to go somewhere and she'd come back to pick her son up in the morning.

She'd drive off, leaving the child alone with her 'friend'. And that, said Marcus, was when what he calls the 'abuse fear factor' kicked in.

And the point at which his memories hit a brick wall.

The following day, she'd turn up and take the child home. Nothing was ever said, and for all their instinctive communication, Alex and Marcus never uttered a word to each other about any of it. They'd carry on as if nothing had happened, and visitors to the house continued to be struck by how happy the twins were: 'always cheerful'.

6

'Normal'

Alex and Marcus often state that they spent a lot of their childhood in their own little world, so that for all they knew their family was perfectly normal.

Their dyslexia was a factor in their isolation, since the world of books was closed to them, and on television fantasy and reality are so often intermixed. They didn't make friends during their first years at secondary school, so never went back to the homes of their classmates. This made it possible to think that maybe all boys were sent to live in an unheated shed, and that all children had to serve their parents at meals and clean up after them and their guests. As Marcus explained when Alex asked why they had never recognised their mother's destructive side: 'When you live in a house with all this shit going on, it's just how your life is. You can make children think anything is normal.' The two families who took them on holiday were always impressed by how helpful they were and how hardworking: for the twins, it was automatic. For all the twins knew it was those families who were unusual in their kindness and generosity; 'normal' was anybody's guess.

Gradually, as Amanda and Oliver got older and were treated so differently, the twins sometimes started to feel resentful. But it was only when they were sixteen and went to the New Year's Eve party at Long Copse where they met Sam and Ellen and their family and friends that the doubts really kicked in. And it wasn't until their travelling years that they realised just how far from normal life at Duke's Cottage had been. But by that time Alex had no memory except for what Marcus told him, and Marcus had buried all the negatives so deep he hardly ever accessed them.

And Jill's behaviour, increasingly bizarre as it was during her last years, was excused by everyone who knew her as 'eccentricity'. She might be grotesquely embarrassing to her sons, turning up at their parties and entertaining their friends with comments about their 'willies', but that was just Jill being outrageous and only to be expected.

The upper-class English eccentric – that phrase can hide such a multitude of secrets. Alex commented that he always knew his parents were strange. 'Eccentric's a lovely word, isn't it? Mad and eccentric – what's the difference? It's just a posh way of saying mad. Or ill.' Besides, Jill had unique style.

Laura Hudson had the Dudleys over to her home every Christmas, and at other times during the year as well. She was usually in the kitchen during these large gatherings, but she remembers the peculiar quality of Jill's laugh. Jack referred to it as 'Jill's Billingsgate laugh': it was loud, distinctive, and highly infectious, so that within a short space of time everyone round the table would not just be laughing along with her, but laughing in the same manic, whooping way. It was, said Laura, like having 'a whole lot of parrots in the room, so when she was saying things about the twins and their girlfriends and all that personal stuff, everyone in the room was doing this mad laughter.'

It would be so much easier to tell Jill's story if she could be neatly filed away under 'monster' because of the damage she inflicted on her children, but the truth is more complicated and far more unsettling. One of their friends, when he heard about the sexual abuse that had taken place in that apparently normal situation, wanted to know what he should look out for among his own friends. How could he know who was a potential abuser so he could protect his own children?

'You can't,' Marcus told him. 'That's the whole point. A paedophile doesn't come with a neat label attached. They are ordinary people, like you and me. Just they have this side to them that is not so nice.'

It is important: the truly terrifying thing about Jill's behaviour is how like the rest of her circle she was in so many ways. If we could demonise her, then she'd pose no serious threat to our peace of mind. She did some terrible things, but she was capable of kindness, and cared for Jack when he was dying. And many observers thought that, in her contorted way, she really did love her children too.

As they loved her. Partly, they loved her because they had no choice. She was their mother and there was no other parent to fill the gap. 'You have to cling on,' says Marcus. 'If you take children in any situation, they will still cling onto something nice: their mother smiled at them, or whatever it is, and that is the memory they will cherish.' Their childhood was not all misery by any means, and on some level the happiness that visitors noticed was genuine.

Marcus says, 'It's wrong to say we hated her, every breath and everything she did, because we didn't. She was our mother and we tried to love her best we could.' He believes all children have the ability to do that.

Even now, knowing all they know, many of her friends remember Jill's excesses with an affectionate smile. Her way of trilling, 'Here we all are!' in her that uniquely fluting voice which instantly transformed a humdrum gathering into a fun event; her delighted 'coo-eeing!' as she sat large and middle-aged and topless on the stern of a friend's yacht and attracted the attention of every passing boatman. 'Oh yes!' said one friend who had not seen her since he was a teenage boy thirty years before, 'Jillikins! What a character!'

The twins may not want to label her a monster, but they don't intend to let her off the hook either. She wasn't mad and she wasn't so befuddled with drink that she didn't know what she was doing. Jill knew the difference between right and wrong and she knew that her actions were criminal. On the surface her behaviour might have seemed random and spontaneous, but there was a calculating mind at work throughout, keeping everything separate, making sure her secrets were safe. For instance, she made absolutely sure Jack never knew about any of it.

Which leads to the question: why, if she wanted the harm she had done to her twin sons to remain secret, did she never accept Alex's memory loss? Surely that made it less likely she would ever be found out.

Those who knew Jill well believed that not being recognised by Alex was the ultimate rejection and she simply couldn't bear it. Jill was unable to see her children as in any real sense separate from herself, as individuals rather than possessions. Having a child who didn't even know who she was threatened her very survival. Right from the start, when Alex came round from the coma, her desperation to be recognised overrode any concern for his well-being.

She did not give the twins the love they needed, but she would not let go of them either. Friends commented on the way she 'boysied' them, treating them as younger than their age, encouraging them to be dependent on her and trying to stop them from leaving. And of course, it is always harder for children to develop a sense of independence when they are still waiting for the unconditional love that never comes.

Alex is clear that he was never able to connect with his mother after the accident in the way he did with his little brother and sister. This might have been simply because children are somehow easier to forge a bond with; or it might have been because some part of him, deep down, remained wary of Jill.

At times both Alex and Marcus have wondered if it is possible that Alex in some strange way chose to erase his memories during the coma. Marcus said at one point that Alex lost his memory legitimately while he lost his deliberately. But supposing there was an element of choice in Alex's memory loss as well? Maybe, as Alex conjectured, 'I was in a coma, and I decided: this is the moment to get out. Press the delete button. On purpose.'

The out-of-body experiences which came to a climax during the workshop with Vivien might simply have been a result of the injury to his head. But it is also a well-documented strategy that children and adults resort to at moments of extreme trauma, such as sexual abuse. Perhaps Alex had already learned to cope in his childhood by absenting himself from particular scenes and blocking the horror of what was being done to him from his consciousness.

Perhaps, deep in the safety of his coma, some still-functioning part of his mind made the decision to blot out the traumas for ever.

Both Alex and Marcus admit it seems far-fetched, and something that could never be proved, but it remains a tantalising possibility. Who knows what the mysterious brain can do?

7

A Different Person?

Not all the discoveries were negative. Right at the bottom of the enormous box of papers that had been salvaged from Duke's Cottage lay a small colour transparency. It had been taken in Charing Cross Hospital shortly after their birth. One of the newborns is being held by Jill, who is still in her hospital gown, and the other is in the arms of their father, John. The first-time parents are turned slightly away from each other, and whichever child John is holding is crying lustily.

Neither Alex nor Marcus could remember ever having seen it before. Jill had never spoken to them about their father. They had seen very few photographs of him, and this was the only picture that showed the little family together. A few days, or maybe only a few hours, after an unknown person took the picture, John had been fatally injured. For a moment, when they looked at it, the twins were amazed, and briefly subdued. Then, almost at once, the humour took over.

'Why did Mum never show us?' demanded Marcus. 'We haven't got a picture of him holding us, have we? I want it, and we can cut Mum off!'

'He's holding me anyway!' insisted Alex, and they both laughed and admitted that unless Alex is wearing his glasses, they can't tell who is who in photographs before the age of about fifteen. With two pink newborns, distinguishing one from the other was completely impossible.

Alex was eighteen when he lost his memory, just the age when, in the natural course of events, the twins would have been leaving home, heading off in different directions and establishing separate identities. In some ways, this process continued anyway: Marcus went to Scotland, Alex to Morels in Haslemere and then the *QE2*. But at a deeper level their separation was delayed. Alex remained dependent on Marcus in a way that was hardly affected by geographic proximity, and Marcus in turn came to rely on that dependence. It was only in their thirties that they really started to establish separate lives; though they continued to work together, their social activities and interests were separate, and their conversations were mostly centred on practical aspects of their work.

Creating the book together in some ways reversed this process of separation. They were back to sharing stories and opinions on a deeper level than they had done in years – perhaps ever. But a lot of Alex's questions were for him alone, and in particular his need to discover how and in what way his personality had been altered by the accident in 1982.

He knew there had been profound changes during the first months and years after the accident. Caz, who had been his girlfriend at the time, confirmed this. She told him that when she'd first met them both at Long Copse she had been struck by how self-confident they both appeared. They were good at talking to adults but found it easy to connect with their peers as well. (Marcus puts this apparent confidence down to the dyslexic's need to overcompensate.) Whatever its cause, Alex had given an impression of easy assurance. As Caz said, 'Nothing seemed to faze him. He just got on with life.'

Not so, when she first saw him again after he came back from the hospital; he had become 'half the person' he was before. Thin and nervous, he had trouble following even the simplest conversation. And though he seemed to make an almost full recovery over the next couple of years, that earlier easy confidence never completely returned.

Talking to other friends who had known him before the accident, Alex was able to put together a fairly consistent picture. Most people, including their mother, had regarded him as the more responsible one. He worked harder at school and in spite of all the difficulties of the dyslexia, and with almost no help from home, he persevered with his studies. According to Marcus, Alex was always the more conservative of the two, and the more biddable.

Alex was regarded as the more thoughtful, and the one who was always concerned for his siblings. Mrs Taylor at Bramley Grange remembered being struck by his sense of responsibility towards Marcus and Oliver. He had been the first to leave home, and to strike out on his own, but she got the impression he was troubled at leaving his siblings and would have been happier if he could have brought them with him. To some extent this sense of being the custodian of the family continued even after the accident. For instance, when their mother died it was Alex, together with Ian Hudson, who dealt with the paperwork and the bureaucracy for the other three.

On reflection, all those who knew him before and after the accident told Alex that he was essentially unchanged, in spite of some superficial differences. Alex remained Alex, even without all the memories that most of us believe to be necessary building blocks for our sense of self. In some subconscious way, all that seemed to have survived.

8

The Children's Home

'The more you dig,' said Alex, 'the stranger it becomes.'
Towards the end of their work on the narrative, there was a revelation that had a profound impact on both the twins, and most especially on Marcus. Amongst Jill's papers they discovered a short typed letter from her London GP, dated June 1965, when Alex and Marcus were just over a year old. The doctor writes that she hopes 'Marcus and Alexander are back with you now from the Children's Home, because I see from my notes that they are due for their triple antigen booster.' The doctor suggests that Mrs Lewis makes an appointment or brings them to a convenient surgery.

In the same box they unearthed two handwritten sheets, presumably compiled by his secretary for 'Wok', who had been one of Jill's most loyal admirers during the 1960s. It provides information about two possible children's homes, one in Worthing, which is described as '*very* satisfactory', and another, Glebe House in Mersham near Ashford in Kent, run by Mrs Bennison, which cared for 'normal healthy babies aged 0–2 years' and was keeping two places provisionally for the twins for one to two months' stay as required.

There was also a reference in a letter from their father's sister saying that his family would have much preferred to give a home to the babies rather than letting them be sent to a children's home. Alex and Marcus had remained in Charing Cross Hospital until they were two months old, when, according to their discharge papers, 'their mother was ready to take them home'.

All this tallies with the memory of Jill's god-daughter, who went to stay with her after John's death. She remembered helping out on the antiques stall, feeling well looked after and enjoying the glamour and sophistication of London life. She also remembered Jill waking her up one evening and telling her to get dressed so they could go together to a coffee bar where Jill was meeting up with a male friend. She did not remember the babies.

There's no way of knowing how much of their first year the little boys spent in the children's home. A handful of photographs from their early months show that Jill must have had them with her some of the time, and maybe they did only go away for a month or two. Glebe House is an elegant eighteenth-century building and was probably at the smarter end of the children's home spectrum, though hardly close to either Jill's London home or to her parents in Newbury. But for Marcus and Alex this final piece of the jigsaw felt like proof that they had been rejected right from the beginning.

They discovered that their mother had spoken about the children's home to her Rudgwick friend Miriam: Jill said it had been necessary to park the twins somewhere while she sorted out her finances and got the antiques business going.

She did not seem to think it was particularly exceptional, and she had come from a social group in which infants were traditionally cared for by wet nurses and nannies.

Perhaps her decision to put the boys in a home had been caused by the trauma of seeing her husband killed in the car crash? Though both Alex and Marcus would have liked to give her the benefit of the doubt, they decided that was unlikely. For one thing she had told close friends that John's death had not been as tragic for her as it might have been if the marriage had been in good shape. And now that they were both fathers of small children, they felt her reaction was inexplicable. Most parents, having lost their spouse, would cling all the more to what was left. As Marcus said, 'If that happened to Vito, she wouldn't think for one minute to put her children in a home.'

But perhaps her action did make a horrible kind of sense. Whether because of the time they were in hospital and the shock of losing her husband, or whether it was simply because of an absence in her personality, they realised she had never properly bonded with her babies. Thinking about it, Marcus concluded that 'it fits in with her ability to have done what she did, because she clearly didn't have a mothering instinct.'

He must have been aware of that for years, but nonetheless, this fresh evidence of Jill's inability to mother her boys hit Marcus hard. He had always been clear about the child's need to believe in a loving parent against all the odds, even if the loving part is just a fraction of that parent, but this news eroded that belief.

Worse followed. A couple of days later, he learned that Oliver was not certain that their mother had known he'd been abused by Patrick, one of her friends. His brother thought that maybe Jill had simply been too trusting when she let her twelve-year-old son go and stay with him. Maybe Marcus had been exaggerating it all. Maybe she hadn't been as bad as they were saying.

The twins were already aware that strangers might find their story hard to believe: the idea that their own brother was doubting them pushed Marcus to the edge.

One evening he drove past the mansion block on Gloucester Road where his mother's friend Cynthia and her husband had held their parties, and where he and Alex had often handed round drinks and canapés. He had driven along that road many times before but this time was different. He looked up at the familiar Edwardian block, white stucco and red brick, with tall French windows opening from the first-floor flat onto a little balcony. Suddenly, he found he was unable to carry on. He pulled over to the side of the road and stopped the car. He was shaking uncontrollably.

The lid flew off the jar he had kept sealed for so long, and a toxic flood of horrifying images burst through his defences. He was overwhelmed. In great distress, he managed to steer the car into a side street where he parked and telephoned Alex. They talked together for a long time.

By the time Marcus was composed enough to continue his journey home, Alex had learned things about his childhood he was going to have to live with for the rest of his life.

9

'Out Is Better'

Maybe it had always been inevitable that Alex's journey into his family history would open up old wounds. He was surprised to find that this was true not only for his own family, but for some of the ones whose lives they had touched, friends who were reminded by his story of all the problems that had been unresolved in their own lives.

But his greatest concern was for Oliver.

Five days after Marcus's breakdown outside Cynthia's home, the three brothers met to see if it was going to be possible to continue to forge a narrative that felt true for them all. So much had still not been talked about openly. Oliver had first talked about the abuse more than a decade before, but Marcus had never really spoken about it with him. When they had got together with Amanda the year before, it had been referred to, but nothing had ever been made explicit. Alex had no memory, and Marcus sometimes maintained it never happened to him. For all Oliver knew, he might have been the only child who suffered. That possibility left him feeling isolated and unsure. His sense of isolation was intensified by the fact that Marcus and Alex had not talked to him about their present project until they were several months into it.

The result of all this was that when they met up, Oliver was still feeling deeply hurt. But Alex and Marcus were also feeling raw and vulnerable, and were struggling to come to terms with the revelations of the previous week. The relationship between Oliver and his brothers had never been so precarious. But what emerged during their meeting was not just the enduring affection between the three brothers, but their determined efforts to care for each other. Their struggle to find a way of relating so different from the way they had been brought up was heroic.

Oliver began their conversation by saying that his main objection to this part of Alex's journey had been the secrecy, that recently it had felt to him as though there was 'a blanket of radio silence' over the whole venture.

Alex and Marcus apologised, but then Alex responded by venturing, 'Oliver is always envious of us being together. Alex and Marcus do this, Alex and Marcus do that. But I don't think you've ever sat down and thought we might be envious of you. *You* are very good at what you do. You can achieve anything. You're clever: we're stupid.' Oliver started to protest, but Alex explained, 'I'm just saying how we've been brought up. Daddy introduced us as "Jill's dim twins". Oliver is the clever one.'

Alex spoke in a matter-of-fact way, working it out as he went. He said, 'I've never really contemplated it before. When you get to the root of the problem, Marcus and I have always had an actual subconscious envy of *you*. We've always seen you as the achiever.'

Because Oliver had always been so much the golden boy, better at schoolwork and more athletic than them, it had taken

Alex a long time to realise that *Oliver* might possibly envy *them* for their closeness.

'I think you put me on a pedestal,' agreed Oliver. But he wasn't prepared to accept that he had ever been envious of their closeness. Frustration, he said, would be a more accurate description of his feelings towards his brothers, 'or feeling invisible.'

Alex explained that he had discovered this sense of exclusion was common among siblings of identical twins when they were all the same sex, so that a boy in a family with identical twin boys will always feel like the odd one out. As he said, 'We're genetically built as identical twins to stick together.'

Oliver agreed. They had always presented themselves as a single unit, which made it impossible for him to have a relationship with them as individuals. The reason his frustration burst out was because 'you will back each other up regardless of the truth'. Alex admitted that the way he and Marcus always take each other's side must be hard for others.

They talked some more about the handicap imposed by their dyslexia and how it impacted on every aspect of their daily life, another reason why they might have often felt envious towards their younger brother.

Marcus then went further, and said that even though it is irrational, seeing how Oliver was apparently able to achieve whatever he set his mind to had created 'an irrational fear'. He emphasised the word 'fear'.

He said, 'We lived in fear. We grew up in a house full of fear.'

Alex and Oliver were listening intently.

'We have a fear of Oliver, same as we have of everyone else. I don't know how we get rid of that. We can only try and conquer our fears one step at a time. This should have been dealt with a long time ago. But our way – Alex's as well – is to stick our heads in the sand and not deal with issues. I've been doing it my whole life. I did it with the abuse from Mummy. I should never,' Marcus's voice cracked as he emphasised the words, '*never* have let Oliver *be* in that situation. I *know* what she did to us. I *know* what she did to Alex and me. I've never told Alex, never. I don't really want to tell him now. I've never told you, Oliver. I've just acknowledged that it happened. But I . . . I have to live with that . . . I never told you, because I wasn't mature enough. I didn't think clearly enough. I should have stood up and been a man. I didn't do that. I went to Scotland and I left you there. Knowing that would happen. I didn't even know because I was so shut down. I was so immature. I couldn't even read and write. I barely got to Scotland in the car!'

Almost worse than remembering what he and Alex went through was the thought that Marcus had not been able to protect his little brother. 'I've always had that feeling,' he said. 'Always.' Given how bad he felt about leaving Oliver behind at Duke's Cottage, it's hardly surprising that his brother's doubts now were devastating.

Marcus went on, 'I drove past Cynthia's house last week because we'd been talking about it, and this has been buried in the sand my whole life and . . . I try not to remember. I keep these things away from my brain and I protect Alex which is . . . right or wrong, I don't know. I almost refused to tell him. And I was sitting outside Cynthia's house last week, in the van, and I had a massive memory.'

Marcus was choking with emotion as he spoke of his sudden, vivid memory of an evening at Cynthia's flat. The occasion had been a large drinks party, for probably about fifty guests. He said, 'I was standing in Cynthia's[20] hall when I was twelve years old and I could see a man in the drawing-room who had done . . .' He hesitated, then said, '. . . *unbelievable* things to me. And I had to go and serve him a drink. And I was so frightened that I peed myself in her hall right in front of everyone, frozen on the spot, age twelve. My mother must have known what that was about. I can see him now, in the corner of the room by the window. And I went into the kitchen and I threw food over myself so I could disguise what had happened.'

With the memory of his terror at the sight of one of his abusers, details of the abuse surfaced as well. He experienced the panic and the shame, the child's utter helplessness, the physical and mental pain, all the horrors he'd worked so hard to suppress. The memory sensations, once unleashed, wouldn't go away.

He said, 'These are emotions, and feelings, I don't *want* to think about! I don't *need* this in my life! These things have not been part of my life for many, many years. I thought I was strong enough to deal with stuff and it's . . . coming up like

20 Although some of the abusers were part of their social circle, Marcus is clear that neither Cynthia nor her husband were involved in any of the abuse; nor did it ever happen in their home.

sick to my throat, all the time. And I don't really know what to do about it. Hiding things from Alex, hiding things from Oliver . . . I didn't protect you. I left you on your own. It's all me. It comes back to me. I feel . . . sorry . . .'

He was weeping now. 'You know what?' he asked. 'You know what drives me? I know I have to write this. I know people need to read this, and I know that people like my mother can't keep this quiet our whole life. That's what they want to do . . . And I know, Oliver, you had some horrific experiences, but you don't really know what happened to me. But we're pretty much on a level, I'm afraid to say. And I'm afraid you were as well, Ali, and . . . stop it there, if that's OK . . .'

For a short while, he was unable to continue.

The room was quiet. Alex was profoundly moved by all Marcus had been saying. He turned to Oliver and said, 'Marcus phoned me from the car, and I had to calm him down. And I'm still finding it very hard to believe the details of what the men were doing . . . and everything else. He told me, and I'm going to have to deal with that for the rest of my life. And Mummy was there watching them do it in front of her and—' Alex let out a wail of despair. 'For fuck's *sake*! What was she *doing*? How could she do that? And give us away as well. It's just mad! *Mad!*'

Marcus was devastated by the thought that he had let people down. He said, 'I don't understand why . . . how could I not know? . . . How could I not help Oliver and Amanda?'

Their younger brother had remained silent throughout. Over the years Oliver had developed his own strategies for coping

with challenging situations; he was able to step back and disconnect mentally and emotionally, survival techniques that had
been hard learned. But now, suddenly, he intervened.

Calmly, and with total conviction, he told Marcus, 'It
would have been miraculous if you'd been emotionally capable
of helping me. There's not a psychologist in the land who'd
have thought you'd be able to help. When you've had a significant trauma the reaction is: head in the sand.'

'Are you shocked to hear all that, Oli?' asked Alex.

'I was shocked when you told me,' he replied, 'because I've
always believed that I was the only person. Nobody's ever told
me anything else.'

They were both remembering the time when Oliver first
talked to Marcus about the abuse. It had taken him weeks of
anguish before he could screw up the courage to speak about
of his haunted truth, a moment of catharsis he's never forgotten. For Marcus it had seemed like a cruel coincidence that
both of his brothers raised the taboo subject within weeks of
each other. As he said, 'All I did was to confirm it did happen.'

After what Marcus had told him, Oliver saw the past differently. He said, 'It was rape. There's a huge difference between
being indecent and rape. Somebody fiddling with you, your
mother fiddling with you – it's pretty bad but it's not as bad as
what you've told us. That is a game changer for me.'

Marcus found it impossible not to keep blaming himself. He
should have protected his siblings. He should have been more
defiant.

Oliver disagreed. 'It's not relevant. I think the norm is to go
into freeze mode.' It was what he did. When his mother's

friend abused him, 'I'd be lying there, paralysed. There is chronic fear, and the only way to deal with it is be like a rabbit in the headlights.'

Marcus agreed. When he remembered what he had experienced, the overwhelming emotions were helplessness and terror. And an appalling sense of shame.

'I've never wanted to talk about it,' said Marcus, 'because I've never wanted Ali to know.'

'I know,' said Oliver.

'It's breaking my heart,' said Marcus.

'No,' Alex told him. 'I can handle it.'

'I'm telling you,' said Marcus, 'I made a vow never to tell you and I would never break it for the rest of my life. It's what has made me strong all this time, never to tell you. Never to tell anyone. Therefore you would never know and therefore you were protected. And—' his voice wavered, 'I've just broken that.'

'We're older now,' said Alex. 'I have to be able to accept this as part of my real story. So much of my life has been not real. Mrs Taylor's memory of me before the accident was of how worried I was, how disturbed I was about leaving Oliver and Amanda, even though I was so happy to be away. She said I couldn't cope with leaving you two. Of course, I hadn't lost my memory at that point, so for me that helps clarify . . . I must have been in a terrible place before the accident, she says I was in a mess.'

'In a way,' said Marcus, 'the accident was probably the only thing that saved me.'

'And it saved me,' said Alex.

'I realise now that without Alex losing his memory it would have been much more of a live concept to me. So my job, in my brain, was to protect Alex from knowing anything about it. And the only way to do that was to put it . . . over there. Which I've always done very successfully.'

'And it had a massive impact on our family,' said Alex.

They talked more about the way the sexual abuse could only happen within a family where other kinds of abuse were commonplace, what Oliver referred to as 'the whole love versus ownership' aspect. He had always maintained their mother loved them as possessions rather than as individuals.

'We weren't abused every five minutes.' said Marcus.

'But the fear, and the consequence of the abuse was there every five minutes,' Oliver said.

The twins were surprised to discover that Oliver had been as frightened of Jack Dudley as they were. His father, he said, shouted and undermined his confidence all the time. 'I've lived all my entire life in fear. I lived my childhood in fear. The safest place to be is on your own.'

'And the safest place for us to be,' said Marcus, 'was together.'

Alex was still trying to take in the enormity of what Marcus had been telling them. 'This was calculated, organised abuse. There's no other way to say it.'

Alex had always found it hard to take in, but he had known, in theory, about the passing around for a long time, but for Oliver this information was new. And it brought him back to the query that had haunted him for years: did Jill know what he himself suffered when she left him with her friend?

Alex said, 'I would say the answer is yes.'

Marcus agreed.

'The only evidence I've had prior to today,' said Oliver, 'is that after it happened with Patrick, I called her up and she came to pick me up. And I cried all the way home. She never asked me what was wrong. No conversation of: *Why are you crying?* Or: *Are you all right?*'

'What could she say to you?' asked Marcus.

'She knew why you were there,' said Alex.

'And it never happened again after that,' said Oliver.

They talked about how to deal with it now. Oliver was a great believer in talking it through; Marcus wanted only to find a way to put it back in its box as soon as possible.

He said to Alex, 'You losing your memory, and protecting you, was the padlock on the box. I've driven past Cynthia's house thousands of times in the last twenty years. Oliver opened the box and,' he snapped his fingers, 'instantly it came out and I'm having a *fit* outside her house! It's instant shit! I couldn't drive.'

Alex said, 'Oliver's been on his journey for years. I've been on this journey for years . . .'

'I don't want to go on this journey, that's my point!' Marcus said. He'd been prepared to expose the fact that their mother had been an abuser, but had hoped it would be possible to do that without having to remember the details. He said bitterly, 'You've been wanting to open the box, Ali. So your gain is my loss.'

Oliver said he never had any choice. He said, 'I was forced to break the padlock because I was going to throw myself under a train. It was either/or.'

Alex said, 'If it hadn't been for the accident—'

'Absolutely,' said Marcus. 'I'd be in the same place Oliver is now, without a doubt, Ali. You were given a free pass. I've always been jealous of that.'

This was too much for Alex. He said the memory loss had been anything but a 'free pass'. Especially now that he had children who were embarking on their schooling, and he had no idea about any of it. 'I don't remember *anything*, Marcus. It's all new, everything is new to me. And now I've got children I'm having to find more things out. I'm like a kid still. Is this what you do with homework? All new. Every day. I still have problems.' And the memory loss was behind his drive to find out the truths in their family. He said, 'I *have* to find out all this stuff!'

Still grappling with his guilt at having kept silent for so long, Marcus turned to his twin and asked, 'Are you saying I've been in the wrong, holding it away from you all this time? I'm beginning to think ... have I done it out of selfishness? I thought I was doing the right thing—'

'We were so young: why would you tell me?' asked Alex. But he admitted that the first question he was always asked was: why didn't your brother tell you about the abuse? Aren't you cross with him? And I said, 'No, why would I be cross with him? He's my twin brother. He had this opportunity not to tell me, and he didn't.'

Marcus could see where this was leading. 'But as my life's gone on,' he said 'it's clear I've been using that as my shield. It's become a selfish act.'

At this moment, unexpectedly, Alex changed tack, and

challenged him. 'I think it *has* become a selfish act because I think you've used me to help you bury it. You've used me to cover your tracks.'

'Completely,' said Marcus.

'And that was wrong Marcus. If you want me to be honest. Perhaps not at the beginning, but I think you could have given me more information than you did. Perhaps not all the details . . .'

'You asked, Ali . . .'

Marcus protested, but he was crushed by Alex's accusation. Almost for the first time, a gulf opened up between the twins. Suddenly Oliver came to Marcus's defence, and said, 'I don't think Marcus was wrong. I feel very strongly that the human reaction to abuse is—' He covered his face with his hands. 'That! There is a massive, massive trauma. And the reason is very simple: survival. How many times, Marcus, have you actually admitted, silently, to yourself in your lifetime, until the last few days, that this has happened?'

'Very rarely.'

'So there you go, then. If it was that rare, how could you possibly—? There's no case to answer, from my point of view, that you should have said anything.'

'Thank you, Oliver,' said Marcus in a low voice.

'The courage . . .' said Oliver. 'How many people go to their graves and keep their mouths shut?'

They talked some more about their hope that their story might be useful to people who perhaps have never spoken about what happened to them in their own childhoods.

For Marcus, the horror of the memories that had surfaced

was still overwhelming. He had never imagined that accompanying Alex on this journey would be so traumatic, and now he didn't know how he was going to be able to live with what he knew.

Alex too, had been appalled by the revelations. But he said, 'The more I am learning, the more we do it, I'm thinking, *yes, we should tell this story*. We're not going to change the world, but we can change a few people's lives in it. And say to people: out is better.'

'Out is much better,' said Oliver, and then he added, 'in can kill you, is the bottom line.'

Oliver's championing of Marcus had changed the dynamic between the brothers, perhaps permanently. Until this conversation, he had always seen the twins as indivisible.

Marcus and Oliver continued their conversation together alone over a meal, and later while walking together in the park. For both of them it was transformative. Oliver was able to place his own experiences in the context of the family, which meant that the terrible sense of isolation he had always felt was, for a while at least, lessened.

10

Repercussions

For Marcus, the events of that momentous week, though almost unbearably painful at the time, marked an important step forward. Deep down, he had always known when he agreed to join Alex for this part of his journey that details of the trauma were bound to emerge. And although Alex was appalled by the details, he later admitted that his imagination, in his darkest moments, had painted pictures that were even worse. Knowing the truth, however bad, was for him a strange kind of relief.

Later, Marcus explained why the possibility that his story was being questioned had been the trigger for the memories that had emerged outside the Gloucester Road flat. One of the effects of the contorted reality imposed by his childhood, where the little boys were 'always happy', was that he sometimes didn't even trust his own sense of truth. To present a false impression to the outside world, it was necessary, superficially at least, to believe the lies himself. Just as the best conmen are the ones who convince themselves, so the adaptive child is forced to believe in two contradictory realities at the same time.

His confidence in his real memories was not as firm as another person's might be. He had to dig deep to find the proof.

He explained that having his story doubted was 'so disturbing that it made me open the box just to let myself know that it had happened at all. It was almost like I had my doubt. Like Fundu. I often say to people I don't think I built Fundu. I just dreamed it. Because it's so removed from my life now that unless I look at the photos, it could be a story. I didn't actually do it. I sometimes think that about a lot of things.'

For Marcus, the dividing line between fact and fiction had often been blurry. He'd been acting as the custodian of Alex's memories, but most of the time his grasp on his own felt uncertain. Perhaps this is one reason why survivors of abuse are so utterly devastated if, when they finally summon the courage to speak about it, their stories are met with scepticism. But it also goes some way to explaining why they are often what the law calls 'unreliable witnesses' – the glossed memory and the reality overlap, so their accounts can be inconsistent.

When he talked about what had happened to him, Marcus sometimes talked about 'faceless men'. Erasing the features of the abusers was another way to attempt to depersonalise the experience: the memories of being hurt by men with no recognisable faces became just that little bit easier to suppress.

He had no intention of going down that road again. He had remembered enough to satisfy himself that the experiences had been real and that the 'passing around' had happened on many, many occasions throughout his and Alex's childhood. He had re-experienced his feelings of helplessness and shame, and he had remembered that his mother had been present on at least a few occasions. It was enough. There was nothing to be gained by going over and over the traumatic memories; on the contrary, his instinct told him that might well make things worse.

The real gain for Marcus after confronting the trauma and talking about it with his brothers was that he was finally able to dislodge his burden of guilt. He had always blamed himself – not just because he failed to stay at home and protect Oliver when he was a child, but because he chose to remain silent when first Oliver talked to him about the abuse, then Alex came and questioned him about what their mother had done. 'I should have sat them both down and said, "This is how it is," but I didn't. I stuck with the programme . . . because at thirty, I still needed the programme. I don't think I could have handled all that then.'

Now Oliver had absolved him. 'He said in no uncertain terms: "You can't feel responsible for that in any way." It was a lot of guilt to be carrying around and now it's lifted. Not that I thought about it on a daily basis or even on a monthly basis. But it was there. Underneath. I know now I was just not emotionally strong enough. That releases something out of me.'

'And now,' added Marcus with a laugh, 'the bad memories are back where they belong. In the box.'

But with a crucial difference. The guilt and the silence have gone, and he is freer.

II

A Public Outcry

By a hideous coincidence, the Jimmy Savile scandal broke a couple of days later. Suddenly the media was showing wall-to-wall coverage of sexual abuse: who had known what and when, who was covering up, how long had it gone on and how it had operated. The exposure of such widespread abuse was disturbing, especially for Marcus who was still shaken by all that he had remembered and now had to find a way to come to terms with the memories. Alex had to fly out to Zanzibar a week later for the annual VAT negotiations for the hotel. As well as haggling with officials, he allowed himself some time to swim and relax, and generally considered he was well out of it.

As the Savile saga unfolded, parallels with their own story emerged. Here was another flamboyant, over-the-top personality who had created an 'eccentric' façade behind which they could indulge in all manner of transgressive behaviour.

The concept of grooming took on a new meaning. It was already well known that abusers groom vulnerable children: it is not the weird stranger who poses a threat so much as the kindly family friend who gives comfort and affirmation when the child is unhappy or alone; the benevolent priest or the schoolteacher or godfather who offers extra coaching. And perhaps this is one of the most hideous legacies of this betrayal of trust: generous actions become suspect. Who can be trusted?

But the scandal revealed that it is not just children who can be groomed. Savile was able to groom whole institutions, and big ones at that. As the extent of his outrages was revealed, some commentators even went so far as to say that 'Savile groomed the nation'.

Jill's area of operation was smaller, but she used similar techniques to groom her social circle. Kind neighbours might have been uncomfortable when Alex and Marcus were bullied and shouted at by their stepfather and generally treated like skivvies; they might be surprised at some of the friends Jill encouraged her sons to spend large amounts of time with – but Jill didn't just claim that all this was acceptable. She insisted that her children were in fact the lucky ones, and that her parenting was especially fine. In her world, only good things happened. She waxed lyrical with her friends about her great love for all her children, 'as though she absolutely idolised them'.

She went further still, and succeeded in undermining the confidence of other, less outgoing parents. Laura Hudson commented, 'She always made out that her upbringing of the children was the best.' She told anyone who was interested that her children loved helping out on the stall at Portobello Road, their lives were wonderful in every way and it was other parents who were failing their own children, not her. And of course, Alex and Marcus had learned to reinforce this image of their family life. How was anyone to know how different the reality really was?

As soon as the Savile scandal broke, it was difficult to find anyone who'd admit to having enjoyed his programmes or been taken in by his bizarre style. Jill's friends were more honest. Most of them were shocked, but not entirely surprised, when Alex talked to them about the murky events he was uncovering. Most people had known that all was not well in the household, but Jack's unkindness had given Jill a useful smokescreen: he was the problem parent, not her. When they thought back, friends now saw how a lot of Jill's behaviour fitted this new picture of events. They remembered how sexual her references to her sons often were, how sex seemed to dominate so much of her conversation. But however appalled they are now, they have tried not to demonise her. Even now they often remember her ebullience with a smile: she did some terrible things, but she could also be life-enhancing. Holding both elements of the person at once is hard.

The Savile scandal was also a useful reminder of how attitudes towards paedophilia have changed over the last thirty years. The general public, in the 1980s, had needed educating. Everyone knew that 'interfering' with children was wrong, but few people realised how lasting the consequences could be. Most assumed that it was wrong because it was unpleasant, like going to the dentist, but that once it was over, no real harm was done.[21] One of the surprises when ChildLine phone lines were opened was how many adults got in touch to pour out their stories. At the time there were murmurings of

21 The groundbreaking study *Sexuality and the Human Female* (Kinsey, 1953) stated that 24% of his sample had experienced the sexual attentions of adults when children. His opinion was that this was not always harmful and might, in some cases, 'be good'.

disapproval. Why were grown-ups clogging the phone lines that were intended for children who were actually suffering and needed help right now? Gradually the message got across: inside many adults a suffering child is still waiting to be heard.

But there is one major difference: Savile abused other people's children, but Jill not only abused her own sons, but allowed her friends to do so as well. Time and again, Marcus and Alex puzzled over the question: why? What was in it for her? She obviously derived intense gratification from her own sexual interaction with her sons, but what could she possibly have gained from leaving them with paedophile friends?

To begin with, they assumed that she had herself been sexually abused, perhaps by her own mother, or a carer, and therefore she dished out what she'd learned to the next generation – but after a while they decided that was too simplistic. Many adults who were abused as children grow up, as Alex and Marcus and their siblings have done, with a profound sense of what children have a right to expect of the adults in their lives. They were treated harshly; if anything, according to Camilla and Vito, the twins can be too indulgent towards their own children and find it almost impossible to set down clear boundaries. And they are fiercely protective towards them.

They think it is possible that their mother was so highly sexualised herself that she believed everyone else was just like her: that they were driven by sex just as she was. Paedophiles often exploit children's natural curiosity about their genitals and their changing bodies to justify their own actions. Grotesquely, they sometimes claim that the children were willing partners and that what took place was consensual, which only compounds the shame and confusion for the child. Maybe she did the same. But if her sons' desire for her approval allowed her to deceive herself that her abuse of them was not harmful, it's hard to imagine she could do the same when it came to passing them about.

One observer, who knew her when he was a teenager in the sixties, remembered noticing that she had an exaggerated need for male approval – almost any male approval, but especially that of men who were aristocratic or famous or wealthy. She cultivated her male friends in 'high society' and would do almost anything to keep her position in the group. Were her sons perhaps a way for her to win status among men whose friendship she craved?

There is one other possibility. It's unlikely that it was ever a financial transaction, but there may have been an element of barter. If the paedophiles in her circle came to recognise each other and help each other out, then it's possible she gained access to boys outside her family in return.

This is speculation. There is no way of knowing how this secretive and hidden system worked. Or how it is almost certainly working still.

Marcus was always clear that he was not interested in naming names, even though some of the men who abused him are still alive. What he had wanted to do from the beginning, apart from helping Alex, was to shed light on how the system operates, for the child as well as the adult, and show how children may be powerless, yet can still find ways to escape the traumas.

Revenge was never part of his agenda. Speaking clearly was.

12

Closure?

Alex was in no doubt. Though the revelations had been horrific, he did not for a moment regret learning the full truth. As he said, 'I think it is better, because it fills in the gaps. For me, it's been an extraordinary journey. A lot more shocking than I'd been expecting.' Because, he admitted, he had not expected to be so shocked. 'A bit like Oliver,' he said, 'in my naivety, even after years of researching, I still wondered how severe it was, or whether it had been embellished as the years went on.'

Now he had learned that far from embellishing the truth, Marcus had downplayed it. Alex said: 'I'm truly shocked at the magnitude, and the realness of it. And the organization behind it.'

It took him several weeks properly to absorb what he had learned. He considered that the timing had been helpful: ten years earlier he might not have been in a place where he could accept what he had heard. And he felt that although there was plenty he still didn't know, he'd learned enough for his original purpose: to get a working narrative, a sense of self.

But he was aware that with a story as complex and far-reaching as his family's there was no knowing what new perspectives might emerge in the future. 'How many skeletons can you fit in a cupboard?' he asked, and then smiled. His question sounds a bit like a joke. 'This cupboard is endless!'

He and Marcus always refused to be trapped by their childhood. 'This book will be closure,' he said firmly. 'Close the book. Finish the book. And then leave it alone. And I'm going to put the book on a shelf and leave it there. I can look at it later, as can my children when they're adults. I think that's important. After all,' he said, 'we have nothing to be ashamed of.' He realised it might be troubling for them to read but it was the only way he could see to break the mask of silence.

'It stops,' he said.

Now that the chains of secrecy have been broken, he was ready to move on with his life. 'When this is put to bed, I can stop being consumed with finding out who I really am.'

Now he knew. He knew enough.

For the first time since that summer night when he was eighteen, Alex had a sense of the person he was before the accident, how much of his original, pre-accident self had continued to exist all the way through, no matter what. A definitive truth about something as complex and fluid as a family can never be created once and for all, but Alex had done what he set out to do: he had uncovered the secrets and the reasons for the secrets and the way the system of secrets had operated in his family. And by so doing, the sibling with no memory became the person who created a memory they could all share.

It was a massive achievement, and now that it was accomplished he was ready to get on with the next stage in his life.

After Dukestonbury and travelling, Twin Decs and Fundu Lagoon, there was no knowing what new challenge he and Marcus would take on.

Perhaps nothing so dramatic. Once, when commenting on the way his friends said how boring their families were in comparison with his, Marcus said wryly, 'Boring is good.' The need to prove themselves, to blot out the memories of being introduced to people as 'Jill's dim twins', had eased as they notched up successes, not simply in their work but in their personal lives as well.

Vito wrote a moving tribute to her husband, in which she set down that Marcus was a loving father, respected among his friends. 'But mainly,' she said, 'he is such a good person. I have never met someone so giving with his own time and effort with no expectation of anything in return. Both of them are real fighters, having had to jump obstacles all their lives and finding resources to make their lives as they are, successful and rich in integrity.' A friend from their Long Copse days echoed this sentiment when he said, 'They have friends who would do anything for them.'

Amanda and Oliver were profoundly affected by Alex's quest. They too had been on different journeys and, still in their thirties, they were at a different stage. Amanda was at last finding ways to develop her remarkable artistic gifts, and Oliver was harnessing his own experience to help others find their potential. As he says, 'using endurance challenges to transform extreme personal darkness into a sense of light through achieving what seemed impossible.'

It is inevitable that the sexual component of the abuse, once revealed, becomes the focus of the narrative. But the sexual abuse was only able to take place in a family context where all boundaries were routinely trampled on, where the children were regarded as accessories, where they existed to meet their mother's needs, where truth was undermined and where fear was constant, fear that existed behind a smokescreen of laughter and jollity. Amanda suffered from the mental cruelty and the constant rows, the chaos and the neglect, just as much as her brothers did.

What is remarkable is not so much the horror of their childhood and the inevitable tensions between the brothers, but the way they have emerged with courage and compassion. And with an ability to look beyond the darkness of their early years, and make something different of their adult lives. They might talk about their formative time at Duke's Cottage as a series of funny stories, or as a nightmare experience, but they refuse to let that be their dominant narrative.

Looking back on the twins' story, it sometimes seems to share elements with the narratives recorded by the Brothers Grimm. There are the children who are kept in hardship, dressed in old clothes and forced to work as the servants of cruel adults. There is the long sleep from which the sleeper emerges to a changed world. There is the wicked woman – the witch or stepmother of fairy tales. There are the challenges to be met, and the unexpected helpers along the way. And through it all, the children emerge, perhaps not unscathed – that would be a fairy story – but with values and lives very different from the narrative they grew up with. Values they have chosen for themselves.

For all the sadness at its core, the twins' story must ultimately be one of hope and of love. Jill made some bad choices: most of theirs have been good. As children they attached themselves to caring adults who were able to give them the affection and the positive experiences they didn't find at home. They made and kept loyal friends and they were generous in their appreciation and support for others. They were determined their own children would have lives very different from theirs. They knew how to give.

The final word goes to Alex and Marcus.

Soon after the discovery that their mother had parked them in a children's home for at least a part of their first year, they were baffled by what seemed to them like the final proof, if proof were needed, of her lack of any maternal instinct.

Marcus was puzzling it all out, and said, half in jest, to Alex, 'How did we turn out . . . I know we're not normal . . . but how did we turn out so *slightly* normal?'

Alex didn't hesitate for a moment.

'Because we had each other, Marcus.'

Epilogue

It has been quite a journey for me to write this book as some one how had buried my head in the sand for so many years and quite frankly intended to do so for many many yeas to come But out of love for alex how has been pushing this agenda for more years then i car to remeber I reluctently got involved and as you can see it has changes my world!!

Living in the shadowy world of a paedophile mother and an emotionally abusive father and pretending out of sheer fear that I must keep the Secret at all costs which i swore to my self i would never brack I now realise that this is what all paedophiles feed on and it is time we all stop and be counted and break the spell acknowledge the elephant in the room and talk about it,

Dilerax has ruled and dictated our lifes in a way only dilesaxa can, it continues to bring good and bad in equlel mesher and i am shore will continu to do so for the reat of our lifs this is an ongong stugle

I have many regrets in my life but keeping quirt for so long is by far the biggest of them all. The more we speak out the harder it is for them to win and to feed on their addiction

Before we went to print i gave this book to a great friend of mine a clumban named Andres

and asked him whot he thought of it His reply amazed me his first thing was we had made our mouther to NICE and we must tone it down to make her into more of a mosnster !!! my reply was infatec "Andres you are missing the point of the book"

At this point i have to point out he had had a happy life and so not had enay exsprence of the subjet

Nice people can be paedophies too it is not just men in flasher coats it is every where. It is at this point i should tell you that if my mother were still alive now and i had the courugh i have now i would be compeled to do every thing in my power to put her behined bars.

I furmly belive we are producks of whow we are in side not producks of the things that have happen to us along the way the glass is half full all the time no mater who you are.

I have had so far a fasanating life and done so manry amazing things alone the way

I have a fantacic wife Vito and two amazing kids that i love with all my hart Vito, thank you

i am a very lucky man and will endever to keep it that way

I would like to thank Jo for helping us though this jerneny thank you

Marcus

For further help and support:

National Society for the Prevention of Cruelty to Children (NSPCC)
www.nspcc.org.uk
0808 800 5000

Childline
www.childline.org.uk
0800 IIII

Dyslexia Association
www.bdadyslexia.org.uk
0845 251 9002

National Association for People Abused in Childhood (NAPAC)
www.napac.org.uk
020 3176 0560

Readers wishing to share their thoughts and experiences can email:
tellmewhoiam@hodder.co.uk

An invitation from the publisher

Join us at www.hodder.co.uk, or follow us
on Twitter @hodderbooks to be a part of
our community of people who love the very
best in books and reading.

Whether you want to discover more about a book
or an author, watch trailers and interviews, have the
chance to win early limited editions, or simply browse
our expert readers' selection of the very best books,
we think you'll find what you're looking for.

And if you don't, that's the place to tell us what's missing.

We love what we do, and we'd love you to be a part of it.

www.hodder.co.uk

@hodderbooks

HodderBooks

HodderBooks